SABBATH AND SECTARIANISM
IN
SEVENTEENTH-CENTURY ENGLAND

BRILL'S STUDIES IN INTELLECTUAL HISTORY

SABBATH AND SECTARIANISM
IN
SEVENTEENTH-CENTURY ENGLAND

BY

DAVID S. KATZ

E.J. BRILL
LEIDEN · NEW YORK · KØBENHAVN · KÖLN
1988

Library of Congress Cataloging-in-Publication Data

Katz, David S.
  Sabbath and sectarianism in seventeenth-century
England.

  Includes bibliographical references and index.
  1. Sabbatarians—England—History—17th century.
2. Sabbath—History—17th century. 3. England—Religious
life and customs. I. Title. II. Series.
BX9680.S3K38 1988   286'.3'0942   88-2849
ISBN 90-04-08754-0

ISSN 0920-8607
ISBN 90 04 08754 0

PRINTED IN THE NETHERLANDS BY E.J. BRILL

To
Dana and Rafi

CONTENTS

ACKNOWLEDGEMENTS

In writing a book an author accumulates debts both intellectual and material. My chief intellectual debt since 1980 has been to Professor Richard H. Popkin, now of UCLA. We share numerous research interests, which he examines from the point of view of the history of philosophy, while I see them from that of the history of religion. His quite unique generosity in sharing references, photocopies, notes, and ideas brings reality to the notion of a republic of letters.

Professor Hugh Trevor-Roper, the Lord Dacre of Glanton, was very helpful throughout the writing of this book, and answered several important queries from his extraordinary sense of where the historical search should be going.

Others who helped in various ways include: Prof. Chimen Abramsky, K. Arms, John Creasey, Dr Brian Golding, David Harley, Sarah Kochav, Prof. Raphael Loewe, Prof. Jean Séguy, Dr David Wasserstein, and Dr Blair Worden.

My thanks for material assistance is also deeply felt. Some of the expenses in the research were met by the School of History, Tel-Aviv University. I would like to thank Professor Zvi Yavetz for this, and for much else. I am very grateful to Mr G. Heppel, the Domestic Bursar of New College, Oxford, for always making rooms available to me during my return visits.

The book was revised during my time as Visiting Fellow at Wolfson College, Oxford, between 1984 and 1986. I would like to thank the Fellows for electing me to that honour, and Sir Henry Fisher, then President, for his constant hospitality.

This book is published thanks to the efficiency of Elisabeth Erdman-Visser of E.J. Brill, with whom it is always a great pleasure to work.

My final debt, both intellectual and material, is to the Upper Reading Room of the Bodleian Library, where from Seat U151 most of the research was accomplished.

PREFACE

A Frenchman, writing home in 1659, confessed that he had failed to understand why the English Calvinists believed themselves to be following a form of that religious doctrine laid down in Geneva. "The religion of England," he remarked, "is preaching and sitting still on Sundays."[1] This observation points to one of the most distinguishing features of English religious life, the English Sunday, devoted to religious edification and complete abstinence from ordinary weekday activity. The strict English attitude towards the Sabbath was and always has been radically different from that which prevailed even in Protestant areas on the Continent. Indeed, it has been argued that Sabbatarianism is perhaps the only important English contribution to the development of Reformed theology in the first century of its history.[2] Strict Sabbatarianism was also one of the permanent effects of the Puritan rule in England. Even after the Restoration, when the Interregnum was regarded as a period of temporary national insanity, the almost Judaic observance of the Lord's Day continued to be a deeply rooted part of English life and culture. Most importantly, the general question of Sabbath observance itself reflects the way in which the biblical text was understood in post-Reformation England.

This book is a study of the practical application of a religious idea: the belief in the continuing literal validity of the Ten Commandments, entailing as it does the observance of the Sabbath on the seventh day. For English Protestants who believed in the absolute authority of the divinely inspired Bible, the text of the fourth commandment was a significant obstacle which was never satisfactorily overcome, since it ruled unequivocally that "the seventh day *is* the Sabbath of the Lord". Theologians like Archbishop Whitgift remained unconvincing when they postulated that Christians had "nothing to do with Moses's ceremonial and judicial laws" which were given to the Jews alone.[3] Certainly the Ten Commandments at least were universally regarded as binding on Christians, and in any case the Mosaic law did come into play not only for Saturday observers, but as early as the debate over Henry VIII's divorce, and discussions about witchcraft, usury, and heresy, in what has been seen as a general drift towards legalism

---

[1] [Anon.], *A Character of England* (London, 1659), repr. *Harleian Miscellany*, ed. T. Park (London, 1808-13), x. 192. Cf. George Herbert's description of the "Parson on Sundays" in *Works*, ed. F.E. Hutchinson (Oxford, 1941), pp. 235-6.

[2] M.M. Knappen, *Tudor Puritanism* (2nd edn, Chicago, 1970), p. 442.

[3] John Strype, *Life of Whitgift* (Oxford, 1822), i. 152.

in Protestant theology.[4] The negotiations during the Interregnum about an English parliamentary Sanhedrin, and the enactment of an almost biblical code of law in Puritan New England, may perhaps be seen as the high-water mark of Mosaic legalism in early modern English society.

This book traces the growth and development of the most radical of English Sabbath observers, those who worshipped on Saturday, the seventh day that God rested after Creation. But this is by no means a house history of the Seventh-Day Baptists or even of the Seventh-Day Adventists who came after them. Rather, this is the story of the remarkable persistence of a revolutionary religious belief in seventeenth-century England, powerful and convincing enough to survive the Restoration and continue into modern times. The Saturday-Sabbath gradually became institutionalized in a non-conformist sect in which the ideological foundation was sufficient to unite men who on political grounds should have been the most bitter of enemies, including millenarians, Fifth Monarchists, neutrals and Royalists alike. That those men and their followers could amicably join forces after the Restoration is testimony to the power of religious ideas which might overshadow the political affiliations of the Civil War.

In this book we look at the religious radicals who refused to compromise the word of God as written with His own finger on the Tablets of the Ten Commandments. The first chapter discusses the evolution of the English attitude to the Old Testament, and its particularization in the Sabbath question of the seventeenth century, especially for those who took the Bible literally and observed the day on Saturday. The next chapter tells the story of the False Jew, the scandal that rocked the Baptist movement during the 1650s and led to the establishment of a Saturday-Sabbatarian commune in Germany. Henry Jessey, a founder of the English Baptists and himself a Seventh-Day man, was forced with his followers to disassociate themselves from this new John of Leyden who threatened to make all biblical literalists seem the intimates of dangerous religious fanatics. In the third chapter we follow the career of Dr Peter Chamberlen, the royal physician of Charles I and II and their queens, who helped found the mother church of Seventh-Day men at Mill Yard, and who was among the first to demand a serious hearing for Mosaical views. But his incessant pursuit of financial gain and personal glory eventually crushed his persona as radical religious leader. The establishment of Saturday-Sabbatarianism as a non-conformist sect after the Restoration was accomplished through the tire-

---

[4] See esp. P.D.L. Avis, ''Moses and the Magistrate: a Study in the Rise of Protestant Legalism'', *Jnl. Eccl. Hist.*, xxvi (1975), 149-72; C.H. & K. George, *The Protestant Mind of the English Reformation* (Princeton, 1961), pp. 231-2; D.S. Katz, ''The Jewish Advocates of Henry VIII's Divorce, 1529-36'' (forthcoming).

less efforts of Francis Bampfield and his circle, who saw the Bible as the book of answers for all of mankind's queries, theological and otherwise, and thereby set the Seventh-Day movement on the course it would take into the nineteenth century.

The penultimate chapter deals with the transplantation of Saturday-Sabbatarianism into English America, to Rhode Island, where thanks to a motley coalition of Quakers, Freemasons, and Jews the sect would flourish as the Seventh-Day Baptists. The epilogue describes the apotheosis of the problem of the Old Testament and the Saturday-Sabbath by means of the solutions proposed in the eighteenth and nineteenth centuries. First among these came from the followers of John Hutchinson, who provided the dominant theological influence in mid-eighteenth-century Oxford. The Hutchinsonians were extreme Old Testament literalists, and by rejecting the Jewish vowel points imbued the original Hebrew text with manifold new meanings. Their views spread particularly to America, where they united in the next century with both the millenarian revival and the Saturday-Sabbath to produce the Seventh-Day Adventists and to provide a profound influence in the development of Fundamentalism.

But far more important than the institutional survival of the Seventh-Day men are the ideas which had been highlighted by their struggle against disintegration, and which continue to run through English Protestantism in the following centuries. It is well known that one of the most important theological results of the Protestant Reformation was that the Old Testament regained a place of honour next to the New, but the precise application of this distinction was never satisfactorily resolved, and at different points in religious history the problem of the Old Testament and the Mosaic law erupted with disturbing clarity. In the seventeenth century, in a culture which prized linguistic precision and confessional allegiance, this issue became centred around the observance of the Seventh-Day Sabbath, that day of rest that had been ordained in the Ten Commandments, the central text of the Old Testament which was revered by Christians of all persuasions. Those worried by the need to observe all of the Ten Commandments literally, found the problem of the Old Testament brought home with terrifying clarity, for they were forced to make a public demonstration of their faith by putting aside Saturday, a working day, as the day of rest.

A good deal has already been written on the persistence of certain social and political creeds from the period of the English Civil War, through the American and French Revolutions, down to 1917, concepts revolving around a wider franchise, land reform, and other views especially associated with the Levellers, the Diggers and other radicals. But the Jewish Sabbath in a Christian context became a potent unifying theme to bring within the fold men whose political views differed so dramatically: Jessey the millenarian and Fifth Monarchist fellow-traveller, Chamberlen the self-seeking fence-sitter, and Bampfield the staunch Royalist, reputedly the last man in England to keep using the Book of Common Prayer. What needs to be looked at again is the *religious* bequest of that sparkling period, by taking the conviction that the Old Testament, and especially the Ten Commandments, was given to all mankind, in all its severity, including the Seventh-Day Sabbath, and examining its institutional and historical consequences.

For many religious radicals, the Bible, including the Old Testament, provided a model for conduct, religious observance, and even for solving intellectual and scientific problems. This was more than irrational bibliolatry, but rather in their eyes the practical application of the divine knowledge revealed in the word of God. So too had Thomas Münzer and his rebellious German peasants raised the cry of "God's word, God's word". "But my dear fellow", Luther objected, "the question is whether it was said to you".[5] The Saturday-Sabbatarians of seventeenth-century England thought they knew the answer.

---

[5] Martin Luther, "How Christians Should Regard Moses", in *Works*, ed. J. Pelikan & H.T. Lehman (St Louis & Philadelphia, 1955-67), xxxv. 171, from the sermon of 27 Aug. 1525.

CHAPTER ONE

SABBATARIANISM AND SATURDAY-SABBATARIANISM

I

The explanation for the phenomenon of English Sabbatarianism must in the first instance be sought in the light of the Puritan emphasis on a direct understanding of the word of God as it appears in the Bible, without priestly intermediaries. Furthermore, although it was during the sixteenth and seventeenth centuries that the Old Testament regained a place of honour beside the newer partner that was thought to have superseded it, the extent to which the Mosaic law might be binding on Christians was still a thorny question. The Elizabethan religious settlement included among its thirty-nine articles the affirmation that "the Law given from God by Moses, as touching Ceremonies and Rites do not bind Christian men, nor the Civil precepts thereof ought of necessity to be received in any Commonwealth."[1] But it was extremely difficult to find convincing theological justification for the partial exclusion of Old Testament injunctions, especially for Puritans who found in both biblical books the ultimate authority for their actions. According to Bishop Sandys of London, as early as 1573 the "foolish young men" of the Presbyterian party were claiming that "the judicial laws of Moses are binding upon christian princes, and they ought not in the slightest degree to depart from them."[2] Archbishop Whitgift worried that if the Bible came to be used too widely as a code of law, then at some point there would be an inevitable restriction on the power of the prince. "To be short," he wrote, "all things must be transformed: lawyers must cast away their huge volumes and multitudes of cases, and content themselves with the books of Moses: we of the clergy would be the best judges; and they must require the law at our hands". In Whitgift's view, slavish devotion to the precise wording of the Old Testament "not only tendeth to the overthrowing of states of commonwealths, but is contrary also to the truth."[3]

Yet even for moderate Puritans, the Old Testament was still seen as a useful model, perhaps somewhat inexact, for the ordering of temporal af-

---

[1] H. Gee & W.J. Hardy, *Documents Illustrative of English Church History* (London, 1896), p. 477; E.C.S. Gibson, *The Thirty-Nine Articles* (London, 1898).
[2] *The Zurich Letters*, ed. H. Robinson (Cambridge, 1842), i. 295-6.
[3] John Whitgift, *Works*, ed. J. Ayre (Oxford, 1822), i. 201, 270.

fairs. This turn of mind was given fullest rein at the high-water mark of the English revolution, in 1653, when Cromwell forcibly dissolved Parliament and prepared to put to the test godly notions about the best way to reorder government and society. But the ideas expressed then were hardly new: when the radicals sought guidance from the past, they turned to sacred history and the books of Moses.

Among the most interesting ideas which emerged during the period of uncertainty between the dissolution of the Rump Parliament and the calling of Barebone's Nominated Assembly was a plan to model the new parliament on the Jewish Sanhedrin of seventy members. The father of this notion seems to have been the Fifth Monarchist John Rogers, who first put it forward at a mass meeting at St Thomas Apostles on 25 April 1653. Alternatively, Rogers suggested, the new assembly could consist of one member from each county.[4] The radical Major-General Thomas Harrison also favoured a parliament of seventy members on the precedent of the Sanhedrin.[5] The plan for an English Sanhedrin soon became widely known and discussed.[6] The main obstacle seems to have been that seventy members alone would comprise an assembly which would be much too small to represent adequately all of the English counties, Scotland, Ireland and Wales. Cromwell later claimed that he had suggested 140 members on this basis, because until the last stage it was intended to summon 130 men to the nominated parliament.[7] The idea of a parliament based on the Jewish Sanhedrin was dropped towards the summoning of this Barebone's Parliament, but it appeared again in the manifesto of the Fifth Monarchy rebels in April 1657, and once again in meetings of junior officers and saints between the fall of Richard Cromwell's parliament in April 1659 and the return of the Rump.[8]

A very strong biblical element appears at the very outset of the short life of Barebone's Parliament, then, and illustrates, like Sabbatarianism itself, the penetration of the Old Testament ideas and values into the realm of political action. This turn of mind is also apparent in the debates over legal reform which threatened to divide Barebone's Parliament. The ultimate hope was that "the great volumes of law would come to be reduced into

    [4] John Rogers, *To . . . Cromwell. A few Proposals relating to Civil Government* (London, 1653), brdsht; B.S. Capp, *The Fifth Monarchy Men* (London, 1972), p. 63.
    [5] Edmund Ludlow, *Memoirs*, ed. C.H. Firth (Oxford, 1894), i. 358-9.
    [6] See, e.g., *Staffordshire and the Great Rebellion*, ed. D.A. Johnson & D.G. Vaisey (Staffordshire, 1964), p. 72; *Clarke Papers*, ed. C.H. Firth (Camden Soc., 2nd ser., 49, 54, 61, 62, 1891-1901), iii. 4; *Thurloe State Papers*, ed. T. Birch (London, 1742), i. 240; *Cal. S.P. Dom., 1652-3*, pp. 339-40.
    [7] Anthony Morgan to Henry Cromwell, 3 Mar. 1657: *The Writings and Speeches of Oliver Cromwell*, ed. W.C. Abbott (Cambridge, USA, 1937-47), iv. 418-19.
    [8] Capp, *Fifth Monarchy*, pp. 117-18; *Clarke Papers*, iv. 21.

the bigness of a pocket book, as it is proportionable in New-England and elsewhere".[9] The reference was to the radical code of laws which had been enacted in Massachusetts in 1643 and revised the following year as "The Laws and Liberties".[10] One of the comprehensive plans which was not finally accepted in Massachusetts was John Cotton's "Moses his Judicials", so called because it aimed at being a synthesis between the biblical commandments and common law practice. Although other plans were thought to be more workable, Cotton's code was printed in England and appealed to radical instincts everywhere.[11] As it was, the final code had numerous biblical overtones: the list of capital offences included idolatry, blasphemy, witchcraft, adultery, rape, sodomy, kidnapping, and cursing or smiting a parent. As Professor Woolrych puts it, "the Bible and the Statutes at Large were almost equally consulted in the framing of it", this "first modern code of the Western world".[12]

Certainly, then, the Old Testament was widely regarded as a legal authority with a divine claim on the obedience of Christians. Yet even the faithful of New England argued that not all the injunctions of the Jews applied to them. These were the "ceremonial" laws whose authority had ended with the coming of Christ. Jewish dietary regulations and the prohibition against mixing linen and wool fell into this superseded category, which included many of the 613 commandments in the Old Testament.

But what was one to do about the Sabbath? Its authority derived from the very central text of the Old Testament, the Ten Commandments, to which was accorded special respect even by those who argued that Christ had fulfilled and abrogated the Mosaic law. Nine of the commandments could easily be incorporated into existing codes of behaviour: murder, theft, and adultery were sins in any man's law. But the fourth commandment proved more difficult to assimilate by New England-style Puritans and more moderate churchman alike. The first problem was that God had ruled that on the Sabbath "thou shalt not do any work, thou, nor thy son, nor thy stranger that *is* within thy gates". Before the Civil War, both Church and State positively encouraged recreation and sports after Sabbath prayer; this sacreligious state of affairs was somewhat ameliorated afterwards. The second and insurmountable difficulty was the divine defi-

---

[9] L.D. [Samuel Highland], *An Exact Relation* (London, 1654), repr. *Somers Tracts*, ed. W. Scott (2nd edn, London, 1809-15), vi. 266-84, esp. p. 278; A. Woolrych, *Commonwealth to Protectorate* (Oxford, 1982), p. 271.

[10] *Ibid.*, p. 272.

[11] [John Cotton], *An Abstract or the Lawes of New England* (London, 1641). The 1655 edn included a preface by William Aspinwall the Fifth Monarchist. Others who advocated adopting the Mosaic law included John Brayne, *The New Earth* (London, 1653) and John Spittlehouse, *The first Addresses* (London, 1653).

[12] Woolrych, *Commonwealth*, p. 272.

nition that "the seventh day *is* the sabbath of the LORD".[13] The Commandment stated very clearly that Saturday was the Sabbath, not Sunday, and
the intention of this Mosaic rule was hardly disputed at any time. The Sabbath question in early modern England was two-fold, therefore, both in
regard to the manner and the day of observance.

Let us look first at the more widespread problem of the proper way in
which the Sabbath day should be honoured, whenever it occurred. Strict
Sabbatarianism in its earliest English form was a doctrine associated with
the unreformed Catholic Church. Even in medieval England the assump-
tion remained that there was a moral core to the fourth commandment
apart from its ceremonial husk.[14] The notion that Sunday should be spent
in good works was eventually codified in legislation prohibiting Sunday
markets. This Roman Catholic Sabbatarianism aroused the hostility of
the Lollards because no justification could be found in the New Testament
for this practice.[15]

So too did the Continental Reformers reject Sabbatarianism as another
evil papistical invention, along with pilgrimages and prayers to saints. The
Church's habit of linking the Sabbath with saints' days in ecclesiastical
legislation only reinforced this view.[16] "If anywhere the day is made holy
for the mere day's sake," Luther advised, "then I order you to work on
it, to ride on it, to feast on it, to do anything to remove this reproach from
Christian liberty."[17] Calvin made a point of playing at bowls on Sunday
to demonstrate his own attitude to the question.[18] Tyndale protested that
"we be lords over the Saboth and may yet change it into the Monday, or
any other day, as we see need ... Neither needed we any holy day at all,
if the people might be taught without it."[19]

Until the later sixteenth century, the English Protestant position regarding the Sabbath was similar to that which prevailed in Reformed circles
on the Continent. During the reigns of Henry VIII and Edward VI the
Church in England took a middle ground: with the Lutherans they denounced the superstitious observance of the Lord's Day, but with the
Catholics they promoted Sunday as a day given over in normal circum-

---

[13] Exod. xx. 8-11.
[14] M.M. Knappen, *Tudor Puritanism* (2nd edn, Chicago, 1970), pp. 443-4; S. Bacchiocchi,
From Sabbath to Sunday (Rome, 1977), pp. 16-55.
[15] E.g. 12 Rich. II, c. 6; 27 Hen. VI, c. 5: see J. Wigley, *The Rise and Fall of the Victorian
Sunday* (Manchester, 1980), pp. 204-8 for a list of statutes.
[16] Knappen, *Puritanism*, pp. 444-5.
[17] Quoted in C. Hill, *Society and Puritanism* (2nd edn, New York, 1967), p. 210.
[18] R. Cox, *The Whole Doctrine of Calvin about the Sabbath* (Edinburgh, 1860), p. 91.
[19] William Tyndale, *An Answer to Sir Thomas More's Dialogue*, ed. H. Walter (Parker Soc.,
xxxviii, 1850), pp. 97-8.

stances to worship, good works, and religious education.[20] By 1573, however, Richard Fletcher, a future bishop of London, could complain that it "is said crediblelly in the countrie that . . . it is no greater a sinne to steal a horse on Munday then to sell him in fayre on the Sunday; that it is as ill to play at games as shoutinge, bowlinge on Sundaye as to lye with your neyghbors wiffe on Munday".[21] Learned theological treatises provided the academic jusitification for this increasingly popular view. Richard Greenham led the way in 1592 with his *Treatise of the Sabbath*, followed three years later by his son-in-law Nicholas Bownde's study of *The Doctrine of the Sabbath*. By the Civil War fifty years later, it could even be claimed that "England was at rest . . . till they troubled Gods Sabbath".[22]

It is clear that this change in attitude was not officially inspired. Elizabeth vetoed a bill for "the better and more reverent observing of the Sabbath day" in 1585 and ensured that a similar or identical measure would not escape the Lords' committee when the issue came up again in 1601. J.E. Neale points out that these were not Puritan measures: the first attempt at passing the bill was probably the legislative result of the collapse of the old scaffolding about the bear pit in the Paris Garden during a crowded Sunday performance, killing eight people and injuring many more. This tragedy seemed to confirm a growing popular feeling that Sabbath abuse might have unforeseen and unpleasant consequences. "Her action may have been determined mainly by a resolve not to let Parliament interfere with any religious questions," Neale suggests, "but there can also be little doubt that she preferred a Merry to a Puritan England. What she had done was to veto a measure on which both Houses had set their hearts; and her chief statesman, Burghley, had been on the committee that steered it through the Lords."[23]

When James I passed through Lancashire in 1617 on his way back from Scotland, he had occasion to "rebuke some Puritans and precise people" for the "prohibiting and unlawful punishing of our good people for using their lawful recreations and honest exercises upon Sundays, and other

---

[20] Knappen, *Puritanism*, pp. 445-6; Hill, *Society*, pp. 149-50: see e.g. 5 & 6 Edw. VI, cap. 3 (repealed under Mary but re-enacted in 1604) which authorized harvest labour on Sunday "or at any times in the year when necessity shall require to labour, ride, fish or work any kind of work, at their free wills and pleasure".

[21] Dr Williams's Lib., MS Morrice B II, f. 9ᵛ: quoted in P. Collinson, "The Beginnings of English Sabbatarianism", *Stud. Ch. Hist.*, i (1964), 208.

[22] Thomas Shepard, *Theses Sabbaticae* (London, 1649), preface, sig. B; W.U. Solberg, *Redeem the Time* (Cambridge, Mass., 1977), pp. 1-2. A similar viewpoint can be found in William Gouge, *Gods Three Arrows* (London, 1631), p. 5; and from John Dod, preaching in Coggeshall: *Cal. S.P. Dom., 1636-7*, p. 514. Cf. W. Hunt, *The Puritan Moment* (Cambridge, Mass., 1983), pp. 259, 274.

[23] J.E. Neale, *Elizabeth I and her Parliaments* (London, 1953-7), ii. 58-60, 394-5.

Holy-days, after the afternoon sermon or service". James took advice with the local bishop and decided that every man was free to amuse himself on Sunday afternoon unless the Puritans could convince him otherwise.[24] The following year, in 1618, James extended this proclamation for Lancashire to the entire kingdom as the Declaration of Sports, where he positively encouraged traditional recreations on Sunday, excepting "bear and bull-baiting, interludes and at all times in the meaner sort of people by law prohibited, bowling." The hope was that all able-bodied men would engage in sports that had some military value, especially archery. His son Charles I reissued the Declaration in 1633, noting that if Sunday sports were banned, "the meaner sort who labour hard all the week should have no recreation at all to refresh their spirits". Charles ordered that the Declaration be read from the pulpits of all parish churches, a step which his father had abandoned in the face of stiff opposition, even from the archbishop of Canterbury.[25] The popular sort of Sabbatarianism, on the other hand, is best illustrated by the possibly apocryphal story of the London clergyman who first read the Declaration of Sports and then the Ten Commandments: "Dearly beloved," he told his congregation, "ye have heard the commandments of God and man, obey which you please." Measures for enforcing Sabbath observance appeared in the parliaments of 1621, 1624, and 1625 as well, and some of them became law.[26]

The explanation for this popular support of strict Sunday observance has long puzzled historians. "The good and evil effects of this self-imposed discipline of a whole nation, in abstaining from organized amusement as well as from work on every seventh day," wrote Trevelyan, "still awaits the dispassionate study of the social historian."[27] The Victorian historian S.R.

---

[24] J. Tait, "The Declaration of Sports for Lancashire (1617)", *Eng. Hist. Rev.*, xxxii (1917), 561-8. Tait located a copy of this hitherto lost document in *Manchester Sessions, i*, ed. E. Axon (Rec. Soc. Lancashire & Cheshire, xlii, 1901), pp. xxiv-xxvii.

[25] *The Constitutional Documents of the Puritan Revolution*, ed. S.R. Gardiner (3rd edn, Oxford, 1906), pp. 99-103: declaration of sports re-issued 18 Oct. 1633. For the background to this action, see S.R. Gardiner, *History of England . . . 1603-1642* (2nd edn, London, 1883-4), iii. 248-52; vii. 318-23; *Vict. Cnty. Hist., Somerset*, ii (1911), 43-6; T.G. Barnes, "County Politics and a Puritan Cause Célèbre: Somerset Churchales, 1633", *Trans. Roy. Hist. Soc.*, 5th ser., ix (1959), 103-22; R.C. Richardson, "Puritanism and the Ecclesiastical Authorities", in *Politics, Religion and the English Civil War*, ed. B. Manning (London, 1973), pp. 15-16.

[26] Gardiner, *History*, vii. 322; C. Russell, *Parliaments and English Politics 1621-1629* (Oxford, 1979), pp. 96-7, 157, 183, 234, 276; *idem*, "The Parliamentary Career of John Pym, 1621-9", in *The Elizabethan Commonwealth*, ed. P. Clark *et al.* (Leicester, 1979), p. 152; *Commons Debates 1621*, ed. W. Notestein, *et al.* (New Haven, 1935), ii. 96; iii. 299; iv. 377-8.

[27] G.M. Trevelyan, *History of England* (3rd edn, London, 1945), p. 453. The two most thoughtful pieces of work are Hill, *Society, cap.* 5: "The Uses of Sabbatarianism"; and Collinson, "Beginnings". See also R.L. Greaves, "The Origins of English Sabbatarian Thought", *Sixteenth Cent. Jnl.*, xii (1981), 19-34; K.L. Sprunger, "English and Dutch Sabbatarianism and the Development of Puritan Social Theology (1600-1660)", *Church Hist.*,

Gardiner thought that one of the features of the Puritan Sabbath which was attractive to religious radicals was that it was incumbent upon them as individuals, not as members of any congregation. They could therefore observe the strict Sabbath quietly at home, and avoid any legal or social reprisals.[28] M.M. Knappen, the religious historian, saw the rise of Sabbatarianism as the natural result of a social need for orderly religion. In his view, the notion of a strict Sabbath worked its way up from the bottom and was in origin the medieval Catholic doctrine which had survived in Anglican teaching and religious legislation. Only in the seventeenth century, especially after the tragedy at the Paris Garden, did Sabbatarianism become a characteristically Puritan issue.[29]

A more dramatic explanation of popular support for Sabbatarianism concentrates on the economic utility of a regular day of rest. Margaret James was the pioneer of this approach more than half a century ago, and no doubt drew some measure of inspiration from Weber's remarks on the Protestant ethic. Margaret James noted that although Puritans were anxious to observe the day of rest with great severity, and though "religious exercises might be reserved for Sundays, the week was fully occupied in the work of economic salvation." The Puritan obsession with work was one of the reasons that they campaigned for the suppression of saints' days, which were economically unproductive. Parliament could therefore be assured of support from business interests when it passed an ordinance in 1647 abolishing festivals and declaring the second Tuesday in every month as an arbitrary secular holiday. The religious enthusiasm which had been distributed over a large number of festivals was now concentrated on the strict observance of the Sabbath.[30]

This economic approach to the Sabbath question was utilized by Dr Christopher Hill in his study of pre-revolutionary English society. Dr Hill argues that the Puritans promoted the Sabbath as a *regular* day of rest, in contrast to the haphazard hundred or so saints' days which were compatible with the agricultural society of medieval England. The newly emerg-

---

li (1982), 24-38; K.L. Parker, "Thomas Rogers and the English Sabbath: The Case for a Reappraisal", *Church Hist.*, liii (1984), 332-47 and his 1984 Cambridge Univ. Ph.D. thesis, "The English Sabbath, 1558-1649", which unfortunately could not be consulted until this book was already written. An older work, still useful, is M. Levy, *Der Sabbath in England* (Leipzig, 1933). More generally, see Wigley, *Victorian Sunday*. The writings on the subject are meticulously catalogued in R. Cox, *The Literature of the Sabbath Question* (Edinburgh, 1865). See also M. Weber, *The Protestant Ethic and the Spirit of Capitalism*, trans. T. Parsons (New York, 1958), p. 167.

[28] Gardiner, *History*, iii. 247.

[29] Knappen, *Puritanism*, pp. 447-9.

[30] Margaret James, *Social Problems and Policy During the Puritan Revolution* (London, 1930), pp. 9, 14-15, 21.

ing industrial society, on the other hand, required a more regular framework in order to develop further. The Puritan objection to saints' days,
then, was part of their general assault on the existing social and economic
order. Following Margaret James, Dr Hill notes that the fourth commandment also enjoins us to *work* on the remaining six days of the week; the Sabbath day was meant to be a day of recovery from a hard working week. Sunday sports would continue to be popular in the countryside, where the medieval agricultural life was still dominant. In the modern industrializing cities, however, the emphasis would be on Sunday rest. Soon, the Puritans
came to see this Sabbath day of rest as a time for religious edification, and
began to argue that *rest* days should be deducted from ordinary work days,
as would be done in the legislation of 1647 which created the Tuesday secular holidays. Generally, then, Hill claims, we should see the Puritan attack
on Sunday sports as an attempt to impose the ethos of an urban civiliza-
tion, particularly the new concern for labour discipline, on the whole
realm, especially its dark corners. The Crown here again supported the
economically backward areas of the country, which would be Royalist in
the civil war, against the values of the "industrious sort of people".[31]

On this basis, Hill is able to explain why nothing like the English Sunday developed in other Calvinist countries. Hill argues that the answer is
to be sought in the peculiar features of economic and social development
in England, where an industrial and urban way of life was established on
a national scale earlier than elsewhere. The "industrious sort of people",
the early capitalists, required a new ethos and protection from overwork,
which they could obtain by championing the Sabbath as a day of rest. The
monarchy and the medieval landed ruling class, however, encouraged traditional sports as a harmless occupation for idle agricultural workers. In
Dr Hill's view, the Bible had little influence on the creation of strict Sabbatarianism, which derived from the pressures and demands of society, only
afterwards justified by an apposite biblical text. "There were plenty of
Bibliolators among the Puritan Sabbatarians;" Dr Hill explains, "but
there was also a rational case for the Sunday rest. It was the habit of the
age to find Biblical texts to justify men in doing what they would have done
even if no texts could be found."[32]

Yet certainly not all biblical interpretation was utilitarian. As is often the
case, one finds the most sensible approach in the writings of unfashionable
classic authors. J.R. Tanner, writing about James I's Book of Sports, insisted that the Sabbatarian controversy is "vastly more important than it
appears at first sight. The fundamental conflict was after all between those

---

[31] Hill, *Society, cap.* 5, *passim.*
[32] *Ibid.*, esp. pp. 146, 159, 167, 172, 209, 213, 216.

who contended for the exclusive authority of the Bible and those who contended for the co-ordinate authority of the Church." This debate, Tanner continues, was part of the controversy which included the question of whether the Church might institute ceremonies not mentioned in the Bible, provided they were not contrary to the spirit of the law. It was only another application of their principle when the Puritans claimed for Sunday the characteristics of the Jewish Sabbath.[33] So too Gardiner emphasized the biblical origins of the Puritan's strict Sabbath observance: "The precepts of the Fourth Commandment were, according to his interpretation, of perpetual obligation. The Christian Lord's Day was but the Jewish Sabbath, and it was the duty of Christian magistrates to enforce its strict observance." The opponents of the strict Sabbath, on the other hand, argued that the Christian Sunday was a human rather than a divine institution, handed down by oldest Church tradition, and that therefore the Church was free to determine the exact form of its observance.[34]

II

Tanner and Gardiner bring us back again to the Old Testament and the second part of the fourth commandment. If, as they argue, the Sabbath question was primarily religious in nature, why have historians consistently revealed a blind spot towards the most radical of Sabbatarians, those who followed the commandment to the letter of the law and observed God's holy Sabbath on the seventh day, on Saturday? James I noted with distaste that "all such kind of people . . . encline to a kind of Judaism".[35] Indeed, the determination of the time of Sabbath observance was not a dilemma that began with the Puritans in seventeenth-century England. Only about one hundred years after Jesus made his dramatic declaration that the "sabbath was made for man, and not man for the sabbath", Christians began using the expression "Lord's Day" as their exclusive designation for Sunday.[36] Certainly by the fourth century the Sabbath was no longer observed on Saturday in accordance with Jewish law, but had been transferred to Sunday, perhaps in commemoration of the Resurrection, but more likely as a means of distinguishing Christians from Jews.[37]

---

[33] *Constitutional Documents of the Reign of James I*, ed. J.R. Tanner (Cambridge, 1930), p. 49.
[34] Gardiner, *History*, vii. 318-19.
[35] Tait, "Declaration", p. 565. Dr Hill claims that it is especially in "the fierce discussions as to whether God intended Saturday or Sunday to be observed as the day of rest" that an element of "mere irrational Bibliolatry" enters into the Sabbath question: *Society*, p. 146.
[36] Mark ii. 27.
[37] Bacchiocchi, *Sabbath*, p. 17.

We need to pay careful attention to the important distinction between the acceptance of the Church's institution of Sunday as the Sabbath day and the belief in the continuing existence of a morally binding Sabbath. As we shall see, many churchmen and indeed less educated practitioners of the Christian faith were quite willing to accept the second principle, while finding no conclusive scriptural authority for the first. Most of these, like Archbishop Whitgift, who recognized that the Sunday-Sabbath had been "appointed by the Church", would nevertheless concur with him that "that which the church hath once determined, and by long continuance proved to be necessary" should not be altered without great consideration.[38]

Another official expression of disapproval of the Saturday-Sabbath and the devotion to Jewish law which seemed to underlie it can be found in the Book of Homilies. The homily "of the place and time of prayer" faces squarely the two related questions regarding the nature and the timing of the Sabbath, attempts to answer them, and by an almost occult assertion of the validity of Sunday worship seems to resolve the entire issue. The quotation from the fourth commandment is in itself crucially selective: "*Remember*, saith God, *that thou keep holy the Sabbath day*." God's definition of that day as the seventh has gone completely. The mode of keeping the day holy is also considered:

> And, albeit this Commandment of God doth not bind Christian people so straitly to observe and keep the utter ceremonies of the Sabbath day as it was given unto the Jews, as touching the forbearing of work and labour in time of great necessity, and as touching the precise keeping of the seventh day after the manner of the Jews; (for we keep now the first day, which is our Sunday, and make that our Sabbath, that is, our day of rest, in the honour of our Saviour Christ, who as upon that day rose from death, conquering the same most triumphantly;) yet, notwithstanding, whatsoever is found in the Commandment appertaining to the law of nature, as a thing most godly, most just, and needful for the setting forth of God's glory, it ought to be retained and kept of all good Christian people.

The homily goes on to discuss the implications of this principle, and parenthetically returns several times to the assertion of "the Christian Sabbath day, which is the Sunday". Afterwards the rationale and history of the alteration of the letter of God's most holy commandments is given. Two New Testament references follow, and the assurance that "Sithence which time God's people hath always in all ages without any gainsaying used to come together upon the Sunday".[39]

---

[38] Whitgift, *Works*, i. 200-2.
[39] *The Two Books of Homilies*, ed. J. Griffiths (Oxford, 1859), pp. 339-51, esp. pp. 339-41. The biblical citations were to I Cor. xvi. 2; Rev. i. 10.

As might be expected, such bland assurances from the Church were not uncritically accepted. At some point during Elizabeth's reign, "a sermon was now preached at Cambridge *ad clerum* by one John Smith, M.A. venting therein a doctrine for keeping the Christian sabbath according to the law and practice of the Jews." According to John Strype, since this doctrine was "new to many of the scholars that heard him, he was informed against to the vice-chancellor and heads."[40] In the Dedham classis, one of the first organized cells of the Presbyterian movement during the reign of Elizabeth, the question came up for discussion several times, and could not be satisfactorily resolved. Henry Sands, a local minister, proclaimed "That ther is a Sabboth I do alsoe frely confesse; that the churche is at liberty to change the day, although I professe myself ready to be informed yet me thinkes yt wch is said doth not satisfy me." Sands thought that the strongest part of the Church's argument for altering the day of the Sabbath was that Sunday commemorated Christ's resurrection: this is why Sunday, "this daie wch we now hold hath his especiall name thapostles themselues putting it upon it and is called the lordes day".[41] As Sands suggests, the very religious name of Sunday was also controversial. Many moderate churchmen worried that even the use of the term "Sabbath" would imply agreement with a strict interpretation of the fourth commandment and all that went with such a view. They insisted on the exclusive use of the term "Lord's Day" as much less problematic. This can be seen quite clearly in the drafting of the Sabbath bill during the parliament of 1601: the original text of one of the bills emphatically used the word "Sabbath" throughout, but when it returned from committee, the word was everywhere deleted and "Sunday" inserted in its place.[42]

This dilemma of the inconvenient text of the fourth commandment clearly continued to trouble the Bible-worshippers of these years. Churchmen had little choice but to find more convincing explanations for the change in day when parish officials like those in the church of St Nicholas at Warwick painted the actual text of the Ten Commandments on the wall in 1582.[43] Some of this confusion is even apparent in the treatises of the proponents of the strict Sabbath. Nicholas Bownde, for example, stressed that we are enjoined to observe the seventh day as a Sabbath, presumably any day in seven, but was reduced to arguing that the Sabbath itself was a divine rather than specifically Jewish institution, "nay, that it was 2000.

---

[40] John Strype, *Annals of the Reformation* (Oxford, 1824), iii. 495-6.
[41] *The Presbyterian Movement in the Reign of Queen Elizabeth as illustrated by the Minute Book of the Dedham Classis 1582-1589*, ed. R.G. Usher (Camden Soc., 3rd ser., viii, 1905), pp. xlvi, 75.
[42] Neale, *Parliaments*, ii. 395. The disagreement over the use of the term "Sabbath" continues throughout the period: see, e.g., below, n. 63.
[43] *Vict. Cnty. Hist., Warwick, viii* (1969), p. 531.

yeeres and more, before euer they were a people''. Bownde agreed that the
Jewish and Christian Sabbaths were very similar, however:

> Wherein though wee differ from them in the limitation of this day, both the
> beginning and ending of it: we holding that it beginneth not at the evening,
> but at the morning, according to the time of Christs resurrection, which
> brought in this day . . . yet they agree with vs in this, that an whole day ought
> to bee sanctified, consisting of 24. houres, when they say, from euening to
> euening.[44]

So too did John Dod and Robert Cleaver, the high-priests of Jacobean
Sabbatarianism, ask provocatively, ''For, goe through the whole Commandement; what one word in all of it hath any note of ceremony? what
reason sauours of any speciall thing to the Iewes, that the Commandement
should be tied onely to them?''[45]

The promulgation of the Book of Sports in 1618 only intensified the general Sabbatarian debate and with it the problem of justifying Sunday as
the day to observe the word of God in all its Mosaic rigour, for one could
hardly obey one part of the commandment with uncompromising strict-
ness while altering the other part completely. The first attempt to eliminate this ambiguity in a dramatic and highly public way was that of John
Traske (1585-1636), the famous Jacobean Judaizer, whose story has been
told at length elsewhere. By the beginning of 1618, Traske and his sect of
Judaizing Saturday-observers could no longer be ignored, even though the
king seemed to be rather more amused than incensed at Traske's well-
known practices. He was sentenced in Star Chamber on 19 June 1618 to
be kept close prisoner in the Fleet for the rest of his life, given a monetary
fine of unpayable proportions, and was finally whipped across London,

---

[44] Nicholas Bovvnd, *Sabbathum Veteris et Novi Testamenti* (London, 1606), sig. A^r; pp. 36,
103, 110, 120, 372. Later on, see Daniel Cawdrey & Herbert Palmer, *Sabbatum Redivivum:
or the Christian Sabbath Vindicated* (London, 1645), p. 68; [Anon.], *The Doctrine of the Sabbath*
(London, 1650); William Pynchon, *The Time when the First Sabbath was Ordained* (London,
1654), p. 85; William Prynne, *A Briefe Polemicall Dissertation . . . of the Lords Day-Sabbath* (London, 1655), pp. 64-7, 94-7, written twenty years before while imprisoned in the Tower (sig.
A2^r). Milton argued that although God hallowed the seventh day of Creation, the Sabbath itself was not instituted before the giving of the law to Moses; this Judaic rule was
revoked with the rest of the Judaic law and no particular day put in its place: W.R. Parker,
Milton (Oxford, 1968), p. 492. So too did Robinson Crusoe "set apart every seventh day
for a Sabbath; though I found at the end of my account I had lost a day or two in my reckoning." (Penguin edn, Harmondworth, 1965), p. 117. Thomas Edwards, *Gangraena* (2nd edn,
London, 1646), p. 30 thought this view to be mistaken. As for the use by Christians of the
Judaic notion that the Sabbath begins on the previous eve, cf. Boccaccio's bogus holy man
who could only find to confess that "I recall that I once failed to show a proper respect
for the Holy Sabbath, by making one of my servants sweep the house after nones on a Saturday": *Decameron*, trans. G.H. McWilliam (Penguin edn, Harmondsworth, 1972), p. 77.
[45] Iohn Dod & Robert Cleauer, *A Plaine and Familiar Exposition of the Ten Commandments*
(London, 1615), p. 126: the same quotation appears on p. 62^v of the 1603 edn.

branded in the forehead with the letter J, and nailed to the pillory by his ears. Traske recovered, renounced the open observance of the Saturday-Sabbath, and eventually joined the Baptist Church led by Henry Jessey, who in many ways was the central figure of Saturday-Sabbatarianism, as will be seen in the next chapter. One of Traske's followers seems to have converted to Judaism in Amsterdam.[46]

But the silencing of Traske and his little band by no means put an end to those who were willing to cut the Gordian knot of biblical fidelity, or who were brave enough to air their doubts in public. Indeed, the local historian of early seventeenth-century Gloucestershire tells us that the only instance in which heterodoxy affected town government was a dispute in 1620 over the meaning of the fourth commandment. Three men were removed as burgesses because they refused to "acknowledge the fourth commandment to be a perpetual moral law of God, and the Christian Sabbath or Lord's Day to be God's holy ordinance, and that it is not in man's power to alter the number of one day in seven for a Sabbath to any other proportion of time." The Council of Wales insisted that the men appear before High Commission; later they made public recantations and only then were restored as burgesses.[47]

Apart from reminding Englishmen about the existence of contemporary Jewry, men like the Traskites were also important in providing a public warning for the authorities of what might happen if the problems of the moral character of the fourth commandment and the time for Sabbath observance were left unresolved. A bill for regulating Sabbath observance progressed unimpeded in the parliament of 1621, except for the protestations of John Shepherd, who was regarded as being of Roman Catholic sympathies. "He was censured to be cast out of the House as an unworthy member", noted a fellow parliamentarian, "and so he was." Wallace Notestein reminds us that the "punishment of Shepherd was a parliamentary gesture against the opinions of the Sabbatarians, particularly the Traskites whose doctrines had caused recent excitement and were to influence the amending of this very bill against which Shepherd spoke." In the Lords, the archbishop of Canterbury affirmed that

> we desyre the title may be altred to the Lords day, for which we have good warrant. We desyere the word *Saboth* showld be left oute, because many of late times have runn to Judaisme, as somm have written for the very day; a booke

---

[46] See D.S. Katz, *Philo-Semitism and the Readmission of the Jews to England, 1603-1655* (Oxford, 1982), cap. 1.

[47] W.B. Willcox, *Gloucestershire: A Study in Local Government 1590-1640* (New Haven, 1940), p. 220n.

or two ther is lately sett forth of the Jewes ruleing over the world, etc. For the suppressing of this we desyre this name to be taken away.[48]

John Pym the parliamentary firebrand gave his maiden speech regarding this case, and recorded in his diary that as far as the Sabbath bill was concerned,

> To the body of which there was noe Exception but only to the word Sabboth in the Tytle. The Reasons whereof were declared by the Arch Bishopp, First the aptness of divers to Enclyne to Judaisme as the newe sect of the Thraskites and other oppinionists concerninge the terrene Kingdome of the Jewes. That therefore their desire was that it might be called the Lords daie.[49]

Shepherd's criticism of the Sabbath bill was directed at the strict observance of Sunday: he pointed out in the course of his objection that the Sabbath was Saturday and that David had danced before the ark of the Lord on that day.[50] When Mandeville spoke in favour of a similar bill in the parliament of 1625, he was careful to refer to it as the bill of Sunday.[51] But the problem of justifying both the moral nature of the fourth commandment and its removal to Sunday was well and truly out, and theologians applied themselves to resolving it, against a background of a small but persistent refusal to accept the assurances of the official Church on these points.

Such attempts were never totally convincing, and were sometimes even counter-productive. Thomas Broad of Oxford, for example, published a short pamphlet during the debate over the Sabbath bill in the parliament of 1621 designed to prove that "What God hath put asunder, let no man ioyne together, Lords day and seventh day". Yet his discussion of the point is more than a little ambiguous. He himself notes that were "it a law of this kingdome set forth long agone in these words: *Remember to fast vpó Thursday*; We in these times faring well vpon Thursday, & fasting vpó friday; . . . who hearing this, would not be much moved at the strangeness of the matter, & presently demand; How shall this be, seing the Statute speaketh of Thursday?" Later on, in an imaginary dialogue between a Christian and a Jew, Broad's Christian is reduced to the following argument:

---

[48] Notes by Sir Thomas Barrington for 24 May 1621: *Commons*, ed. Notestein, iii. 299. The book referred to is [Henry Finch], *The Worlds Great Restavration* (London, 1621): see Katz, *Philo-Semitism*, pp. 95-7. Generally, see *Commons*, ed. Notestein, ii. 96n.; Russell, *Parliaments*, pp. 96-7; J.P. Kenyon, *The Stuart Constitution* (Cambridge, 1966), p. 131; J.D. Eusden, *Puritans, Lawyers, and Politics in Early Seventeenth-Century England* (New Haven, 1958), p. 83.

[49] Pym's diary: *Commons*, ed. Notestein, iv. 377-8.

[50] *Ibid.*, ii. 82; iv. 52-3.

[51] Russell, *Parliaments*, p. 234.

The fourth Commandement is partly morall, & partly Ceremoniall or shadowish: the morall part bindeth to sanctifie one day of the weeke: the Ceremoniall or shadowish part bindeth to sanctifie the seauenth day only. Now
to sanctifie the seauenth day in obedience to the morall part, is tolerable: but
you keepe it in obedience to the shadowish part, for you take your selues
bound to sanctifie the seauenth day alone: and so you keeping the seauenth
day, obserue a shadow; whereas did we keep the same day, we should not;
for we would keepe it in obedience to the morall part: and then wee might
sanctifie the seauenth day, as well as any others

As the Jew remarks, "Had your Apostles taught such doctrine in the Synagogues, J beleeue our Rabbins would haue smiled at it". Indeed, either
Broad's work was meant to be satirical, or it may be that he himself imper-
fectly understood the doctrine of the Sabbath.[52]

A far safer, and perhaps more effective method of justifying the alteration of the Sabbath day by the Church was that of axiomatic postulation.
This was the plan of William Whately, who asserted in 1622 that in spite
of the text of the fourth commandment, in reality it "appoints the conse-
crating of a speciall time, *viz.* one day in seuen (without nominating any
date or time whence the computation must begin, for that must be knowne
to vs by some other meanes, and is a thing alterable, not vnalterably setled
by the commandement)".[53] So too did Peter Barker, a Dorsetshire preacher, condemn without demonstration "they which ouerkeepe it as the *Iewes*
which are too nice and too strickt in obseruing this day". He went on to
make the amusing claim that "the *Iewes* thought that on this day no body
might in publicke scratch where it itched".[54] Such arguments would hardly have laid any doubting minds to rest.

On the contrary, what one does find is a continuing thread of Saturday-
Sabbath murmurings, often accompanied by other Jewish practices. This
may be what lies behind the case of "James Whitehall, master of Arts of
Chirst-Church in Oxford" who "preached publickly in that University
many thinges tending to Judaisme". Whitehall was examined before both
the University authorities and High Commission and was finally imprisoned, but managed to escape to Ireland where he was incarcerated in Dublin Castle.[55] John Etherington, the London box-maker connected with the
Family of Love, was said to have held Saturday to be the Sabbath, but he

---

[52] Th. Broad, *Three Questions Ansvvered* (Oxford, 1621), pp. 9, 13, 16, 18-19, 27-33. For a
more successful attempt at justifying this position, see e.g. George Walker, *The Doctrine of
the Holy Weekly Sabbath* (London, 1641), pp. 79-80.
[53] William Whately, *A Pithie, Short, and Methodicall opening of the Ten Commandments* (London,
1622), pp. 87-8.
[54] Peter Barker, *A Iudicious and painefull Exposition vpon the ten Commandments* (London, 1624),
p. 174; *idem, A Learned and Familiar Exposition vpon the Ten Commandments* (2nd edn, London,
1633), pp. 226-7.
[55] n.d. (c. 1624): SP. 14/180, f. 101.

thought that all the other days of the week were the Sabbath as well.[56] Even Laud as bishop of London was not above turning the argument on its head. When John Vicars, a Lincolnshire conventicle-keeper, ''did preach and affirme it to be a sinne to receive the sacrament upon any other day than the Saboth-day'', Laud teased him that ''I am noe enimy to the word, but if you meane the Saboth day that is nowe in the newe testament, then your opinion is for receiving on our Satturday, for in all our returnes of lawe and statutes before the reformation the Satturday is called the Sabbath''. Laud suspended the vicar for seven years and deprived him of his living.[57] So too was Laud present when another minister was deprived of his benefice for having ''justifyed heere'' Traske and others, ''all lewd fellowes''.[58] Even more dramatically, when in the 1630s the churchwardens in Batcombe, Somerset painted on the wall of the church the verse, ''If thou turn away thy foot from the Sabbath'', Bishop Piers sent his chaplain to wash over the inscription, saying that a Jewish piece of Scripture should not be allowed in a Christian church.[59]

But of course it was Theophilus Brabourne (1590-1661) who, after Traske, did the most for propagating the belief in the Saturday-Sabbath in England before the outbreak of the civil war. Brabourne, a native of Norwich, the son of a Puritan hosier, began to write on the Saturday-Sabbath in 1628, but was not committed to prison until six years later. Brabourne appeared before Laud and High Commission, and was pronounced ''a Jew, a heretic and schismatic, and adjudged him worthy to be severely punished.'' During the Interregnum he was free to promote these doctrines once again, although he seems to have steered clear of the organized churches which observed the Saturday-Sabbath. After the Restoration he wrote several pamphlets concerning liberty of conscience, while upholding the royal supremacy in religious affairs. Some of Traske's followers may have migrated to Brabourne's circle of acquaintances after 1636, but in any case in contemporary minds the two men were inextricably linked. As Peter Heylyn the royalist hisorian of the Sabbath wrote, ''their Opinions, so farre as it concerned the *Sabbath*, were the very same; they onely making the conclusions, which of necessitie must follow from the former premisses''.[60]

---

[56] Stephen Denison, *The White Wolfe* (London, 1627), pp. 54-64; A. Hamilton, *The Family of Love* (Cambridge, 1981), pp. 136-7.

[57] *Reports of Cases in the Courts of Star Chamber and High Commission*, ed. S.R. Gardiner (Camden Soc., n.s., xxxix, 1886), pp. 202, 236, 238: the case came up in Nov. 1631.

[58] *Ibid.*, pp. 320-1: case agst. John Etsall in High Commission, 21 June 1632.

[59] *Vict. Cnty. Hist., Somerset, ii* (1911), p. 43: from a petition of Bastwick, Burton and Prynne to Charles I complaining about Bishop Piers. The offending quotation is from Isa. lviii. 13-14.

[60] Heylyn, *History*, pp. 259-60. On Brabourne, see Katz, *Philo-Semitism*, pp. 34-8.

By Brabourne's time, then, the practice of the Saturday-Sabbath had become a recognized element in the debates over the true meaning of that day. After the re-issue by Charles I of his father's controversial Book of Sports in 1633, it seemed to many that the debate itself had gone rather out of control. Robert Cleaver, one of the most prominent of Sabbatarian theorists, pleaded that he would "humbly intreate both *you*, and all other *good Readers*, not to regard the *Sabbath* the lesse, because there is *contention* about it."[61] John Prideaux's old Latin sermon on the doctrine of the Sabbath was also dusted off and published in England after the Book of Sports, with the aim of disposing of those "who either seeme to tend, on the one side to *Atheisme*, or on the other side to *Iudaisme*". Prideaux thought that "some men most *superstitiously* perswaded" cited the Old Testament texts in favour of strict Sabbath observance and only had the effect of restricting Christian liberty and charity unnecessarily. Even Hebrew and other etymologies were brought to bear to make the point, Prideaux lamented, a practice he thought superfluous: the Hebrew word for the Sabbath might be fancifully derived from many supposed origins, "nor last of all, from any foule disease in the privie parts, by the Ægyptians called Sabba". The chief aim, Prideaux asserted, was to free ourselves from "the Toyles of Iudaisme".[62]

Even in the last few years before the Civil War, the terms of the objections to the Saturday-Sabbath changed very little, and continued to be concerned primarily with the right of the Church to alter the day of worship, and the validity of the use of the term "Sabbath" for Sunday.[63] By that time the objections to the strict observance of Sunday had acquired much greater force and were already a recognized weapon in the dogmatic arsenal against the Puritans. Robert Sanderson's work of 1636, meant to clear up questions of Sabbatarian doctrine, repeated the view that the Apostles used "to celebrate their holy Assemblies the first Day of the weeke in honour of Christ and his Resurrection". One reason for their practice, he asserted, was "for avoiding of Iudaisme". In any case, the

---

[61] Robert Cleaver, *A Declaration of the Christian Sabbath* (2nd edn, London, 1630), sig. A4ᵛ.

[62] [John] Prideavx, *The Doctrine of the Sabbath* (London, 1634), pp. 2-15, 19, 24, 30, 32, 35, 41. R. Cox, *Literature*, i. 164 notes that the translator was Peter Heylyn who sought support for the Book of Sports, and at the same time hoped to do damage to his old rival Prideaux in the eyes of the Puritans. Prideaux's original Latin work was said to have been "Delivered in the Act at *Oxon. Anno*, 1622", but according to William Twisse, *Of the Morality of the Fourth Commandement* (London, 1641), sig. Crʳ (1st ser.), it "was neither delivered (as I am perswaded) by word of mouth, nor afterwards set forth in print" until it finally appeared in English in 1634. Twisse's book was an extended rebuttal to Prideaux.

[63] The final official word was had in the Directory for Public Worship, 4 Jan. 1644-5, meant to replace the Book of Common Prayer, which ruled that the Lord's Day "is to be celebrated as holy to the Lord . . . as being the Christian Sabbath": *Acts and Ordinances*, ed. Firth & Rait, i. 598-9.

Christian Sabbath had been celebrated for so many centuries on the first day of the week that it would be unwise to change it now, "not to dispute what she may or may not do *ex plenitudine potestatis*". As for the use of the term "Sabbath" for Sunday, although objections might be made to it, Sanderson thought, those who favoured it "(otherwise sober and moderate) ought not to be censured with too much severity, nor charged with Iudaisme, if sometimes they so use it."[64] For John Pocklington, sometime president of Sidney Sussex College, Cambridge, admitting the very use of the Judaic term Sabbath was to concur with the entire range of Sabbatarian vices: "For this name *Sabbath* is not a bare name, like a spot in their foreheads to know *Labans* sheepe from *Jacobs*; but . . . allow them but their *Sabbath*, and you must allow them the service that belongs to their *Shabbath.*" Pocklington clarified this last point as well: "What Service then must you allow them for their Sabbath? Why nothing but preaching."[65] This was the sort of line taken by Christopher Dow, who worried that "men may not be deceived with shewes, and mistake Iudaisme for Christianity". The Sabbatarians, he argued, little realized the implications of their emphasis on the morality of the fourth commandment, as "they unawares bring in *Iudaisme.*" This was not a polemical point, Dow thought, but "is generally confessed by all, whom the heresie of *Iudaisme* hath not infected". But of course, as Henry Burton the collector of divine judgements noted wryly, the books of these authors, "though they condemne the very name of Sabbath, as Iewish, yet they are all characterised with that name and title."[66]

Perhaps even more worrying than the views expressed was the belief that too much unlicensed discussion would cast unnecessary doubt on accepted teaching. George Vernon writes in his biography of Dr Peter Heylyn, the Royalist historian, that Charles I specially commanded the scholar to produce the ultimate history of the Sabbath question which would silence all critics from both sides of the religious spectrum. Vernon writes that Hey-

---

[64] Robert Sanderson, *A Soveraigne Antidote Against Sabbatarian Errovrs* (London, 1636), pp. 5-8, 20-1.

[65] John Pocklington, *Sunday No Sabbath* (London, 1636), pp. 6-7, 11, 12, 16. In 1641, Pocklington was ordered to appear before the Commons sub-committee on religion to "answer the exhorbitancys of his booke"; others connected with its publication were also sent for: *Proceedings . . . with the Parliaments Called in 1640, and especially with the Committee of Religion*, ed. L.B. Larking (Camden Soc., 1st ser., lxxx, 1862), pp. 83, 84, 95. Pocklington was also condemned by Henry Burton, *A Divine Tragedie* (n.p., 1641), p. 27.

[66] Christopher Dow, *A Discovrse of the Sabbath and the Lords Day* (2nd edn, London, 1636), pp. 1, 17, 25; Burton, *Tragedie*, sig. A3ʳn. Cf. John Collinges, *Responsoria ad Erratica Piscatoris* (London, 1653), p. 88. For more on Burton and other examples of "warning literature", see L.B. Wright, *Middle-Class Culture in Elizabethan England* (2nd edn, Ithaca, N.Y., 1958), pp. 459-63. The classic of the genre was Thomas Beard, *The Theatre of Gods Iudgements* (London, 1597).

lyn finished the two-volume work of nearly five hundred pages within less than four months, and put out a second edition three months later.[67] Heylyn's work is indeed an impressive effort, despite a certain tendency to use his learning in order to confuse simple objections to his theories. The point, Heylyn asserted, is that the Christian Lord's Day and the Jewish Sabbath are two completely different institutions: "that the *Lords day is not founded on divine Commandement, but the authority of the Church:* it is a point so universally resolved on, as no one thing more". In Heylyn's view, the two began to be connected about the eleventh century:

> Indeed the marvaile is the lesse, that these and such like *Iewish-fancies*, should, in those times beginne to shew themselves, in the Christian Church: considering that now some had begunne to thinke, that the *Lords day* was founded on the fourth *Commandement*; and all observances of the same, grounded upon the *Law* of GOD. As long it was taken onely for an *Ecclesiasticall institution*, and had no other ground upon which to stand, than the authoritie of the *Church*; wee finde not any of these rigours annexed unto it. But being once conceived to have its warrant from the Scripture, the Scripture presently was ransacked; and whatsoever did concerne the old *Iewish Sabbath*, was applied thereto.

What was most distressing, Heylyn lamented, was that people should have becomes slaves not only to the strict observance of the Lord's Day in an almost biblical fashion, but that some should have taken the fourth commandment as purely moral and applying literally to them. "Of these," he noted, "one *Traske* declared himselfe, for such, in King *Iames* his time; and therewithall tooke up another *Iewish* Doctrine, about Meates and Drinkes". For Saturday-Sabbatarians, as unto "so strange a bondage are the people brought, that, as before I said, a greater never was imposed on the *Iewes* themselves, what time the Consciences of that people were pinned most closely on the sleeves of the *Scribes* and *Pharises*."[68]

---

[67] George Vernon, *The Life of . . . Dr. Peter Heylyn* (London, 1682), p. 88.

[68] Heylyn, *History*, i. 25-7, 73; ii. 163-4, 185, 256, 259-60. Heylyn was gracious enough to acknowledge that as for the Jewish practice regarding manna on the Sabbath, "I must ingenuously confesse my selfe obliged to *Theophilus Braborne*, the first that ever looked so neare into *Moses* meaning", to which Hamon L'Estrange, *Gods Sabbath* (Cambridge, 1641), p. 25 would add "that in Optiks, amongst other requisites to perfect discerning, *justa distantia*, a fit distance, is one; and Mʳ Brabourn might perhaps by looking too near see to little". Among those who seem to be drawing on Heylyn are George Hakewill, *A Short, But Cleare, Discovrse, of the Lords-Day* (London, 1641), esp. pp. 20, 37-8; John Bramhall, *The Controversies About the Sabbath* (Dublin, 1677), pp. 907 (blaming Brabourne), 910, 916, 917 (citing White and Brerewood), 918, 928-9, 934; W[illiam] G[ouge], *The Sabbaths Sanctification* (London, 1641), sig. A2ʳ⁻ᵛ; pp. 23-5, 33-4; Iohn Lavvson, *For the Sabbath* (London, 1644), pp. 2-3; Geo. Baitman, *The Arovv of the Almighty* (London, 1653), pp. 32-7, 40. Selden even denied that others of the Ten Commandments applied to Christians as well as to Jews: *Table Talk of John Selden*, ed. F. Pollock (London, 1627), p. 123.

By the time Heylyn wrote his comprehensive history of the Sabbath, however, the validity of the seventh-day Sabbath was already an idea that had taken root in the fertile soil of the English religious landscape during this period. For in that year Henry Jessey the pioneer of English Baptism was appointed pastor of the Jacob Church, the mother church of the Baptist movement and of the English semi-separatist tradition. And Henry Jessey observed the Sabbath on Saturday. His adoption of that straightforward understanding of the fourth commandment would be crucial for the later development of Saturday-Sabbatarianism into an organized religious sect during the period of the civil war. Jessey's own interests in Hebrew, biblical studies, contemporary Jewry, millenarianism, and in the Baptist movement itself ensured that these would be the controlling themes of Saturday-Sabbatarianism as a whole even after the Restoration.

CHAPTER TWO

THE CASE OF THE FALSE JEW AND AFTER

Belief in the Saturday-Sabbath is as old as the Jews, and as we have seen, entered into English Protestant thought soon after the Reformation. Most of the early practitioners of the seventh-day Sabbath, however, tended to be rather isolated figures, lacking in supporters and persecuted by the church authorities who found their mode of religious observance to be wholly objectionable. Even John Traske, who did command a certain number of followers and did attract widespread attention, was important for the issues of Sabbath observing and Judaising that he raised, rather than for any genuine threat that his beleaguered sect imposed. But we do know that the idea of the seventh-day Sabbath eventually does become institutionalized in a Restoration sect; what needs to be done is to complete the lines leading into that non-conformist fellowship from its earliest antecedents, and away from them as well, to determine if a genuine personal link can be found to more modern groups such as the Seventh-Day Adventists and other Fundamentalist denominations. For it is not enough merely to show that someone, somewhere had similar ideas about the Sabbath; the historical influence of these beliefs can only be demonstrated either through direct personal contact or by testimony relating the expression of the idea to its eventual implementation. At the same time, such a search often becomes ends-oriented in such a way that it takes on the worst characteristics of Whig history, isolating those elements in the story which in some way "contributed" to the final design, as if only that final destination could have been reached.

But all this having been said, there definitely *is* a prehistory of the Saturday-Sabbatarian movement, a boiling pot of ideas from which the emerging institutions established their controlling ideologies. Very clearly, the first Seventh-Day men of this group were Baptists, and it is to the beginnings of that movement that we need to go when looking for the evolution of the Saturday-Sabbatarians in England. The most influential founder of the English Baptists, Henry Jessey, was himself a Seventh-Day man:

> As for what he held (in his latter days) concerning the seventh day Sabbath, to be kept by Christians Evangelically; without Jewish Services or Ceremonies he managed his Judgment and practice therein with great caution; that there might be no offence or breaches among Professours; for at first for some considerable time, (near two years) he kept his opinion much to himself, and then afterwards (when he had communicated it to others) he observed the

day in his own Chamber, with only 4 or 5 more of the same mind, and on the first day of the week he preached, and met publickly and privately as before.

One of these men may have been John Traske the notorious Jacobean Judaiser, who was a member of the flock which Jessey led. Jessey even believed that "the Lords *Sabbaths* begins on the *Evening* before", in Jewish fashion. Jessey was careful to keep this aspect of his private belief concealed from most of his followers so as to avoid yet another split in the already fragmenting world of the gathered churches in London.[1] Jessey would have preferred to leave the thorny theological question of the Sabbath for some very future discussion, but was unable to keep quiet the erratic and even bizarre career of Thomas Tillam, who left the organized Baptist Church after being duped by a fraudulent convert in the north of England where Tillam had been sent as a Baptist missionary. Tillam eventually led a group of followers to the Continent where he established communal settlements devoted to the exaltation of the Saturday-Sabbath and the keeping of the Ten Commandments in their entirety.

Tillam's decision to forsake a society that defiled the word of God had a great effect on all those associated with him. The Baptists were ridiculed out of the north, which was largely lost in this period to the Quakers. Henry Jessey himself, a man with very numerous contacts with Jews and an ardent millenarian, never revealed publicly his devotion to the Saturday-Sabbath and thus denied the doctrine the respectability which it dearly needed.[2] Most importantly for the other Seventh-Day men who made the Saturday-Sabbath their creed, Thomas Tillam and the Case of the False Jew was a calumny that they were never allowed to forget, and which seemed to link them inextricably with fanatics of every undesirable variety.

I

Tillam's early life remains obscure. He has been claimed to have been of Jewish extraction, although no evidence for this exists.[3] Tillam avowed himself to have been originally a Roman Catholic, and to have travelled on the Continent.[4] Like Oliver Cromwell himself and many other Englishmen during the years of extreme political and economic hardship in the 1620s and 1630s, Tillam had looked towards the New World and the possi-

---

[1] D.S. Katz, *Philo-Semitism and the Readmission of the Jews to England, 1603-1655* (Oxford, 1982), pp. 32-3.

[2] See generally, D.S. Katz, "Menasseh ben Israel's Christian Connection: Henry Jessey and the Jews", in *Menasseh ben Israel and his World*, ed. R.H. Popkin *et al.* (forthcoming).

[3] W.T. Whitley, "The Rev. Colonel Paul Hobson", *Bap. Qly.*, ix (1938-9), 307.

[4] See below, p. 28.

bility of migration. He arrived in America on 29 June 1638 and commemorated his freedom with a poem "Uppon the first sight of New-England" which still appears in anthologies of early American verse.[5]

Tillam returned to England during the 1640s, and eventually became a member of the Baptist church in London under the leadership of Hanserd Knollys, the man who had baptized Henry Jessey. Tillam seems to have distinguished himself in this society, for by the end of 1651 he was selected by his church to be their "messenger", a minister of the gospel, in the town of Hexham, about twelve miles up the Tyne from Newcastle.[6] "In the name of the Lord Christ, I came to Hexham the 27th day of [December] 1651," he explained, "and so wonderfully hath God appeared in this dark corner, that . . . a living temple began of these living stones". Thereupon follows in the church records a list of eleven men and five women to whom "Thomas Tillam, minister, and a messenger of one of the seven [Baptist] churches in London, did administer the holy ordinance of baptism."[7]

Tillam's task was not only to found a Baptist church in this Northumberland town, but also to spread more general Puritan light into a "dark corner of the land". To this end, he was appointed to one of the Puritan lectureships which had been established during the dark days of piecemeal subversion against the Established Church. In 1625, a member of the Mercers' Company in London had bequeathed a large sum of money for the purpose of buying church livings in some "northern county or counties of this land, where . . . most want of preaching of the word of God [was found] to be." The pious merchant warned his executors, "for God's sake . . . be very careful from time to time to make choice of such as be well known to be honest, discreet, learned men, fearing God, and painful in their ministry, that by their life and doctrine they may win souls to Christ Jesus."[8] This lucrative lectureship, which seems to have been worth about £80 a year, was in the gift of the parliamentary Commission for the Propa-

[5] Autograph MS., Mass. Hist. Soc., Davis Papers, I, 15: repr. H.S. Jantz, *The First Century of New England Verse* (N.Y., 1962), p. 115 & *Seventeenth-Century American Poetry*, ed. H.T. Meserole (Garden City, N.Y., 1968), pp. 397-8. Several other poems by Tillam appeared in print: Thomas Tillam, *The Seventh-Day Sabbath Sought out and celebrated* (London, 1657); Samuel Hutchinson, *A Declaration of a Future Glorious Estate* (London, 1667), pp. 3, 18-19. On this basis, Tilliam is referred to as "an early pioneer of hymn-singing" in I. Mallard, "The Hymns of Katherine Sutton", *Bap. Qly.*, xx (1963-4), 24.

[6] J.F.V. Nicholson, "The Office of 'Messenger' amongst British Baptists in the Seventeenth and Eighteenth Centuries", *Bap. Qly.*, xvii (1957-8), 209-10.

[7] Hexham Church Book: repr. *Records of the Churches of Christ, gathered at Fenstanton, Warboys, and Hexham, 1644-1720* (Hanserd Knollys Soc., 1854), pp. 289-90.

[8] Will of Richard Fishborn, 30 Mar. 1625: J. Wallis, *The Natural History and Antiquities of Northumberland* (London, 1769), ii. 99-100.

gation of the Gospel in the Northern Counties.[9] So Tillam enjoyed this more formal support which gave substance to his role as messenger from Knollys's Baptist church in Coleman Street.

Tillam published an exposition of the eleventh chapter of the book of Revelation at the time of his appointment to the post in Hexham which shows him to have held unequivocally millenarian views, especially with regard to the Jewish people. Tillam prophesied that at the end of days "the Jews (the Kings of the East)" would return to the Holy Land, where they would come under attack from "these great Enemies, Turk, Pope, &c. that have so long kept the poor Jews in slavery". The Jews in the Holy Land, "this poor distressed unarmed people", trapped and surrounded with no hope of escape, await the slaughter, when suddenly "up stands *Michael* the great glorious Prince, discomfits this great and mighty Host, and delivers his distressed ancient people out of their hands". Tillam's emphasis on the part to be played by the Jews in the final cosmic drama was more marked than in conventional millenarian prophecies and foreshadows his later Mosaic interest.[10]

Despite this promising start, by March 1653 certain reservations were being openly expressed in London about the suitability of Mr. Tillam to be a Baptist pioneer in the north. When the Hexham Baptists asked that Tillam be promoted to full pastor, the Baptist divines of Coleman Street showed themselves unwilling to support his interests any longer. They stressed that Tillam had only been appointed "messenger", and even that solely on the basis of "that little knowledge we had of him whilst he was with us". Meanwhile, the Coleman Street church promised to be ready to help in any further way, "especially when our brother Tillam hath given us an answer to our letter, that we have now sent to him, concerning our judgment of our brethren's charge of Newcastle against him, and his answers thereto."[11]

By March 1653, then, Tillam was already under attack from the neighbouring Baptist church at Newcastle, which may have had cause to resent the spectacle of a newcomer reaping the fruits of their spiritual labour. The congregation at Newcastle seems to have become organized sometime between the garrisoning of the town by the army in 1649 and the establishment of Tillam's church at the end of 1651. The presence of the army was

---

[9] A.B. Hinds, *A History of Northumberland, III. Hexhamshire*, Part I (Newcastle & London, 1896), p. 167. See generally C. Hill, "Puritans and 'the Dark Corners of the Land'", *Trans. Roy. Hist. Soc.*, 5th ser., xiii (1963), 77-102; rev. version repr. in his *Change and Continuity in Seventeenth-Century England* (London, 1974), pp. 3-47.

[10] Thomas Tillam, *The Two Witnesses* (London, 1651), title p.; sig. A3^r; pp. 69-70, 135-6.

[11] Coleman St. to Hexham, 24 Mar. 1653: *Records*, pp. 319-21, signed by eight church members, Knollys not among them.

essential to its foundation, for Newcastle was notoriously backward in religious matters, and had hardly felt the influence of Puritanism before the Civil War. But among those stationed with the army in Newcastle were a number of Baptists, including Colonel Robert Lilburne the governor of the town, and Colonel Paul Hobson his deputy. By the time Tillam arrived in the north, the Newcastle Baptists were well established, and enjoyed the leadership of their minister Captain Thomas Gower.[12] During the Protectorate, they were permitted by the ministers of the town to meet at the chapel of St Thomas on Tyne Bridge, and were allowed to worship undisturbed.[13] Relations between the Baptists of Hexham and Newcastle were therefore strained at the best of times, but the summer of 1653 proved to be much more troublesome, and indeed it was the decisive moment in Thomas Tillam's life. The church book of the Hexham congregation recalled the events of that summer succinctly:

> [4 June 1653], a child of the devil came from Rome to ruin this church, and with great subtlety made a most glorious confession of Christ, pretending that he had been a Jew, and that his name was Joseph Ben Israel. After his declaration in the parish house, he was baptized. But the Holy One of Israel, our gracious Protector, brought the hellish impostor to light before he had any church communion. Ever blessed be His glorious name for this great deliverance.[14]

Tillam and his followers tried to gloss over this terribly embarrassing incident as insignificant and even trivial because the ruse was discovered before Joseph ben Israel had desecrated their communion. In fact, the Case of the False Jew destroyed Tillam's credibility and reputation, severely damaged the Baptist movement in the north, and helps explain the comparative ease which other dissenting sects had in establishing themselves later on in that part of England.

Joseph ben Israel arrived in Hexham from Newcastle on 4 June 1653 and made a declaration and confession in the congregation's church the next day, and at the parish public meeting house the following Sunday. The man claimed to be a Jew of the tribe of Judah, born in Mantua, conversant in eight languages, and educated in philosophy as well as in the religion of his ancestors. Joseph recalled that he came to Christ following the realization that the word for God in Hebrew appears in the plural

---

[12] No original records of this first congregation survive: see R. Howell, *Newcastle Upon Tyne and the Puritan Revolution* (Oxford, 1967), pp. 218-19, 247-9; F.G. Little & E.T.F. Walker, *The Story of the Northern Baptists* (Newcastle, 1945), pp. 7-10; D. Douglas, *History of the Baptist Churches in the North of England* (London, 1846). pp. 4-7.

[13] M.R., *Memoirs of the Life of Mr. Ambrose Barnes*, ed. W.H.D. Longstaffe (Surtees Soc., L, 1866), p. 150: ded. dated 19 June 1716.

[14] Hexham Church Book, p. 292.

form, even if the verb is expressed in the singular, as in the phrase "God created the heaven and the earth". Joseph came to reject the first tenet of the Jewish faith that the Lord is one. He soon "resolved to leave my Countrey, and Friends, and to goe over the Alpes to finde a people professing the true *Messiah*". Joseph found the Germans obsessed with tangential questions of consubstantiation; the wicked lives of the Calvinists stood in contradiction to their lofty ideals. Eventually he arrived in Hamburg, where he heard of the judicious principles of the "Anabaptists" and determined to make his way to England, in spite of the prohibition of Jewish settlement in that country. "I made a lye my refuge, and sought selfe-preservation under falshood, by denying my Nation and Descent, and giving out my selfe to those in the Ship with me, to be an English-man."[15]

Joseph ben Israel landed at Newcastle, where he "repaired to some of the Ministers in the Towne for reliefe, and presently after went into the Countie of *Durham*" to the house of Lieutenant-Colonel Paul Hobson, the deputy-governor of Newcastle. There he described himself as a converted Jew anxious to become acquainted with the Baptist interpretation of the Protestant message.[16] Hobson was one of the pioneers of English Baptism: he was a signatory to the first London Particular Baptist Confession in 1644, and after the Civil War ended he helped found the Baptist church at Newcastle. Thus, by the time that the False Jew appeared at his door, Hobson was a well-known figure in the north of England whose fame may indeed have spread to certain circles in Germany.[17]

Joseph ben Israel was entertained by Hobson for three weeks to a month, after which time he expressed a wish to visit the saints at Hexham. "In answer to my desires", Joseph related, Hobson "recommended me by his Letter to the Minister of the Baptized Church, who, together with the whole Church, received me gladly, and in a way becomming their profession."[18] Tillam baptized Joseph ben Israel in Hexham a few days later,

---

[15] Joseph Ben Israel, *The Converted Ievv*, in the version repr. in Thomas Tillam, *Banners of Love* (Newcastle, 1653), pp. 3-7; Thomas Weld, Samuel Hammond, William Durant, *et al.*, *A false Jew: Or, A wonderfull Discovery of a Scot* (Newcastle, 1653), p. 11. R. Welford, "Early Newcastle Typography, 1639-1800", *Arch. Aeliana*, 3rd ser., iii (1907), 14, 57-8 notes that all of the pamphlets regarding the False Jew were probably printed by the same man, Stephen Bulkley, who had a press at Gateshead in 1653, although only *The Converted Ievv* bore his mark.

[16] Weld, et al., *false Jew*, p. 11; cf. Joseph Ben Israel, *Converted Ievv*, p. 7.

[17] On Paul Hobson, see A. Laurence, "Parliamentary Army Chaplains, 1642-51" (Oxford Univ. D. Phil. thesis 1981), pp. 60, 91, 377-9; Howell, *Newcastle*, pp. 248-9, 252, 333; Whitley, "Hobson"; M. Tolmie, *The Triumph of the Saints* (Cambridge, 1977), pp. 59, 60, 63, 127, 147, 156, 158-9, 164, 167; H. Roundell, "The Garrison of Newport Pagnell during the Civil Wars", *Recs. of Bucks.*, ii (1870), 357-60; A.G. Matthews, *Calamy Revised* (Oxford, 1934), p. 186.

[18] Joseph Ben Israel, *Converted Ievv*, p. 7; cf. Weld, *et al.*, *false Jew*, p. 11.

in part on the recommendation of Paul Hobson, who did warn Tillam that "the Ministers at *Newcastle* are discontented at him, and some of them report he is no Schollar; which I doe not beleeve: I am sure his condition calls for love and pitty".[19] Even after baptism, however, Joseph was not permitted to take communion with his fellows. With tears and trembling Joseph smote his breast and "professed that his soule did weep even tears of blood for those lyes", but Tillam was firm: no communion would be administered until he had cleared himself at Newcastle.[20]

Tillam's defiant baptism of Joseph ben Israel in the face of their warnings spurred the Baptist leaders of Newcastle into action. "Having our eares much beaten with the confident report of *a converted Iew*," they announced, they now had reasons for suspecting that he might in reality be a certain Thomas Horsley of their acquaintance who had just recently passed through the city. Joseph ben Israel and Thomas Tillam were therefore invited to present themselves at Newcastle to acquit the converted Jew of these charges, and to face "a deare friend of ours, yet deluded by him" who had brought the issue forward to the ministers. Joseph and Tillam arrived in Newcastle on 21 June 1653 and met at the home of Alderman George Dawson, where other interested parties were also assembled.[21]

One of those present was Christopher Shadforth, the master of the ship which had brought Joseph ben Israel to England. Shadforth identified Joseph as the man who on board had called himself Thomas Horsley. It seemed that the previous April, Shadforth had done some business in Hamburg with an English merchant and the English minister there who were acquainted with Horsley, who claimed to be a native of Newcastle wishing to return to England from Rome. The merchant gave Shadforth a sum of money to take Horsley back to Newcastle, and he agreed. Horsley became sea-sick en route, and confessed that he had been a Benedictine friar in Rome, but fled when he was pressured to return to England in the guise of a tailor in order to promote Roman Catholicism. Horsley told Shadforth that there were many such agitators in England, disguised as craftsmen, utilizing the evangelical method made notorious by the Jesuits during the reign of Elizabeth. Horsley revealed that the Popish plan was to promote at first "Libertie and free-Will, and after to bring them to the notion of a Congregation or Church, and after to Anabaptisme". Though the Baptist persuasion was naturally not as desirable to Rome as the

---

[19] *Ibid.*; Tillam, *Banners*, p. 15. G.F. Nuttall, *Visible Saints* (Oxford, 1957), pp. 112-13 notes that few confessions by candidates for membership in Congregational churches have been preserved, and such a one "none the less valuable as a type for being bogus, is preserved in *The Converted Jew*."

[20] Tillam, *Banners*, p. 18.

[21] Weld, *et al.*, *false Jew*, p. 3.

Catholic faith, this "was as much as they sought after, and all they desired". As for being a Jew, Shadforth related that Horsley had told him that on his way to Hamburg from Rome he was accosted by a group of soldiers who, suspecting him to be a Jew, offered him pork, which he ate to clear himself of this slander. Shadforth said that the last he had seen of Horsley was the twenty-first of April when in the company of two merchants who were also passengers on his ship, the reluctant missionary was ferried across the River Tyne into Newcastle.[22]

Joseph ben Israel *alias* Thomas Horsley denounced Shadforth's story as a complete fabrication, and was defended vigorously by Thomas Tillam, who refused to believe that his prize convert was an imposter. The ministers of Newcastle, here in the presence of the Mayor, rejected Tillam's charge that their investigation was driven by simple jealousy, and that "we had never inquired into the man except hee had beene baptized into their way". They noted that Shadforth's testimony aside, there were a number of weighty reasons which led them to suspect the baptized Jew for a fraud. First of all, they thought it strange that a Jew of Mantua should speak perfect English, especially "in the verie dialect of it (as indeed he doth)" of the Newcastle region. Tillam answered that many Jews could speak perfect English, a fact he discovered when travelling on the Continent. Tillam revealed that he himself had once been a Roman Catholic, and had had many opportunities to meet Jews. Another of Joseph's supporters ventured helpfully that "because the Jews could pronounce Shibboleth: therefore they could speake perfect English". Joseph himself was pressed to demonstrate his command of the English language, and suddenly lapsed into a "broken English in a lisping way", rather different from the manner in which he had spoken earlier in private conference.[23]

Other grounds for suspicion concerned Joseph's immediate address to Paul Hobson. The ministers at Newcastle, one of them in particular, had shown themselves willing to assist him in his search for Christian truth, but Joseph left Newcastle hastily the very day he arrived, claiming falsely that he could find no lodging. It now appeared that Joseph's real reason for seeking out Hobson was that he had heard in Hamburg that the minister seemed to be a man suitable for exploitation. Indeed, it was on the basis of Hobson's declaration that Tillam agreed to baptize Joseph ben Israel after only a few days' acquaintance, "in the presence of some hundreds, accompanying him to the River *Tine.*"[24]

The Newcastle ministers' third argument was that their own inquiries

---

[22] *Ibid.*, pp. 4-5.
[23] *Ibid.*, pp. 6-7.
[24] *Ibid.*, p. 7.

revealed that when he first arrived in the town, Joseph ben Israel immediately headed for the house of a certain Anne Horsley. There he called
himself Thomas Horsley, and referred to people and places in Newcastle
and in that very house "which did evidence to us he was certainly no Jew
borne". Tillam refused to be convinced by this argument either, and Joseph himself, pressed to explain "how a Native Jew, and never in *England*
before, could know so exactly these particulars in a private family",
claimed that he had met a certain Ramsey in Florence and certain sailors
en route who had supplied him with this and other information which enabled him to masquerade as Horsley in order to avoid the prohibition of
Jewish immigration into England. The ministers of Newcastle, however,
refused to believe that Joseph could be ignorant of the fact that "a true
converted Jew might have much freedom and entertainment in *England*".
Tillam remonstrated angrily, and Joseph threatened to go back to Italy
and to "write to the confusion of all Christianity" to repay the Newcastle
ministers for their persecution of him: "at which expression", the ministers dryly noted, "we were persuaded he was a perfect Cheat".[25]

But it was their fourth piece of evidence that finally compelled Joseph
ben Israel to abandon his masquerade. Whether by "a more then or-
dinarie hand of God" or by chance, at that moment a citizen of Newcastle
arrived, carrying with him two letters. The first was addressed to the bear-
er himself, from a Mistress Ramsey, wife to a Doctor Ramsey of Scotland.
The second was directed to the converted Jew, to Thomas Horsley, from
the same Mistress Ramsey, who called the addressee her son, and wrote
that "his Father having received a Letter from him under the name of
Thomas Horsley, knew it was his writing though under a false name". The
ministers of Newcastle confronted the Jew with this new evidence, and
asked him if he had written to that Doctor Ramsey. Joseph replied that he
had, and in the name of Thomas Horsley, concerning Ramsey's son
whom, as he already said, he had seen in Florence. When asked why Mistress Ramsey should write to her son at Newcastle, pleading with him to
come home, the Jew asked permission to step outside with Thomas Tillam. By this time, in any case, the ministers of Newcastle "were abundantly satisfied that he was not a Jew, but some *Jesuited Papist* and an English-
man borne". Joseph and Tillam had never offered any convincing answers
to their four arguments, and Tillam even vaguely threatened the investiga-
tors by mentioning that the Jew was expected by the army.[26]

The two men returned to the Newcastle ministers shortly, and Joseph-
Horsley-Ramsey confessed that he had deliberately deceived everyone

---

[25] *Ibid.*, pp. 7-8.
[26] *Ibid.*, pp. 8-9.

since his arrival back in England. In the presence of the sheriff and a group
of aldermen, the man admitted that he was not a Jew but the son of this
Doctor Alexander Ramsey of Scotland. The name "Joseph ben Israel"
presumably was chosen to evoke some sort of familial connection with Menasseh the famous Dutch rabbi. Ramsey made his confession immediately
under his own hand, and began to tell the story of his plot to infiltrate Baptist circles in England.[27]

Thomas Ramsey told his unmaskers that he was born in London
twenty-two years ago, of Scottish parents, Doctor Alexander Ramsey, physician, and grew up in Scotland. At the age of sixteen he was sent to London, and then to Rotterdam with the aim of studying at the University of
Leiden. His uncle there thought he might do better in a Scottish university, and sent him to the university at Glasgow, where he remained a year
studying philosophy and Greek. The plague drove him to the University
of Edinburgh, where he stayed another year in the study of philosophy. He
was then persuaded to continue his studies abroad again, and travelled to
Bremen and Würtzburg, and finally landed in a Dominican cloister in
Rome. A year there, followed by another year in a Jesuit college completed
his education, although Ramsey denied throughout his examination that
he had ever taken any orders in Italy. The Jesuits sent him north again to
Germany, first to Hildesheim and then to Hamburg, where he was further
instructed to proceed to England "to use his best endeavours there to pro-
pagate their ends". It was in Hamburg that he met Christopher Shadforth, the master of the ship *Elizabeth* of Newcastle. As Shadforth himself
had testified, Ramsey now agreed that he had given himself out to have
been Thomas Horsley, born in Newcastle.[28]

The rest of Ramsey's sorry tale from the time of his arrival in Newcastle
was known to all present. Ramsey revealed that there were other agitators
sent from Rome into England, "particularly into the Army . . . sent over
for dividing the Army, the troubling of the peace both of the Nation and
Church". Ramsey swore that if he should meet up with any of these persons, he would be very willing to make them known to the General,
"though he cannot remember their Names, and further saith not".[29]

Such was Ramsey's official confession as taken down and signed by
Henry Dawson, the mayor of Newcastle; and Thomas Bonner, alderman.

---

[27] *Ibid.* The mayor had already left, but not before telling Tillam that he thought his
Jew to be an imposter.

[28] *Ibid.*, pp. 10-11. Cf. *Dict. Nat. Biog.*, *s.v.* "Ramsay or Ramsey, Thomas (fl. 1653)",
which is very incomplete and less than accurate, although it is surprising that he is included
at all. It is claimed here that Ramsey's name does not appear in the register of the Jesuit
college at Rome.

[29] Weld, *et al.*, *false Jew*, pp. 11-12.

Ramsey added some other particulars in private conversation with New-castle ministers Samuel Hammond and William Durant, themselves op-ponents of the Baptists. He claimed that he was sent from Rome by a special order of the Jesuits with a personal command from the pope him-self; that he had taken an M.A. and was perfectly learned in Hebrew and other languages. Hammond and Durant reported that while in Rome Ramsey was in the employ of the Inquisition, although he tried to conceal this fact once he was discovered in England. Ramsey's plan was said to have been to send his reports to Rome in the Hebrew language. He was to "take up preaching, and cry up notions", as he did in a public meeting sponsored by Hobson, when he told his listeners "some stories of the Rab-bies, and of the Old Testament" and passed himself off as a rabbinical scholar.[30]

Thomas Tillam, the fool of the piece and the unwitting promoter of the False Jew, replied as expected at the end of August. He opened his defence by recounting the numerous lies which had been told about him: that he had baptized a dozen "Apostles" who called him their God; that he took up to a pound for baptizing them; that he had been seen drunk on the road; that he robbed a man near Corbridge; that he had been summoned to Newcastle and to London to be rebuked; that people whom he baptized had gone mad, been struck with palsy, or blindness, had been drowned, had hanged themselves, and so on.[31]

Tillam's argument was that at the time of the baptism he had had no idea that Joseph ben Israel was a false Jew. Tillam claimed that Ramsey's baptism was not done with haste, for in any case he did not subscribe to that "*New-England* way of keeping Persons upon tryall many Moneths". Mistakes will certainly be made, but his way was the only one which could reach out to the dark corners of the land, while his critics rest on their "fat Lots at *Newcastle*" and neglect to reach out, "no not once in a Summer, to hold forth their Light to some thousands of poor soules which sit in darkenesse, and may, for all them, perish without understanding." Tillam's own position was clear: "I must freely declare," he wrote,

> and let all the Saints know it, and well weigh it, That if a Jaylor should pres-ently come from tormenting the tender Lambs of Christ, or a *Symon* from his Sorceries (which are worse then the French Pox, or Adultery) ... if they should professe the Faith of the Gospel, with Evangelicall repentance, and an earnest desire of the Ordinance; I would in the strength of Christ speedily Baptize them, though it were the same *houre of the Night*

---

[30] *Ibid.*, pp. 12-13.
[31] Tillam, *Banners*, sigs. A^v-A2^r.

In this way, Tillam argued, "I endeavour to keep the door, not an Inch narrower after the *New England* way, nor a foot wider".[32]

One man who was not allowed to slip through the door was the False Jew himself, Thomas Ramsey of Scotland. The Council of State issued a warrant for his arrest on 13 July 1653, and Ramsey was imprisoned at the Gatehouse in London.[33] What worried Cromwell's government now in these first few weeks of Barebone's Parliament was not the excitement that Ramsey had caused among the northern Baptists, but rather his own confession to being a Catholic and an agent of Rome.[34] The Council appointed a committee the following month to examine the circumstances of his entry into the country and the activities of other Roman Catholic priests in England, and when they reported Secretary Thurloe was ordered to have their conclusions summarized and published.[35]

Ramsey seems to have remained in prison for about six years, and even there gained some notoriety by participating in a rather good practical joke against a Royalist prophet named Paul Hunt, who rested in the Gatehouse after prophesying the return of the king. Hunt claimed "that he was sent of God, to perswade old *Cromwell* to resign". While Hunt was asleep, Ramsey slipped into the prophet's cell a counterfeit divine order written in Hebrew charging him to put his case to the new Protector at any cost. Hunt awoke to an earnest discussion between Ramsey and two other imprisoned Jesuits speculating on the source of heavenly music heard during the night. When Hunt discovered the letter he excitedly called for his release, but being refused wrote a long epistle to Cromwell, which the prisoners prudently suppressed, "and persued the design much further to the admiration of many worthy Gentlemen, (State-Prisoners there at that time)".[36]

Nevertheless, despite his long imprisonment, Ramsey seems not to have been brought to trial.[37] On his release about 1659, according to William Prynne, Ramsey "twice boldly entered into the University Schools at *Cambridge*, desiring conference with Mr. *Smith* the *Hebrew Lecturer there*, with whom he discoursed in *Hebrew*".[38] Another account makes him a Hebrew

---

[32] *Ibid.*, pp. 8-9; Joseph Ben Israel, *Converted Ievv*, pp. 17, 28.

[33] *Cal. S.P. Dom., 1653-4*, p. 428.

[34] See generally I.Y. Thackray, "Zion Undermined: the Protestant Belief in a Popish Plot during the English Interregnum", *Hist. Wkshp.*, xviii (1984), 28-52, esp. pp. 36-7 and the works cited therein.

[35] *Cal. S.P. Dom., 1653-4*, pp. 73, 101: day's proceedings, 4 & 23 Aug. 1653.

[36] J.S., *The Jesuite Discovered* (London, 1659), pp. 8-10.

[37] Hen. Denne, *The Quaker no Papist* (London, 1659), p. 19. Denne sought to disprove the existence of a subversive conspiracy between Quakers and Roman Catholics.

[38] William Prynne, *A true and perfect Narrative* (n.p., 1659), p. 44. Prynne follows his report of Ramsey with one on Paul Isaiah and Peter Samuel (pp. 44-5), two well-known professional Jewish converts to Christianity: see below, pp. 58-66.

teacher in Cambridge at Christ's College, St John's and elsewhere. Indeed, noted one anti-Quaker critic, "I know his Religion & design from other Reasons, besides his frequenting *Milton* neer *Cambridge.*"[39] This intellectual activity was in any case short-lived: at the end of March 1660, two months before the entry of Charles II into London, the Council of State gave him a passport for France and freedom.[40]

II

It was apparent for all to see by the autumn of 1653 that Tillam's mission to the north, while not quite a failure, had succeeded in bringing shame and disgrace to the Baptist movement as a whole. The support which Tillam's congregation had enjoyed from London was about to come to an end. The Newcastle church was unwilling to pass up the opportunity which the False Jew had presented them to bring down their brethren in Hexham, and made their views known to Coleman Street. There seems to have been a genuine dispute between Tillam and Gower over the question of the maintenance of the clergy, Gower claiming that a minister should not be entirely dependent on the church, Tillam arguing that as preaching was a full-time task, he should be supported by the congregation that called him.[41] But this disagreement was soon subsumed under personal animosity, which (Tillam recorded) was made manifest by Gower's "rugged and unbrotherly carriage".[42]

The Newcastle church eventually succeeded in their efforts to topple Tillam and to initiate the revocation of his commission in the north. The Hexham churchbook notes the following events of 11 June 1655:

> Great storms and commotions, raised by Mr. Gower more than ever, so far prevailing with the church in Coleman Street, as to a disowning of Mr. Tillam, and all that are in the practice of laying on of hands.

Soon afterwards, Stephen Anderton, one of the sixteen founding members of the Hexham congregation in July 1652, himself raised the issue of laying

---

[39] Thomas Smith, *A Gagg for the Quakers* (London, 1659), sigs. B2ᵛ-B3⁴. Smith also notes that Ramsey was never brought to trial; his pamphlet is a reply to Denne's.

[40] *Cal. S.P. Dom., 1659-60*, p. 572.

[41] Hickeringill to Hexham, 15 Mar. 1652-3: *Records*, p. 318. Further information might exist in Thomas Tillam, *A Christian Account of Speciall Passages of Providences* (Colchester, n.d.). The pamphlet is said to include the charges made by the Newcastle church in 1654, Tillam's reply, and other correspondence, including a letter from Hammond to Warren, minister of Peter's, Colchester. The pamphlet appears in a card index at the Friends' House Library, London, apparently clipped from a bookseller's catalogue where it is described as "24 pages, sm. 4to, Very Scarce".

[42] Hexham Church Book, pp. 293-4.

on of hands, "but failing therein, he opened his mouth in blaspheming against Mr. Tillam's doctrine, and plunged himself into other gross evils" and was summarily excommunicated. The last entry in the church book written in Tillam's hand, dated 4 November 1655, refers to the excommunication of two more veteran members. By 18 November 1655, Tillam seems to have already left his post, for the remaining entries in the book were written by another member of the church.[43] His successor as the Mercers' Company lecturer at Hexham was George Ritschel, the Bohemian divine, chief master of the free school at Newcastle, who took up his new post on 18 February 1655-6, and was awarded the town curacy which Tillam had never acquired.[44]

Thomas Tillam was thus driven from his pulpit in Northumberland by the end of 1655, putting an end to a ministry that began in such a promising fashion but collapsed under the weight of scandal, jealousy, and doctrinal disagreement. Tillam's immediate plans and movements during the winter of 1655-6 are unclear, but the revelation during that season of a secret Jewish community in London must have brought back bitter memories.

Yet by the spring Tillam seems to have found himself a fresh audience, far removed from the scene of his humiliation. On 6 May 1656, Ralph Josselin the Essex clergyman was informed that "about 100 dipt at Colchester to Tillam a papist convert as he saith, if not still a Jesuite, oh how giddy and unconstant people are, to condemn us as Romish antichristian, and embrace such as are, and mingle themselves with them for evill ends."[45] Nevertheless, Tillam apparently still had friends and supporters who helped him get his position there regularized. On Thursday, 29 May 1656, the Council of State noted as its first order of business that

> The Lord Presid^t [Lawrence] signified to the Counsell, That his Highness [Oliver Cromwell] hath referred to ye Counsell a Certificate from the Mayo^r, and seurale Aldermen of the Towne of Colchester, on behalfe of Mr Tillam, preacher in the said Towne, and moved that he may haue a Convenient place assigned him in Colchester for him, and his Church to meete in[46]

A letter was issued from Whitehall by Lawrence in the name of the Council of State to the mayor and aldermen of Colchester to this effect, noting

---

[43] *Ibid.*, p. 295.

[44] Hinds, *Northumberland*, pp. 169, 172; *Dict. Nat. Biog.*, *s.v.*, "Ritschel, George (1616-1683)". Ritschel was himself succeeded by his son George in 1683 as lecturer and curate. Howell, *Newcastle*, p. 253, citing the Newcastle City Archives, Common Council Book 1650-9, f. 439, writes that Ritschel's appointment began as late as Michaelmas 1657.

[45] *The Diary of Ralph Josselin*, ed. A. Macfarlane (London, 1976), p. 368.

[46] SP. 25/77, p. 148 (f. 76^v).

that "His Highnesse and the Councell haueing receiued good Satisfaction of the pietie and abilities of Mr Tillam" were interested in seeing him and his church established in their town.[47] Secure once again, and freshly installed, Tillam was free to undergo his final metamorphosis. By 23 January 1656-7, Josselin had heard that "Tillam, an anabaptist pastor had set up the practice of the Satturday Sabbath and indulgeth those of his church that will to use their trades it being their Colchester market and observeth the lords day, this done in regard of the present temper of the state. the lord helpe us." Indeed, Josselin surmised, "I expect the Jewes finger in the apostacy before perfected."[48]

As Josselin testifies, Thomas Tillam was certainly a Saturday-Sabbatarian by 1657, for in that year he published his first pamphlet which called for the "recovery of the long-slighted seventh day, to its ancient glory". Tillam described himself in its preface as the "faithful and affectionate Minister" of the church at Colchester. The work itself is decidedly millenarian. Although Tillam criticized those who would take the Sabbath and "imprison it in *Palestina*", his arguments in favour of the Saturday-Sabbath were clearly based on Jewish sources. "I may with as much reason," he claimed, "question whether my right hand be that the world calls so, as I may question whether saturday be the very seventh day, seeing the Jews also dispersed through the world punctually observe it." Tillam noted that Jesus himself was a Jew, and prophesied that he would shortly return "in his glory to make them a glorious people". Most significantly, Tillam revealed that he had received a letter from a man who had been in contact with the nascent Jewish congregation in London:

> The Jews in London are very much affected with our keeping of the Sabbath, and do frequent our meeting places every Sabbath in the latter part of the day, and truly I hope the Lord will in time awake upon them to imbrace the truth: As yet they keep on their Hats in the time of prayer; I am well acquainted with their Rabbi, He and the rest of the Jews with him were so taken with Brother *Sallars* prayer for the restauration of the Kingdome to Israel, as that they desired that they might have it in writing, promising that they would print it, and send it to all the places where the Jews inhabit; I told them also your resolution to preach up the Sabbath, and they are very much taken therewith, desiring the Lord to prosper you in your endeavours therein.

---

[47] *Ibid.*, p. 851 (f. 432ᵛ).
[48] Josselin, *Diary*, pp. 388-9. Tillam disputed during these months with the Quaker evangelist James Parnell when their mission came to Colchester. The Quaker records give the date as June 1655, but as Tillam was still in Hexham then, this might be an error for 1656: *"The First Publishers of Truth"*, ed. N. Penney (London, 1907), i. 96. Cf. Gerard Croese, *The General History of the Quakers* (London, 1696), p. 48 (first part), who also gives the date as 1655.

The aim in entertaining the Jews was of course to convert them to Christianity, and Tillam's correspondent noted that

> I perceive it as a great stumbling block to them as to believe Christ to be the *Messiah*, because Christians violate the Sabbath; for (say they) if Christ were not a Sabbath-breaker, why are Christians? and if Christ were a Sabbath breaker then he was a sinner, and if a sinner, what benefit can we expect by the death of an evil doer? And thus you see what evil consequents follow the non-observance of the Lords holy Sabbath

Tillam confessed that his heart did tremble when he read these lines.[49]

Presumably the rabbi referred to in the letter is the famous Menasseh ben Israel, who remained in England most probably until November 1657. On the other hand, the mysterious rabbi might well have been Moses Israel Athias, who since 1652 had served as assistant synagogue reader and Hebrew teacher in the religious school of the Portuguese Jews in Hamburg. Athias arrived in London in August 1657 and led the congregation there until the appointment of Jacob Sasportas in 1664.[50] "Brother *Sallars*" is certainly William Saller, later the second pastor of the Mill Yard congregation after the Restoration, who published a short declaration in 1657 calling on the chief magistrates of Englad to recognize Saturday as the Sabbath day.[51]

It was about this point that Christopher Pooley entered into Thomas Tillam's life. Pooley was educated at Cambridge, and took his M.A. there in 1647. He then seems to have spent four years in the army until 1651. By 1653 he was pastor of the church at Wymondham, Norfolk, but he became a Baptist in 1656 and soon emerged as one of the most notable Fifth Monarchy Men in the country. Christopher Pooley, then, was already a known subversive when Thomas Tillam made his acquaintance, sometime between 1656 and 1658.[52]

---

[49] Thomas Tillam, *The Seventh-Day Sabbath Sought out and celebrated* (London, 1657), sigs. A2^r, A4^v; pp. 26, 35, 37, 49, 50-1. The only copy of this pamphlet is in the McAlpin collection of the Union Theological Seminary in New York City.

[50] L. Wolf, "The Jewry of the Restoration, 1660-1664", *Trans. Jew. Hist. Soc. Eng.*, v (1908), 5-33.

[51] William Saller & John Spittlehouse, *An Appeal To the Consciences of the chief Magistrates* (n.p., 1657), pp. 12-14. Spittlehouse was a former soldier, a signatory to the Fifth Monarchist declaration of 1654, and the author of a number of millenarian tracts during the 1650s: see B.S. Capp, *The Fifth Monarchy Men* (London, 1972), p. 263. Their joint effort indeed echoes Tillam's correspondent quite strikingly in their call to shift the Sabbath to Saturday in order to remove that stumbling-block for the Jews.

[52] *Ibid.*, p. 258; J. & J.A. Venn, *Alumni Cantabrigienses* (Cambridge, 1922-54), iii. 379. For more on Pooley, see *State Papers of John Thurloe*, ed. T. Birch (London, 1742), iv. 727; v. 187-8, 219, 220, 371-2; A.J. Kaiber, "Early Baptist Movements in Suffolk", *Bap. Qly.*, iv (1928-9), 116-20; C.B. Jewson, "Norfolk Baptists up to 1700", *Bap. Qly.*, xviii (1959-60), 310, 364; *idem, The Baptists in Norfolk* (London, 1957), pp. 20, 23. A three-volume typescript collected by M.F. Hewett includes much information about every Baptist church in Norfolk: deposited at Norfolk Record Office, MS. 4259-61, T 137 F.

Certainly, Thomas Tillam must have been during this period no less a controversial figure in that part of the country. Unwilling to confine his activities to Colchester alone, we know that at least in the summer of 1658 he brought his strict-Sabbatarian message to Norwich as well. On 11 July 1658, a Sunday, Tillam preached at the parish church of St Giles there, denouncing the local clergy and proving out of his chosen text from Isaiah the necessity of keeping the Saturday-Sabbath. According to one report, Tillam told "his hearers that they might knowe when the Eleaventh the last hower was come when in stead of Hirelings such as himselfe went to labor in the Lords vinyard without making any agreement for hire but depending wholly upon Providence".[53]

Such remarks were bound to make him an unwelcome visitor to the city, and it seems that steps were taken before the day was out. Nevertheless, he was permitted to preach two days later on Tuesday, 13 July at the palace of the bishop of Norwich. According to witnesses, Tillam claimed that the actions taken against him were the work of the devil, acting through the magistrates of the city. Tillam warned the people of Norwich, "this little poore citty know what they doo". Indeed, he announced,

> Christ said to the Apostles goe into that citty & what howse will not receive you then shake the dust off yor feet as a Testimony against them, and so I will say to the Magistrates of this City as I live I will shake the dust off my feet against them as a Testimony as soone as I am out of the gates of this citty[54]

Good as his word, when Thomas Tillam left town shortly thereafter, in the company of his new partner Christopher Pooley, "when he went out of the gates of this Citty did light of his horse backe & tooke his bible in his hand and turned to the 10 Math 13:14 verses & did lift up his foote & did shake the dust of his feete as a witnesse against the Rulers of this Citty".[55]

Tillam's flamboyant campaign on behalf of the Saturday-Sabbath, and the support which it found in certain quarters, quite naturally provoked a certain amount of contempt and antagonism. Tillam appears to have participated in a debate on the question of Sabbath observance on 6 January 1659. Representing Sunday was Jeremiah Ives, who later published the

---

[53] Info. of John Hobart, Esq., taken before Roger Mingay, Esq., mayor of Norwich, 3 Aug. 1658: Bodl. Lib., MS. Tanner 311, f. 39^r.
[54] Info. of Francis Copping, Ingleman Lake, and Benjamin Fisher, taken by the mayor, 2 Aug. 1658: *ibid.*, f. 39^v.
[55] Info. of Fisher, *ibid.* Pooley told his story to a certain Norwich butcher, who passed it on to Roger Mingay, the mayor of Norwich, when an investigation was made into the entire unfortunate affair the following month: *ibid.*, f. 40^r.

text of the disputation. Ives complained that although the others had been willing to argue in a logical fashion, "Syllogistically", Tillam was unwilling or incapable of doing so.[56] The Quaker George Fox himself published an answer to Tillam in a short book which presented the traditional arguments for altering both the day and method of observance of the Sabbath. Fox concluded by reminding Tillam that apart from slipshod theology, "a great deal more confusion is there in thy book not worthy mentioning, but will fall into the mire and the dirt with thy self". He urged Tillam to "give over deceiving the people; for thou art wallowing in the mire thou speakes of".[57] Once again, like all northern Baptists, Tillam found the Quakers at his heels.[58]

III

This world of earnest discussion of the fine points of Puritan dogma came to a swift end with the entry of Charles II into London in May 1660. His Declaration of Breda had promised "a liberty to tender consciences and that no man shall be disquieted or called in question for differences of opinion in matter of religion, which do not disturb the peace of the kingdom". He even proclaimed his hope that this toleration would be confirmed by an act of parliament.[59] But especially in the first decade of the Restoration, strict censorship and persecution of dissenting churches was a characteristic feature of the king's religious settlement. While it certainly is true that the enforcement of uniformity varied considerably, among those arrested were some of the most influential saints, radicals, and Fifth Monarchists.[60]

---

[56] Jer. Ives, *Saturday No Sabbath* (London, 1659), sig. A6ʳ; pp. 1, 3.

[57] G[eorge] F[ox], *An Answer To Thomas Tillams Book* (London, 1659), p. 30: repr. *idem, The Great Mistery of the Great Whore Unfolded* (London, 1659), pp. 190-205. About half of all books published at Newcastle between 1652 and 1662 were concerned with Baptists and Quakers: Welford, "Typography", pp. 57-8.

[58] Tillam himself attended a Quaker meeting on 19 Oct. 1654, where he claimed to have been possessed by the Devil, who caused him to quake with the rest of the worshippers. He then wrote a short paper, never published, denouncing the sect: Frs. Hse. Lib., MS. Portfolio 36, #13 (dated 1654). But when Giles Firmin told the tale in *Stablishing Against Shaking* (London, 1656), pp. 55-6, he referred to the discredited Tillam as an anonymous fellow minister in Essex. The source of the story was soon unmasked by Edward Burrough, *Stablishing against Quaking, Thrown down* (London, 1656), p. 31, who referred to Tillam as a minister "known in all the parts about *Hexam*, to be a deceitful fellow". The story is repeated in Charles Leslie, *The Snake in the Grass* (London, 1696) and J.R. Greer, *The Society of Friends* (London, 1853), ii. 157-8. Cf. *'First Publishers'*, ed. Penney, i. 89-90.

[59] *Sources of English Constitutional History*, ed. C. Stephenson & F.G. Marcham (London, 1937), p. 533.

[60] See generally, Capp, *Fifth Monarchy, cap.* 9; G.R. Cragg, *Puritanism in the Period of the Great Persecution* (Cambridge, 1957).

Thomas Tillam was one of the saints who found it difficult to adjust to the new realities of English religious and political life. He went north at the time of the king's return, but was arrested in London on the way back to Colchester. The London letter office passed on to the authorities two letters which came for Tillam under blank cover. The post official explained to Secretary Edward Nicholas that Tillam himself had called for the letters: "it was 3^d time I ever saw him", wrote the official, "hee is a stranger to me, never eating or drinking nor haueiing any discourse with him but now under standing hee is in restraint, and for some cause deseruing vndoubtedly, I thought it my dutie to sent the inclosed to your Lor^d.[61]

Tillam's was only one of the many arrests which took place during the first year of the Restoration. As a preventative measure they were no doubt effective to some extent, but were insufficient to prevent the notorious uprising of Thomas Venner and his followers on 6 January 1661. The rebellion lasted only three days, and less than one hundred men on both sides were killed, and about twenty rebels captured. From the point of view of the more moderate dissenting sects, what was most significant about Venner's fiasco was that in the wave of government reaction and repression, Baptists, Quakers, and Congregationalists were all swept into the prison cells of London.[62] In spite of the "Humble Apology" and "Renunciation" of these respectable churches, a government ban on conventicles followed soon after Venner's rising had been put down.[63]

Government fears that Venner's rising was part of a nation-wide plot to overthrow the newly restored monarchy were expressed in more vigorous efforts to uncover supporters of radical religion and dissent. Among those under suspicion were Thomas Tillam, Christopher Pooley, and their followers. Fortunately for them, however, Tillam and Pooley seem to have escaped to Holland, but not before publishing a very long devotional work.[64] They appear to have returned to England in August 1661, for information was then received "that Ludloe and Whalley and Tilham, were landed in Essex in a dutch small vessell." It was noted that "Tilham hath a house in Colchester . . . & is often imployed by them".[65] At least part of this intel-

---

[61] James Hickes to Nicholas, 13 June 1660: SP. 29/4, fos. 27^r-28^v.

[62] Capp, *Fifth Monarchy*, pp. 199-200; M.R. Watts, *The Dissenters* (Oxford, 1978), pp. 221-3; C. Burrage, "The Fifth Monarchy Insurrections", *Eng. Hist. Rev.*, xxv (1910).

[63] *A Renunciation and Declaration of the . . . Congregational Churches* (London, 1661); *The Humble Apology of some . . . Anabaptists* (London, 1661); *A Declaration from the . . . Quakers* (London, 1661). On 10 Jan. 1661, a royal proclamation forbade all meetings of "Anabaptists, Quakers, and Fifth Monarchy men": Watts, *Dissenters*, p. 223.

[64] SP. 29/446, f. 139^r: ?29 June 1661; Tho. Tillam, *The Temple of Lively Stones* (London, 1660), with intro. by Pooley.

[65] SP. 29/40, f. 157^r: info. by John Thedam, 27 Aug. 1661. The two regicides were certainly not in Tillam's company: Edward Whalley had escaped nearly a year before to Mas-

ligence was confirmed five days later by Sir William Killigrew, whose letter provided a vivid illustration both of Tillam's activities during these dangerous months and of the way in which he and his followers were regarded. Killigrew reported that Tillam, Pooley, and a certain Dr Love "desired the m^n of the packet boate to Land the other two at a by place & not at Yarmith amongst the rest of the passengers". Furthermore, "Tillam noe sooner was Landed but knowne to bee one Mallit (which is Tillam backward) who had at Colchester for diuers yeares gained diuers proselites vpon ye Judaism . . . where he there not only preached vp but alsoe publisht in print for the Saturday Saboth". Killigrew also reported that

> Pooly though (as Tillam was) wth an ouergrowne beard was knowne at first landing to haue bene a grand Dipper in Noreffolke and Suffolke one there witnessing that he saw him dip 3 women at Norwitch & Loue gaue himselfe out for a Doctor of Phizick at rotterdam

Killigrew had information that Tillam, Pooley and Dr Love ran a private assembly in Rotterdam

> where the regicides & others such like meete together & haue lately Motioned to the Magistrates there for a Ministers allowance for wch they will undertake aboue 200 families shall within a yeare come from England and Liue there.

But this was only a blind which they used while travelling through Holland on the way to England "to avoyd suspition of their right errand", Killigrew thought,

> that is they gaue out that they had bene in the palatinate to settle 100 plantations for soe many families as would remoue out of England.

Their real plan was to establish a settlement of Saturday observers in Germany where they would be safe from the religious persecution of the Restoration government.[66]

Tillam and Pooley are well known to us, and indeed they were long under suspicion by the religious authorities. But who was the mysterious Dr Love, who now made his appearance in the eleventh hour as an organizer of Sabbatarian emigration? He was in reality none other than Paul Hobson, the original magnet for the False Jew, the founder of the Newcastle Baptist church, now with Tillam, Pooley and many more radical dissenters, driven to abandon old quarrels and plan more dramatic action.[67]

---

sachusetts, and Edmund Ludlow made his way to France and then Switzerland at about the same time: *Dict. Nat. Biog.*

[66] Sir William Killigrew to John Garrnis, JP, 1 Sept. 1661: SP. 29/41, fos. 1^r-2^v.

[67] E. Curtis to Bennet, 18 Mar. 1664, from Rotterdam: *Cal. S.P. Dom., 1663-4*, p. 521.

Hobson had left the north about 1654 to become chaplain at Eton College, but naturally was ejected at the Restoration.[68] In July 1661 he was in Rotterdam, and participated with Tillam and Hanserd Knollys at a meeting of English refugees in which William Caton the Quaker missionary demanded the right to put forward his views as well. Caton immediately wrote to George Fox imploring him to warn Quakers against joining Tillam's projected Mosaic colony in Germany.[69] After landing with Tillam and Pooley at Essex several weeks later, Hobson seems to have let them recruit members for the Sabbatarian colony, and to have returned to Durham about November. The authorities were forewarned and Hobson was ordered to appear before the deputy-lieutenants immediately upon his arrival, whereupon he fled to London and kept in contact with the Baptists of Hexham and Newcastle by post.[70] "Paul Hobson", Secretary Nicholas was informed, "is an agent for a German prince".[71] He was arrested in London with Thomas Gower, the former minister of the Newcastle Baptists, on the discovery of seditious correspondence the following year, in November 1662, but at least Hobson was released ten days later.[72] The precise parts played by Hobson, Gower, Tillam, and Pooley in joint resistance to the new government were never made completely clear, but Samuel Pepys heard in a coffee-house in London at the end of January 1663 "of a design in the North of a riseing which is discovered among some men of condition, and they sent for up."[73]

Tillam and Pooley seem to have stayed out of sight for most of 1662 and 1663; they may have returned to the Continent to organize their Sabbatarian settlement. Active resistance in the north of England was left to Hobson and Gower, Tillam's old implacable rivals at Newcastle. Both Hobson and Gower were already severely compromised, and John Cosin the bishop of Durham was on record as having described Hobson as a dangerous person who should be kept in custody and forced to swear the oath of allegiance as a trial of his loyalty.[74]

It is no surprise, then, that the authorities were so willing to believe the accusations brought against Hobson, Gower, and many others on 22 March 1662-3 by John Ellerington, a Baptist servant, that seditious meetings had been held between the Hexham and Newcastle Baptists,[75]

[68] Laurence, "Chaplains", pp. 377-9.
[69] Caton to Fox, 26 July 1661, from Rotterdam: Frs. Hse. Lib., MS Swarthmore I 328.
[70] Cal. S.P. Dom., 1661-2, p. 564.
[71] W. Garrett to Nicholas, 12 Aug. 1661: Ibid., p. 62.
[72] Ibid., pp. 549, 559, 564. Hobson was released on bond for good behaviour.
[73] Samuel Pepys, Diary, ed. R. Latham & W. Matthews (London, 1970-), iv. 22: 23 Jan. 1663.
[74] Cal. S.P. Dom., 1661-2, p. 564.
[75] At Muggleswick Park in the valley of the Derwent, an ancient country residence of

to rise in rebellion against the government, and to destroy Parliament, and murder all Bishops, Deans, and Chapters, and all other ministers of the Church; to break all organs, and further to kill all the gentry that should either oppose them, or not join with them, and to destroy the Common Prayer Book, and to pull down all Churches.

The effects of the "Muggleswick Plot" threw the Hexham and Newcastle Baptists into disarray. Only nine were arrested in the north, all stiffly denying any frequent and seditious meetings, but many fled to Scotland and remote Northumberland, away from the searches of the militia and the deputy-lieutenants of Durham.[76] Thomas Gower "a chief contriver" and Paul Hobson "his great friend" were known to be in London, and the bishop warned the Council of this fact.[77]

Ellerington's information proved to be false, but his accusations seem to have spurred Hobson into further action. Years later, Gower described how he was with Hobson when the warrant came for their arrest, and how they slipped out the back on the landlord's advice. Hobson spent the next few months going from one friend's house to another, moving about only at night with a cloak over his face, now cleverly going under the name of "Dr Smith".[78] This was the much more famous and genuine Yorkshire Plot developed in the summer of 1663. According to one of the conspirators, they intended to force Charles II to honour the promises made at Breda, to grant liberty of conscience to all but Roman Catholics, to take away the excise and hearth money tax, and all taxes whatever, and to reform the ministry. Among those on their death list were the dukes of Albemarle and Buckingham.[79]

But like so many of the Restoration plots and conspiracies, the Yorkshire Plot was rotten with informers and spies. The authorities intercepted letters as soon as they were sent, and about one hundred of the conspirators were seized.[80] Hobson himself was sent to the Tower, then transferred to

---

the priors of Durham, where a lodge with a hall and chapel had been built in the time of Edward I in this remote and inaccessible spot. When Tillam left Hexham his congregation divided: the Derwentside section under John Ward of Muggleswick Park disowned Tillam and became a thriving cause, while the Tyneside brethren under Richard Orde declined somewhat, and met in various farms around the town: Little & Walker, *Northern Baptists*, p. 11.

[76] Generally, see H. Gee, "The Derwentdale Plot, 1663", *Trans. Roy. Hist. Soc.*, 3rd ser., xi (1917), 125-42; *idem*, "A Durham and Newcastle Plot in 1663", *Arch. Aeliana*, 3rd ser., xiv (1917), 145-56; J. Walker, "The Yorkshire Plot, 1663", *Yorks. Arch. Jnl.*, xxi (1934), 348-59; W.T. Whitley, "Militant Baptists 1660-1672", *Trans. Bap. Hist. Soc.*, i (1908-9), 148-55.

[77] On 30 Mar. 1663: *Cal. S.P. Dom., 1663-4*, pp. 91-2.

[78] Hobson to Joplin, ? Aug. 1663: *ibid.*, p. 263; H.W. to Williamson?, 1 May 1668: *Cal. S.P. Dom., 1667-8*, p. 369.

[79] Info. of Capt. Robt. Atkinson, 26 Nov. 1663: *Cal. S.P. Dom., 1663-4*, p. 352.

[80] Walker, "Yorkshire Plot", pp. 352-7.

Cheapstow Castle, and after numerous petitions asking permission to emigrate to Jamaica, was apparently permitted to leave.[81] Gower was still alive and in trouble for preaching at Gateshead in 1669.[82] The smaller fry were less fortunate: about twenty northerners were executed at York and at Leeds.[83]

The Yorkshire Plot was the sort of direct action that must have been near to Tillam's heart, wherever he was during 1663. All we can say is that three years later he was still in contact with Captain Jones, an old Cromwellian soldier and a Yorkshire plotter, who went under the name of "Mene Tekel".[84] But apart from any dim light that it sheds on Tillam's activities in the Restoration underground, the Yorkshire Plot provides a classic illustration of the way in which various sects which had clashed so vigorously during the Commonwealth came together after the return of the king. Indeed, what was so striking to Killigrew when he first reported the landing of Tillam, Pooley and Hobson in Essex was not the fact of the planned Sabbatarian settlement, but that "a Jew a dipper & an Independent all 3 english men of 3 sundry sects of soe vast distance from one another should bee consorted together to Land obscurely in England."[85] This sudden ecumenism of the saints after the Restoration also surprised Secretary Edward Nicholas, who noted the striking fact that Presbyterians, Baptists, and Fifth Monarchy Men could be found meeting together, preaching that deliverance was at hand.[86] This phenomenon, so apparent in the temporary union of Hobson, Gower, Tillam, and Pooley, was one of the last straws that brought in the First Conventicle Act of 1664, which made it illegal for five or more persons not a family to meet for religious service outside a church.[87]

Tillam and Pooley returned to England at the end of 1664, Pooley to Norwich and Tillam to Colchester, and spread reports of success and progress. They soon fled to the Continent, but Christopher Pooley was back in England again by June 1666, this time in the company of one John Foxey: "they came out of Bohemia; and were sent by their Judge or Leader, one Tillam ... into England, to acquainte all of there Judgement". Pooley and Foxey spoke of "what great favours they received from yᵉ Palsgrave there, and what a pleasant part of yᵉ Country hee hath assigned them to

---

[81] *Ibid.*, p. 353n.; Gee, "Durham", p. 156; *Cal. S.P. Dom., 1663-4*, pp. 453, 536, 574, 670; *1664-5*, pp. 22, 186.

[82] Little & Walker, *Northern Baptists*, p. 17.

[83] *Cal. S.P. Dom., 1663-4*, p. 443; Gee, "Durham", p. 155; Walker, "Yorkshire Plot", p. 357.

[84] W.H. to Phillipson, 24 Aug. 1666: SP. 29/168, f. 209ʳ.

[85] Killigrew to Garnis, 1 Sept. 1661: SP. 29/41, fos. 1ʳ-2ᵛ.

[86] Nicholas to Clarendon, 13 Sept. 1661: Bodl. Lib., MS. Clar. 75, f. 191.

[87] See generally, Watts, *Dissenters*, p. 225.

live in and they doubt not but in a shorte time (as they two doe report) but y^t they will gaine him to their opinion''. Pooley and Foxey spent the second half of 1666 travelling in the north trying to convince believers to join their Continental colony and to subscribe to their covenant. Christopher Sanderson of Egglestone, reporting on their activities to London, noted that ''they are very timerous to give a Coppy, but to such as subscribes itt; yet by perswasion & rideing a weeke with them in this County hee gott itt''. Despite the radical beliefs expressed therein, however, it appeared that Pooley and Foxey had no plans for causing any sort of disturbance in England itself.[88]

''The Solemne Covenant'' which Sanderson enclosed in his letter is naturally one of the most important pieces of evidence regarding the beliefs and practices of Tillam's Saturday-Sabbatarian sect. The central clause in the Covenant was the second one:

> Wee doe solemnly swear to ye lord our onely Judge law giver and king whom wee chuse for our God, wth our whole hearts in whose ways through grace wee will walke and religiously obey all his lawes, statutes, and Judgements wch hee haith Commanded for all Jsraell, & perticulerly those first foundation truthes, ye seaventh day sabbath and marriage, and never give our dauthers to ye sons of strangers, nor take their dauthers for our wives.

The term ''strangers'', they clarified, included ''both naturall Jsralites and others y^t are not in ye faith of Christ Jesus.'' Jews were thus expressly excluded from Tillam's community. The group claimed to be obedient to tolerant authorities: ''Wee doe not utterly renounce such powers as are onely different from Christs Goverment though wee cannot subject to them or owne Communion with them.'' On the other hand, however, they did renounce ''all powers y^t ever were, are, or shall bee, opposers and persecutors of ye subjects of Christs kingdome.'' They declared themselves to be in search of ''a place for ye lord an habitation for ye mighty god of Jacob, where wee may advance his holy throne & righteous scepter, as a distinct people dwelling alone & not being reckoned among ye nations''. To this Covenant, they swore, ''wee subscribe our hands to ye lord surnameing our selves by ye name of Jsraell''.[89]

In March 1668, Arlington's secretary Joseph Williamson began to receive information that Pooley and Foxey were about to return to Germany with their new-found converts. Captain Silas Taylor, the storekeeper at Harwich, reported that a small ship was ready to set sail, carrying eight or nine passengers,

---

[88] Sanderson to Williamson, 14 Dec. 1666: SP. 29/181, fos. 193^r-194^v.

[89] SP. 29/181, f. 195^r-v: earlier than 14 Dec. 1666 (?14 Mar. 1665-6). Another copy of the Covenant, damaged but containing the names of Pooley and Foxey, is SP. 29/181, fos. 196^r-197^v.

to be transported to a Monastery granted by ye Duke of Brandenburg to one Tilham heretofore of Colechester & now settled there; where his doctrines are received amongst his disciples of wch he hath plenty both males & females He preaches circumcision; the 7th day Sabbaoth Jewish rites; comunity of goodes (& they say of wiues) but as many concubines as they please; among these departing (as they say for to enjoy the comunion of ye s^ts) is one mayd (in appearance) very handsome; & some that haue well remarked her say it is pitty she should goe &c:[90]

That very day, Taylor saw the master of the ship which was meant to transport the "circumcised Christians", who delayed sailing because of bad weather, and was even forced to turn back once after having set sail. It appears that the vessel finally left in the last week of March 1668.[91]

The ultimate destination and fate of the Saturday-Sabbatarian settlers remains unknown.[92] It may be that they set sail for the Palatinate, as some reports claimed, where the Elector was of English ancestry, the grandson of James I. Taylor thought that they were en route to Brandenburg, where the Great Elector Frederick William was known to support persecuted Protestants. Frederick William had just signed the Treaty of Berlin with France which removed him from the impending conflict in the Spanish Netherlands. After 1681, when Louis XIV began issuing repressive decrees against the Huguenots, many Protestants fled France to Brandenburg where they were warmly welcomed. When Louis revoked the Edict of Nantes in October 1685, the Great Elector issued his own Edict of Potsdam the following month, which publicly invited the Huguenots to take refuge in his territory, promising them employment in the army, land on easy terms, exemption from taxation, and numerous other privileges. It may be, then, that Tillam's group found refuge in Brandenburg even as early as the 1660s, for Frederick William's devotion to persecuted Protestants remained one of the constant aspects of his religious and foreign policy.[93]

---

[90] Taylor to Williamson, 5 Mar. 1667-8: SP. 29/236, f. 28^r-v.

[91] Same to same, 14 Mar. 1667-8: *ibid.*, f. 186^r-v; same to same, 17 Mar.: *ibid.*, f. 302^r-v; same to same, 19 Mar.: SP. 29/237, f. 3^r-v; same to same, 21 Mar.: *ibid.*, f. 52^r-v. A former Saturday-Sabbatarian, John Cowell, *The Snare Broken* (London, 1677), pp. 2-3, also thought that Tillam and his followers practised circumcision.

[92] According to Edward Stennett, the Saturday-Sabbatarian minister, *The Insnared Taken* (London, 1677), p. 7, "Mr. *Pooley* and some of those you now cry out against, have returned and professed their Repentance". Cf. pp. 6, 11, 94.

[93] F. Schevill, *The Great Elector* (Chicago, 1947), pp. 281-6, 357, 381. See also S. Jersch-Wenzel, *Juden und "Franzosen" in der Wirtschaft des Raumes Berlin/Brandenburg zur Zeit des Merkantilismus* (Berlin, 1978).

IV

By the beginning of the eighteenth century, the humorous aspects of the Case of the False Jew were apparent even at the scene of the crime. "From an expectation of the calling of the Jews there is scarce an irreligious imposture set on foot but a pretended Jew must be the Jack-Pudding of the play", explained the anonymous biographer of alderman Ambrose Barnes in 1716. Apart from the False Jew of Hexham, he was reminded of the bogus conversions of Shalom ben Shalomoh and Signior Rigep Dandulo, "said to be of a great family in Venice".[94] Indeed, he wrote,

> Such another ridiculous folly were the Anabaptists of Northumberland guilty of. Their pastor Mr. Tilham and his friends, at Hexham, were not a little flusht with the accession of a Jew supposed to be converted to their Society, whose fictitious name was Joseph ben Israel. They wanted not caveats against too much forwardness and credulity in entertaining strangers. But they would have their own way, and with much ceremony baptized their new comer, imagining it would raise the reputation of their persuasion. But the printing the story brought a shame and contempt upon their party not to this day worn off, by discovery of the fallacy of this new proselyte, who proved to be a knavish Scottsman whose true name was Wilson. Our Author lookt upon these pranks as so many robberies committed upon the holy name of God.

Barnes's biographer may have been mistaken as to the true name of the False Jew, but surely his sentiments were basically correct. The problem was an exaggerated hankering after Jews, in part because of the widely held conviction that their conversion was a precondition for the Second Coming. At the same time, however, he praised Ambrose Barnes for the fact that his "knowledge of the doctrines and opinions of the Jews was by acquaintance in his youth with the famous Mannasseh ben Israel, and was much improved by Victor Amadeus, a Jew well learned in the Hebrew language, who for some time resided in the north parts of England."[95] Contact with Jews was not necessarily a bad thing, provided that they were not False.

But as Barnes's biographer notes, one long-term effect of the Case of the False Jew was that the spread of the Baptist faith in the north of England suffered a considerable set-back, which is apparent when looking at the geography of nonconformity. Indeed, George Fox and the Quakers paid close attention to the scandal and exploited the weakness of the northern Baptists in a second campaign during 1657 and 1658, soon after Til-

---

[94] See *A True Narrative . . . of Shalome Ben Shalomoh* (London, 1699); Tho. Warmstry, *The Baptized Turk* (London, 1658).
[95] Barnes, *Memoirs*, ed. Longstaffe, pp. 17, 149.

lam left Hexham.[96] Later on, Fox published an explicit attack on Tillam in case anyone missed his point that the Baptists were a somewhat less than serious sect and in decline.[97]

Certainly it is true that the Case of the False Jew, and Tillam's activities afterwards, had the effect of giving a tinge of insanity to the quite serious theological question of Saturday-Sabbath observance, and of making its proponents the bedfellows of plotters and fanatics. This is apparent as early as March 1653-4 when the False Jew of Hexham was included in a special list of "Grand Blasphemers" drawn up for contemplation before an official fast day. Also condemned were Thomas Tany, John Robins, and Joshua Garment, all notorious and somewhat violent Judaising religious extremists.[98] It would be the constant challenge of respectable Saturday-Sabbatarianism to live down Tillam and his unfortunate humiliation. Indeed, in 1667 seven prominent Saturday observers clubbed together to publish a "faithful testimony against the teachers of circumcision, and the legal ceremonies; who are lately gone into Germany".[99] Tillam for the Saturday-Sabbatarians was what John of Leyden was for the Baptists: a dangerous fanatic whose memory threatened to blacken the movement for all time to come.

When Charles II opened the new session of Parliament on 21 March 1663, he devoted a considerable portion of his speech to "the late Treason in the North". "I do assure you," he told the House, "we are not yet at the Bottom of that Business."[100] No doubt we never will be. "I shall acquaint y° w^t is come of mr. Tillam", wrote a Sabbatarian Baptist in 1674, "I hear he died in Germany; a very great blemish to the truth he was, I fear he went out as a snuff.'[101] But the author of a short pamphlet published in 1683 speaks of Tillam as if he were still alive, perhaps in England, perhaps in Germany, in Brandenburg or in the Palatinate, leading his band of Saturday-Sabbatarians.[102] It has been claimed that they survived until Napoleon's invasion of Germany.[103] They may be there still.

---

[96] George Fox, *Journal*, ed. N. Penney (Cambridge, 1911), i. 310-11. Fox had already "passed away through Hexam peaceably" in 1653, the year of the False Jew (i. 136-7). Cf. Howell, *Newcastle*, p. 259.

[97] F[ox], *Tillam*, *passim*.

[98] *A List of some of the Grand Blasphemers* (London, 1654), broadsheet.

[99] George Eve, Arthur Squibb, John Belcher, Edward Stennett, John Gardiner, Richard Parnham, Robert Woods in 15 pp. appendix to Edward Stennett, *The Royal Law Contended For* (2nd edn, London, 1667): only copy in Crawford Library, Haigh Hall, Wigan: described in *A Baptist Bibliography*, vol. i, ed. W.T. Whitley (London, 1916), p. 92, from "Copy owned by editor".

[100] *Lords Jnl.*, ii. 582.

[101] Joseph Davis to the Seventh-Day Church in Newport, 5 Aug. 1674: see below, p. 167.

[102] J.B., *The Morality of the Seventh-day-Sabbath Disproved* (London, 1683).

[103] Whitley, "Militant Baptists".

CHAPTER THREE

DR PETER CHAMBERLEN AND THE FRUITS OF FAILURE

Edward Gibbon once remarked that Cambridge Hebraist John Lightfoot, "by constant reading of the rabbies, became almost a rabbi himself." The persistent fear that overexposure to the religious sources common to both Christianity and Judaism would lead to unacceptable beliefs and practices began at least with Erasmus and in England never ceased to be expressed. In many ways it was fortunate that the Case of the False Jew did not produce a sufficient ideological backlash that might have made ridiculous any and all attempts to apply the Old Testament to Christian life. Tillam and his band remained as an uncomfortable warning to Henry Jessey and others in the Baptist movement, who were unwilling to let their beliefs and practices on this issue, especially regarding the Sabbath, create yet another cause for division within the fragmenting Separatist tradition. But it was inevitable that the question of the continuing validity of the Old Testament and the observance of the Saturday-Sabbath should have resulted in a group of men devoted to that cause; separate churches had already been formed over far less significant issues.

The first man who had the opportunity to do so was Dr Peter Chamberlen (1601-1683), physician, projector, and entrepreneur. Both Jessey and Tillam were connected with the gathered Baptist church which met at Lothbury Square in London under his leadership between August 1652 and May 1654, by which time Chamberlen was already a Seventh-Day Baptist. This congregation had its own bogus Jewish convert as well, whose unmasking precipitated the dissolution of the church. Chamberlen thereupon helped to establish a viable Seventh-Day church, by founding the fellowship which would later meet at Mill Yard as the home congregation of the English Seventh-Day Baptist movement until this century.

Chamberlen's failure to remain a leader of the Seventh-Day men in large measure derived from his inability to devote himself wholeheartedly to any single project, especially one which was unlikely to be financially profitable as well as morally uplifting, in a period when all seemed possible. Like Jessey, Dr Peter Chamberlen was hardly part of any lunatic fringe. He was a scion of the distinguished Huguenot family which held the secret of the obstetrical forceps, the source of their professional success and economic prosperity. Chamberlen in his time was royal physician to Charles I, Henrietta Maria and (notwithstanding his radical past) to Charles II after the Restoration, whom Chamberlen himself had delivered. But he was distracted during the Interregnum by numerous brain-storms which competed for his attention. He advocated the incorporation of midwives, promoted a new system of public baths, and called for the establishment of a public bank and self-supporting communities of the poor. On this basis, Dr Margaret James in her book on social policy during the Puritan Revolution even singled out Chamberlen as one of the small handful of essentially practical men who were genuinely anxious to improve the lot of the poor during that period.[1]

Yet despite the failure of Dr Peter Chamberlen to give institutional form to the belief in the continuing validity of the Saturday-Sabbath, his numerous appeals on behalf of the Old Testament, and his prominent if not always revered position in English life ensured that these ideas were given a hearing. It remained for less flamboyant figures in the next generation to transform an idea into a sect.

I

Peter Chamberlen was born on 8 May 1601 in the parish of St Anne, Blackfriars, and was baptized four days later at the French Church, Threadneedle Street.[2] His grandfather, William Chamberlen, had been a French Huguenot who fled to England with his wife and three children and settled at Southampton in 1569. He was probably a surgeon by trade, for this is the profession which attracted his two most famous children, Peter Chamberlen the elder (d. 1631) and Peter Chamberlen the younger (1572-1626).[3] The Sabbatarian Peter Chamberlen was the son of the younger brother, but it may have been his uncle who was the first to use the famous obstetric forceps which became associated with the family name. The elder Peter left Southampton and practised in London from 1596 and indeed became one of the most popular "accoucheurs" of his day. In this capacity he assisted the queens of James I and Charles I (French herself) in the birth of their children.[4]

---

[1] M. James, *Social Policy During the Puritan Revolution* (London, 1930), pp. 275, 281.

[2] *The Registers of the French Church, Threadneedle Street, London*, vol. i, ed. W.J.C. Moens (Pubs. Hug. Soc. Lon., ix, 1896), p. 40. One of the witnesses was Pierre de Laune, his maternal grandfather, "ministre de Norwich".

[3] That Peter the elder and Peter the younger were brothers is clear from their respective entries in the *Dict. Nat. Biog.* The author of the article on Peter Chamberlen the Sabbatarian has unfortunately made them father and son, and William Chamberlen the great-grandfather. Generally, see J.H. Aveling, *The Chamberlens and the Midwifery Forceps* (London, 1882); J.W. Thirtle, "Dr. Peter Chamberlen. Pastor, Propagandist, and Patentee", *Trans. Bap. Hist. Soc.*, ii (1910-11), 9-30, 117-17; iii (1912-13), 176-89.

[4] *Dict. Nat. Biog.*, *s.v.* "Chamberlen, Peter, the elder (d. 1631)"; Aveling, *Chamberlen*, pp. 4-14.

"My birth was in *May*, sixteen hundred and one, in the Precinct of the *Black-friers, London*", related our Dr Peter Chamberlen, the younger Peter's son, "I boast not the *Norman* Familie of *Tankervile*, nor any Lordly extraction of *England*. My rejoycing is to be of the Escapes of Parisian Massacres, and of honest Parents, fearing God, for which beloved, and well reported of by Neighbours." Chamberlen was sent by his physician father to Merchant Taylors' School, one of what Dr Christopher Hill described as the "nurseries of science" in early seventeenth-century England, whose Old Boys included numerous leaders of science and medicine. "At the Vniversitie I piddled in Chyrurgery, amongst my fellow-Pupils of *Emmanuel* Colledge in *Cambridge*", Chamberlen recalled. Here, too, we find him in one of the centres of English medical tradition: other graduates of Emmanuel College included Samuel Ward, Ralph Cudworth, and John Bastwick. Chamberlen took his MD at Padua in 1619, and was afterwards incorporated at Oxford and Cambridge:

> I did Publick Exercises in *Heydelberg* and *Padua*: and (ere nineteen sunnes had measured out my Nativitie) received the Doctorall Robes of that Vniversitie, and wore my Scarlet under that worthie Professour of *Oxford* Doctour *Clayton*, and the next year under the Doctour of the Chair in *Cambridge*. I confesse, my Degree seemed big unto my self, and the pointings of the finger dyed my Cheeks with the reflection of my Robes. Yet I was led into Practice, which God blest with Gifts of Healing.[5]

Chamberlen's study abroad was quite normal in his day. An English MD was supposedly obtained after a long course of study in the medical and arts faculties. A candidate for a fellowship in the College of Physicians was required to have had at least four years of practice in addition to his medical degree. One accepted way of circumventing this arduous path was to spend a brief period abroad, taking an MD at Padua or some other popular Continental centre, and then incorporating at Oxford or Cambridge, the two English universities. This arrangement was financially profitable for the College as well: the fees for graduates of foreign universities were triple those for doctors who qualified in England.[6]

---

[5] Peter Chamberlen, *A Voice in Rhama* (London, 1647), sig. A3ᵛ-A4ʳ. Despite these modest protests concerning his family origins, we find that Chamberlen had already gone to the effort of proving his descent and use of arms described as "Gules, an inescutcheon argent and an orb of cinquefoils or: a label of three points". These arms were confirmed to his son Hugh in 1664: Aveling, *Chamberlen*, p. 5ln., quoting Brit. Lib., MS. Harl. 1476, f. 27b & 1086, f. 2; C. Hill, *Intellectual Origins of the English Revolution* (Panther edn, London, 1972), pp. 63, 312; F.W.M. Draper, *Four Centuries of Merchant Taylors' School 1561-1961* (London, 1962), p. 51.

[6] On the College of Physicians and the practice of medicine in early Stuart England, see C. Webster, *The Great Instauration* (London, 1975), pp. 250-310; R.S. Roberts, "The Personnel and Practice of Medicine in Tudor and Stuart England", *Med. Hist.*, vi (1962),

Chamberlen recalled that the ''vacancy of Schooling was improved to Galenicall and Chymicall Preparations, and some Chyrurgicall Operations, by the assiduous care of an indulgent Father, of known fame and successe in all the Parts of Physick''. He was also instructed by ''others of my Paternall and Maternall kindred'' until finally his ''father added to me the knowledge of Deliveries, and Cures of Women.'' Chamberlen appeared three times before the College of Physicians in 1621 and was deemed a worthy candidate for a fellowship should one become vacant. He appeared and was examined again in 1626, unsuccessfully competed for a fellowship the following year, and was finally elected fellow on 29 March 1628. He was at that time called to be admonished by the president to change his style of dress and to abandon the habits and fashions of the youth at Court. It was ordered that he not be admitted until he conformed to the custom of the College of Physicians and adopted their sober form of dress. On 7 April 1628, apparently having obeyed these instructions, Dr Peter Chamberlen was admitted fellow of the College of Physicians.[7]

In this same year 1628, Chamberlen's uncle Peter the elder attended Queen Henrietta Maria when she miscarried at Greenwich. Chamberlen's father had died two years before, so it was probably the elder Peter who used his influence at Court to have his nephew introduced into the royal birth-room. Dr Peter Chamberlen, only twenty-nine years old, attended the queen in 1630 on the birth of the future Charles II, and two years later his appointment as royal physician was confirmed, after the death of Peter the elder in 1631.[8]

Dr Peter Chamberlen spent the next twenty years plying his trade as a hugely successful man-midwife and the holder of the secret of the obstetrical forceps. Involvement in religious affairs would have to await the coming of the Civil War and the decline in power of the medical monopoly which so opposed his various schemes in the 1630s and 40s. The most notorious of these was his bid, in the words of a critic, ''to get himself created vicar generall of the Midwives in city & suburbs''. Midwives were still licensed by the Church, a vestige of their now abolished power of baptizing dying infants. But the midwives themselves protested to the College of Physicians, to the archbishop of Canterbury and to the bishop of London in 1634, and on 22 October in the presence of Laud and William Juxon, Chamberlen was ordered to give up his plan and to devote himself to the

---

363-82 & viii (1964), 217-34; G. Clark, *A History of the Royal College of Physicians of London* (Oxford, 1964-6), i. 132, 188, 190.

  [7] Chamberlen, *Rhama*, sigs. A3ᵛ-A4ʳ; Aveling, *Chamberlen*, pp. 31-2.

  [8] W. Radcliffe, *Milestones in Midwifery* (Bristol, 1967), p. 30; *Cal. S.P. Dom., 1660-1*, p. 519.

service of women in labour, without further attempts to extort money from rich and poor alike.[9]

Chamberlen seems to have moved to Holland about this time, and remained there seven or eight years until the beginning of the Civil War.[10] There was some talk, quite probably genuine, of his going to Russia as the czar's personal physician, which came to nothing.[11] In any case, his self-imposed exile was ended by May 1642, when the Company of Barber Surgeons awarded him a silver tankard: by September he was invited back to the College of Physicians, which had so sternly admonished him in the previous decade, and indeed caused to have him imprisoned.[12]

For Chamberlen, as for many others, the chief significance of the outbreak of Civil War was that it removed many of the restrictions which had so limited his activities. Chamberlen abandoned temporarily his plan for the incorporation of midwives, and turned to the burning question of public baths, petitioning Parliament in September 1648 for a patent for "the sole Making of Baths and Bath Stones, within the Kingdoms of *England* and *Ireland*, and Dominion of *Wales*, for Fourteen Years".[13] This latest

---

[9] T.R. Forbes, *The Midwife and the Witch* (New Haven & London, 1966), pp. 141-3, 151-2; W. Radcliffe, *The Secret Instrument (The Birth of the Midwifery Forceps)* (London, 1947), esp. pp. 16-19; *idem, Milestones*; A. Eccles, *Obstetrics and Gynaecology in Tudor and Stuart England* (London, 1982), pp. 13-14, 117, 141-2; J.H. Aveling, *English Midwives* (London, 1872), pp. 22-8; H.R. Spencer, *The Renaissance of Midwifery* (London, 1924); *idem, The History of British Midwifery from 1650 to 1800* (London, 1927), pp. i-xxiii; "Philalethes", *An Answer to Doctor Chamberlaines Scandalous and False Papers* (London, 1649), pp. 1-2: Thomason dates the pamphlet as 29 Mar. 1650, which claims that this charge "was proved at the bar of the house of Commons, in the beginning of the Parliament". Perhaps this is a reference to Chamberlen's arrest and release by the House of Lords as "contrary to the Privilege of Parliament": *Lords Jnl.*, vi,. 186b: Aug. 1643; Charles Goodall, *The Royal College of Physicians of London* (London, 1684), pp. 463-6, including "An Historical Account of the College's proceedings against Empiricks and unlicensed Practisers"; "The humble peticõn of divers auncient Midwifes inhabiting w^{th}in the City of London", 27 July 1634: repr. Aveling, *Chamberlen*, pp. 37-9; cf. pp. 43-8.

[10] Chamberlen, *Rhama*, sig. A4^{r-v}. Chamberlen was cited by the college for non-attendance on 28 Mar. 1635 and 28 Sept. 1640: Aveling, *Chamberlen*, p. 59.

[11] W. Munk, *The Roll of the Royal College of Physicians of London* (2nd edn, London, 1878), i. 194-5. Arthur Dee, the son of the famous Elizabethan magus, became the personal physician of Michael Romanov in 1621. Previously he had been one of the physicians to Anne, queen of James I, along with Chamberlen's uncle. Dee left Russia in 1634 and became physician extraordinary to Charles I the following year. Dee would therefore have become acquainted at court with Peter Chamberlen and may have brought him to the czar's attention: see J.H. Appleby, "Ivan the Terrible to Peter the Great: British Formative Influence on Russia's Medico-Apothecary System", *Med. Hist.*, xxvii (1983), 289-304, esp. 289-95; *idem*, "Arthur Dee and Johannes Banfi Hunyades: Further Information on their Alchemical and Professional Activities", *Ambix*, xxiv (1977), 98-9; I. Lubimenko, "Anglo-Russian Relations During the First English Revolution", *Trans. Roy. Hist. Soc.*, 4th ser., xi (1928), 39-59.

[12] Aveling, *Chamberlen*, pp. 32, 59.

[13] G. Doorman, *Patents for Inventions in the Netherlands during the 16th, 17th and 18th Centuries*

scheme, combining public welfare and private profit, came to naught as well, but it was evidently taken quite seriously. A Commons Committee was appointed, which turned once again to the College of Physicians for a medical opinion. The results of the doctors' deliberations were predictably negative, for they were hardly about to condemn one of Chamberlen's opportunistic projects and then support another. But Chamberlen was awarded his patent, despite the College's claim that public baths would lead to "effeminating bodies, and procuring infirmities, and morall in debauching the manners of the people".[14]

Dr Charles Webster has observed that a good indicator of changing conditions at the College of Physicians is its relationship with Peter Chamberlen. Before the Civil War, it had successfully put an end to his scheme for the incorporation of midwives; his project for public baths, although strenuously opposed by the College, received official approval and a parliamentary patent. "This is indicative of the minor role played by the College on matters of public health", Webster explains. At the time, however, this was not an insult to their institutional dignity that the College of Physicians was willing to suffer. Chamberlen by his own admission had been avoiding fellow members and had ceased to attend meetings of the College. At a meeting held on 4 June 1649, the College ordered that Chamberlen be compelled to appear before them. Having disregarded this summons, Chamberlen was dismissed from his fellowship on 23 November 1649. Dr Webster reminds us that non-attendance was a misdemeanour which was allowed to pass unnoticed in the case of other members who attended infrequently.[15]

In any case, by the time of his expulsion from the College of Physicians, Peter Chamberlen had set his sights on even grander goals. The previous April, Chamberlen published a comprehensive scheme for solving at a stroke the problem of poverty in England which would incidentally pro-

---

(The Hague, 1942), p. 142: 11-year patents from 12 Mar. 1644, prolonged for 11 more years in 1663. Chamberlen took out a similar patent from the States of Holland and West-Friesland in Dec. 1663, perhaps in response to another patent for bath cabinets registered the previous July in the name of Mordechai del Monte of Amsterdam: *ibid.*, p. 181; Aveling, *Chamberlen*, pp. 60-4; *Com. Jnl.*, vi. 27 (22 Sept. 1648).

[14] Peter Chamberlen, *A Paper . . . to the Honorable Committee for Bathes and Bath-Stoves* (London, 1648), p. 2: the College replied officially on 16 Oct. 1648, and Chamberlen here prints the text with a reply. Chamberlen also answered the College in his *A Vindication of Publick Artificiall Baths* (London, 1648), charging them with having ignored his plan for years to the detriment of public health; [Anon.], *Pvbliqve Bathes Pvrged* (n.p., 1648), pp. 1, 4, 9-10: the style and opening sentence of this pamphlet are identical to that of the anonymous writer who called himself "Philalethes". Cf. R. Jenkins, "The Protection of Inventions During the Commonwealth and Protectorate", *Collected Papers* (Cambridge, 1936), p. 233; Aveling, *Chamberlen*, p. 60; Webster, *Instauration*, p. 298.

[15] Chamberlen, *Vindication*; Aveling, *Chamberlen*, pp. 68, 77; Webster, *Instauration*, p. 298.

vide funds for paying the arrears of pay in the parliamentary army, the issue which fuelled the rise of the Levellers, who had yet to meet their final repression the following month. Chamberlen's plan was to form a syndicate which would advance money at five per-cent to set a minimum of 200,000 poor to work, cultivating all commons, wastes, forests, and other under-utilized lands, including those of the deans and chapters, which had already been set aside to form the financial basis of a future English Presbyterian Church. Chamberlen calculated that each poor worker could produce a surplus of twenty pounds over and above the costs of his own subsistence. The state would organize these funds through a national bank, and would encourage investors to improve existing methods of production. A new model herring fleet alone could generate enough profit to finance the entire navy. The poor themselves would have the choice either of working as tenants on as much land as they could cultivate themselves, or of working in common teams under discipline while living in the disused palaces of the king and the bishops. The men would do all of the outdoor work and farm labour, while the women would manage the communal household. In this way, Chamberlen thought, the poor might become ''more tractable to all duties and commands'', for there were ''none more untractable, then idle Beggars''.[16]

It was this dramtic programme for solving the problem of poverty in England which made Margaret James include Chamberlen in the troika of practical men who were genuinely interested in improving the lot of the poor in this period.[17] H.N. Brailsford thought that Chamberlen's scheme proves that ''some of the more active minds among the radicals were turning in a socialist direction'', although Chamberlen himself cannot be reckoned as ''a consistent socialist''. ''Superficially these 'public houses' resemble the communal farms (*kibbutzim*) of contemporary Israel,'' Brailsford mused, ''with the all-important difference that they would not be self-governing.'' But even Brailsford thought that the plan was ''unrealistic'', and suggested that ''Chamberlen was a graduate of Cambridge and Padua; to these two schools an unkind critic might add the Academy of Laputa.''[18] Brailsford thought that Chamberlen had been inspired by Lieutenant-Colonel Jubbes; Dr Charles Webster suggests that Chamberlen's ''ramshackle schemes'' owned more to Samuel Hartlib, and Peter Cornelius Plockhoy van Zurick-zee, who in turn was impressed by the Anabaptist communes of Transylvania and Hungary, which may have given Til-

---

[16] Peter Chamberlen, *The Poore Mans Advocate* (London, n.d.), *passim*: dated 3 Apr. 1649 in text, and printed by Giles Calvert.

[17] James, *Policy*, pp. 275, 279-81, 302.

[18] H.N. Brailsford, *The Levellers and the English Revolution*, ed. C. Hill (London, 1961: 1967 edn), pp. 433-6.

lam the idea to establish his Sabbatarian commune on the Continent.[19] Indeed, another such Anabaptist commune had been established in America under Dutch auspices before being suppressed by the English.[20] At the very least, Chamberlen's plan shows him turning away from purely medical improvement projects, towards more universal schemes.

II

Unlike Jessey, Tillam and the other very early Saturday Baptists, Dr Peter Chamberlen, as we have seen, came very late to religious matters at all. His increasing involvement in doctrinal controversy came only after establishing a successful medical career and failing to devise a scheme which would bring in a good deal of money with very little effort. His conversion to Seventh-Day observance may have followed the traditional pattern beginning with a literal understanding of the fourth commandment, but this occurred only after a considerable apprenticeship in the Baptist movement. Significantly, like Thomas Tillam, the catalyst seems to have been involvement with a Jewish figure in his own church. Unlike Tillam's Jew, Chamberlen's was genuine, but he was no more of a sincere convert than the imposter of Hexham. The break-up of Chamberlen's church which followed the Jew's expulsion prompted him to join with other Seventh-Day men and to campaign for the implementation of Old Testament law, while never abandoning yet another combination of profit-making schemes.

Peter Chamberlen seems to have joined the Independent congregation which worshipped under the leadership of Nathaniel Homes since 1643.[21] Homes over the years had numerous contacts with philo-semitic millenarians and with Rabbi Menassah ben Israel himself, and was a close associate of Henry Jessey. Like so many Independent ministers during this period, Homes supplemented his pastoral duties to his gathered congregation by continuing to hold in his legal possession an ordinary parochial living. John Vicars the anti-schismatic described the situation which prevailed in Homes's church when Chamberlen must have been a member. Homes, he said,

> gathered an Independent congregation, excluding all his foresaid loving parishioners from Christian communion in their own parish church, except they would enter into a covenant with him, to walk according to his rule,

---

[19] *Ibid.*, pp. 434-5; Webster, *Instauration*, pp. 261, 368.

[20] W. Schenk, *The Concern for Social Justice in the Puritan Revolution* (London, 1948), pp. 144-8. For other views on Chamberlen's scheme, see B.S. Capp, *The Fifth Monarchy Men* (London, 1972), pp. 145, 148-9; C. Hill, *The World Turned Upside Down* (New York, 1973), pp. 44, 87.

[21] "Philalethes", *Answer*, p. 3.

which they not willing to yield unto he having got the keys of the church from their clerk, keeps all the parishioners out, and will not administer the Lord's Supper to any of them, not baptize any of their children, nor do any act of a minister or pastor to his people, save what he would do to a very Turk or pagan, unless they will dance after his Independent pipe. And thus now the parishioners wander as sheep without a shepherd, glad to run into others' pastures.[22]

Homes was not the only Independent minister who turned his territorial congregation out of their parish church and installed his own private collection of worshippers.[23] Dr Peter Chamberlen apparently was unwilling to submit to such strict discipline and left the congregation under a cloud.

"Philalethes" reports that it was after this incident with Nathaniel Homes that Chamberlen "quitted those quarters, and now turned Anabaptist", like Henry Jessey and Thomas Tillam. Newly converted to the Baptist faith, Chamberlen hastened to write to the distinguished Dr William Gouge, the famous Puritan preacher of Blackfriars, offering to dispute in public the question "Whether the sprinkling of Infants were of God or Man?" Gouge politely replied at the end of January 1649-50 that "the Matter was very weighty, and of Publick Concernment, and that he desired to advise about it with others." He reminded Chamberlen meanwhile that it was not his practice to admit "private men to vent heterodox opinions".[24]

At the same time, Chamberlen did not entirely abandon his plans for the economic and social improvement of England as a whole. On 14 December 1650 he wrote a letter to Cromwell himself, fighting the Scots in the north, now in the latter part of the second Civil War. Chamberlen was especially worried about the grievances of the army, more than a year after the suppression of the Levellers. Chamberlen seems to have known Cromwell personally by that time, for he described himself as one "who hath once had the sweet influence of an attendance nigh your Lordship".[25] He followed up this epistle with an open appeal to the House of Commons on

---

[22] John Vicars, *The Schismatick Sifted* (London, 1646), pp. 26-7. Cf. *idem*, *The Picture of Independency* (London, 1645), p. 9; M. Tolmie, *The Triumph of the Saints* (Cambridge, 1977), pp. 87, 94, 109-10, 123.

[23] Henry Burton, for example, followed the same practice: see *ibid.*, p. 110.

[24] "Philalethes", *Answer*, pp. 1-6; Peter Chamberlen, *To my Beloved Friends and Neighbours of the Black-Fryers* (London, 1650), broadsheet; Thomas Bakewell, *The Dippers Plunged* (London, 1650); *idem*, *Doctor Chamberlain Visited* (London, 1650), pp. 6, 8. Chamberlen also defended his view of baptism to the Seeker expert on Mosaic law: Peter Chamberlen, *A Letter to Mr. Braine* (n.p., 1650): dated in text as 3 Aug. Chamberlen moved house about this time as well, perhaps in order to place himself within the borders of another parish: 11 Nov. 1650, Miles Woodshawe to [Lord Conway]: "I have taken a lease of Dr. Chamberlain's house for six years": *Cal. S.P. Dom.*, *1650*, p. 424.

[25] *Original Letters and Papers of State*, ed. J. Nickolls (London, 1743), p. 36.

10 April 1651, protesting against increased taxation and the recent conduct of Parliament. He also suggested a reform of the electoral system, especially interesting for its provision giving the common soldier a political voice.[26]

But these issues were by now more of a sideline for Dr Peter Chamberlen, who had decided to put his religious views into action by joining and later leading a radical church in Lothbury Square, London, the history of which shows in fascinating detail the centrifugal effect which virtually unlimited religious freedom had on organized worship. The records of the church and more correspondence concerning its leaders have been preserved, and show very clearly Chamberlen's religious evolution and his final emergence as a Seventh-Day Sabbatarian. The first date in this folio volume of about 130 pages is 20 August 1652, but the records begin in earnest only from 5 June 1653 and continue until the final notation for 23 May 1654.[27]

The earliest records of the church were kept by John More, the first "Overseer" of the congregation.[28] More was an apprentice of William Webb, perhaps the man of that name who was Surveyor-General, and was forbidden by his master to join the Lothbury congregation.[29] More had become convinced of the truth of adult baptism, and was himself baptized on 1 February 1652. Webb thereupon had the idea of organizing a public disputation on the issue, and invited Peter Chamberlen and James Cranford the Presbyterian divine to represent the two sides. Four meetings took place between the end of March and the middle of April 1652, each session beginning and ending with prayer. The issues under debate were finally clarified as "1. Whether the Ministers of London, *Presbyterian-Ministers*, be not Ministers of Jesus Christ?" and "2. Whether private men, I mean tradesmen, may preach the Word of God without Ordination in the City of London?". Webb's aim, it seems, was to show that laymen like More and his friend Peter Chamberlen should be forbidden to preach and teach. Chamberlen complained that he was supported only by two or three others, apparently John More and John Splittlehouse, another religious radical, while Cranford's party was unlimited in number. The sessions went predictably, Cranford even admitting that the "Church of *Rome*

---

[26] Peter Chamberlain, *Plus Vltra. To the Parliament of England* (n.p., 1651): broadsheet, dated 10 Apr. 1651.

[27] Bodl. Lib., MS. Rawl. D 828, part. repr. in *Trans. Bap. Hist. Soc.*, ii (1910-11), 129-60, ed. C. Burrage.

[28] Chamberlen refers to More by that title on p. 131 of the records, and Jessey's letter to the church in 1652 was addressed to More as the man in authority.

[29] For more on Webb's religious beliefs, see D.S. Katz, *Philo-Semitism and the Readmission of the Jews to England* (Oxford, 1982), pp. 58-60.

might be a true Church, though full of Errours: as a man may be a true man, though full of sores and Ulcers.'' Chamberlen wanted to publish an account of the proceedings, although Cranford protested that ''there are books enough already of this argument''. Chamberlen's account of the debate appeared in print before the year was out, and appears to give a fair presentation of the two sides, although without any hint of his ''uncivill behaviour there, which not I, but your own party rebuked'', according to one eye-witness.[30]

By the following August, More and Chamberlen were joined together in the church at Lothbury Square. The actual records of the church begin only on 15 December 1652, four months after the congregation was organized and an accounting of money begun. Thus only eleven pages of the Lothbury records are in John More's hand, for ten days later, on Christmas Day 1652, Dr Peter Chamberlen assumed the function, and possibly that of Overseer as well. According to the inscription on Chamberlen's tombstone, the doctor began to ''keep ye 7th day for ye saboth'' from 1651, but similar to the method of Henry Jessey, the Lothbury Church held services on Sunday in accordance with normal Christian practice.[31]

In any case, the Lothbury congregation began to sow the seeds of disintegration from the very first entry in their record book: ''1652 December the 15.th Eliazer Barishaie Baptized at ovldford I.[ohn] M.[ore]''. The following day ''Bro: Eliazer'' married one Rebecca Hounsell, including signed testimonies in the record book. The witnesses to this marriage were John More, Theodore Naudin, John Spittlehouse, John Light, and Richard Ellis, all of whom were members of the Lothbury congregation.[32] Naudin was a French physician who had already published the proceedings of his controversy with ''Sieur Jean Mestrezat, Pasteur de l'Eglise reformee de Charenton les Paris''.[33] John Spittlehouse spent the years 1643 to 1651 in the army, rising to become deputy to the Marshal-General, in charge of military security, but apparently was dismissed at some point.[34] Spittlehouse published in 1652 a work with John More regarding the primitive church, and would become well-known for his numerous pam-

---

[30] [Peter Chamberlen], *The Disputes Between Mr Cranford, And Dr Chamberlen* (London, 1652), *passim*; John Graunt, *The Shipwrack Of All False Churches* (London, 1652), p. 2.

[31] See below, p. 86.

[32] MS. Rawl. D 828, pp. 5, 9.

[33] Capp, *Fifth Monarchy*, p. 256. Chamberlen's congregation may have included other French-speaking Baptists as well: see *A Calendar of the Letter Books of the French Church of London from the Civil War to the Restoration*, ed. R.D. Gwynn (Hug. Soc. Lon., Quarto ser., liv, 1979), p. 13. For Naudin's later involvement in a plot to murder Cromwell, see: *Thurloe State Papers*, ii. 309, 352; S.R. Gardiner, *History of the Commonwealth and Protectorate* (London, 1903), iii. 113, 125-6, 136; *Cal. S.P. Dom., 1654*, pp. 289, 372; Capp, *Fifth Monarchy*, p. 256.

[34] Capp, *Fifth Monarchy*, p. 263; *Dict. Nat. Biog.*

phlets and other writings.[35] Even during his military service he had published a work criticizing the government, which may indeed have precipitated his dismissal.[36] Of John Light we only know that he later became a Quaker.[37] Of Richard Ellis we know nothing at all.[38]

The admission of Eliazer Barishaie *alias* Paul Isaiah into their godly congregation was to prove a disaster no less costly than the Case of the False Jew to Thomas Tillam. When William Prynne came to write the history of the Jews in 1656, he warned Englishmen against Jesuits, "Popish Priests and Friers" who came from other countries to England

> under the title, habit, and disguise of Jews, of purpose to undermine our Religion, Church and State, and sow the seeds of Heresie, Blasphemy, Popery, Superstition, Schisms, and Divisions amongst us; they having formerly sent over some of late years amongst us, under the notion and vizard of *converted Jews*, as *Ramsey* the *Scot*, and *Eleazer*, and *Joseph Ben-Isaiah*, all *Jesuitical*, wicked, cheating Impostors: the two last whereof, have cheated the honest people of the Nation of many thousand pounds, being notorious Villains, one of them formerly a Trooper and Plunderer in *Prince Ruperts* army, as he confessed to his Hostesse at *Dursly* in *Glocestershire* in his drink, where he would have ravished the Maid-servant of the house, locking the door upon her, whiles she was warming his bed in the night, and upon her crying out for help, fled away presently in the night, to avoid apprehension; And yet wanders about cheating the people in other places, instead of being brought to *Tyburne* for his Villanies.

The reference to Alexander Ramsey the False Jew of Hexham is clear, as is that to Paul Isaiah, Eliazer Barishaie. "Joseph Ben-Isaiah" is almost certainly a reference to Isaiah's associate, the notorious convert Abraham bar Samuel *alias* Peter Samuel: Prynne has confused Samuel's Christian name with the pseudonym of the False Jew, "Joseph ben Israel" (which itself probably was meant to echo the name of Menasseh ben Israel) and tacked on Eliezer's surname in its Hebraic rather than Aramaic form.[39] Peter Samuel presumably is the "Trooper and Plunderer in *Prince Ruperts* army" in the Spanish Netherlands during 1647, since if Paul Isaiah's testimony is to be relied upon, during that year he was studying in Prague.[40]

---

[35] John Spittlehouse & John More, *A Vindication of the Continued Succession of the Primitive Church* (London, 1652): xerox copy at Regent's Park College, Oxford.

[36] John Spittlehouse, *Rome Ruin'd by Whitehall* (London, 1650).

[37] J. Besse, *A Collective of the Sufferings of the People Called Quakers* (London, 1753), i. 366, 392, 437, 480, 481; Capp, *Fifth Monarchy*, p. 224, where he describes John Light as a Fifth Monarchist, but omits him from the biographical appendix.

[38] A certain Thomas Ellis was a deacon of Vavasor Powell's church and later became a Quaker, but no record of a Richard Ellis has been found: Capp, *Fifth Monarchy*, p. 223.

[39] William Prynne, *A Short Demurrer To the Jewes* (2nd edn, London, 1656), p. 89.

[40] J. Cleugh, *Prince Rupert* (London, 1634), p. 180; W.S. Samuel, "The Strayings of Paul Isaiah in England, 1651-1656", *Trans. Jew. Hist. Soc. Eng.*, xvi (1952), 78.

The life of Paul Isaiah is well-documented, although the source for his early years is his own autobiography, which was published in the first edition of his *Vindication of the Christians Messiah*. Paul Isaiah was born Eliazer Barishaie in eastern Europe, and in due course like all Jews was "instructed in all their abominable vices, as blasphemie, cursing, and other sinnes". His parents observed with worried eye his reluctance to perfect his abilities in these essential Jewish skills, so "they determined to send me to my Brother in *Prague*, (the Metropolis of the Realme of *Bohemia*) who is yet, if living, one of the learnedest Rabies there". Eliazer was tutored two and one-half years in "the fabling *Talmouth*" while his brother kept him strictly under his care. That is, until "it came to pass in . . . 1648. there arrived a *Rabie*, by name *Elias*, from ארץ ישראל (that is *Jerusalem*) into Dutch-land or *Holland*, who, whensoever he came into the Iewish Synagogues, preached or declared, that their *Messias* should come in during that present year". According to Eliazer, Rabbi Elias was showered with gifts of gold and silver, as a demonstration of faith in this fore-runner of the Messiah. But their prayers were in vain, "for that their *Messiah*, whom they so expected, was either asleep, or had some other weighty business".[41]

Eliazer claimed that it was the failure of Rabbi Elias's preaching that prompted the summoning of the quasi-legendary Jewish Council, supposedly held near Buda in Hungary, to discuss the entire Messianic question. Eliazer's account was probably based on a much-garbled report of the meeting of the Council of Four Lands, the Jewish representative body in eastern Europe, but his version is very different from the others. Eliazer claims that their disappointment in Rabbi Elias was so great that they

> did with the like unanimity confess and acknowledge, that Iesus Christ, whom the Christians worshipped, was the true *Messiah*, and that none other was to be waited upon or expected, until his second coming . . . And thereupon they were sprinkled according to the custome of the Papists, unto whose Religion they betook themselves[42]

Eliazer recounted that he had wished to join them in declaring for Christ, but as he was so carefully watched, his only course was to leave his brother's care and to make his way to a Christian centre where he might convert

---

[41] Eliazar Bar-Isajah P., *A Vindication of the Christians Messiah* (London, 1653): "Epistle to the Reader", sigs. A4ʳ-B3ᵛ. The 2nd and rev. edn appeared in 1654 under the name of "Paul Isajah". No reference to a Rabbi Elias appears in A. Ya'ari, *Christian Emissaries to Palestine* (Jerusalem, 1951), but in 1648 the Chmielnicki massacres began, which left thousands of Jews in eastern Europe dead and their homes destroyed, an ideal climate for messianic preaching: see J.I. Israel, *European Jewry in the Age of Mercantilism* (Oxford, 1985), pp. 121-2.

[42] According to other "reports" of the Council at Buda, the Jews declined to convert because all they were offered was unreformed Roman Catholicism, and knew of no other Christian faith. For more on this very popular story, see R.H. Popkin, "The First College for Jewish Studies", *Rev. Etud. Juiv.*, cxliii (1984), 357-9.

unmolested. His first thoughts were "to take a Voyage to this blessed and prosperous Country of *England*", but went by way of Antwerp, where he fell ill, and was visited by

> a *Jesuite*, hearing that I was a *Jew*, and newly come to that Town, with another young man my Fellow-Traveller, who was also a *Jew*, he comes to our lodging to instruct us in the Christian Faith or Religion, perswading us exceeding much to be Baptized, promising that he would afterward instruct us through-ly in the same; but we purposed not to have tarryed there in hope of his instructions in their belief, our resolutions being for *England*; But it pleased God so to increase my sickness, as that we were forced to abide there; which the aforesaid *Jesuite* perceiving, would never leave perswading us, until he had overcome us to be sprinkled, which they call Baptism

Eliazar Barishaie *alias* Paul Isaiah, and Abraham bar Samuel *alias* Peter Samuel, were both in England by 1651, for in that year Samuel was received by the Baptists in Oxford, and in the following one Paul Isaiah joined Dr Peter Chamberlen's congregation in Lothbury Square.[43]

Their entry into this godly society was lubricated by Paul Isaiah's "Confuting of the Jewish Religion" in a pamphlet which appeared in September 1652. Isaiah testified that he had been converted abroad to Christianity, and "it was to make a full and publike expression of my enjoying the right Christian Faith I arrived here in England".[44] Their religious credentials as potential converts to the Baptist sect assured, Paul Isaiah and Peter Samuel became friendly with one of the members of Chamberlen's group, a widow named Susanne Coveney, who was in receipt of charity from the congregation. It later transpired that during this period they managed to cheat the lady of her plate, and when she complained officially to the church in January 1653-4, it was reported that Samuel acknowledged having received over three pounds in money and plate from the widow, nearly half the amount in dispute. Even then, after both Jews had left the congregation, the Elders left it "for her to take wt means she thought good for recovery of her Money or Goods from . . . ye Jew Eleazar" and declined to take any further action.[45]

It is more than likely that Peter Samuel's aims were matrimonial as well as financial, because his friend and colleague Paul Isaiah during these same months was hard at work at winning the heart of another of the congregation's widows, Rebecca Hounsell, whose husband John had only recently passed away. Isaiah, unlike Peter Samuel, was as yet unbaptized,

---

[43] Isaiah, *Vindication*, p. xx; A. Neubauer, "Additions to Notes on the Jews in Oxford", *Collectanea II* (Oxf. Hist. Soc., xvi, 1890), 2.

[44] Eleazar Bargishai [Paul Isaiah], *A Brief Compendium of the Vain Hopes of the Jews Messias* (London, 1652): Thomason received the pamphlet on 11 Sept. 1652.

[45] Bodl. Lib., MS Rawl. D 828, p. 6.

and this final act of faith was made, as we have seen, on the eve of his marriage to the unfortunate widow. As if to cement his new-found devotion to Baptism, Isaiah published a somewhat longer work, dedicated to Parliament and the Lord Mayor and aldermen of London, which purported to summarize Jewish belief and practice. As might be expected, this work was little more than a collection of European fantasies about Jewish habits, but it left no doubt as to the religious sympathies of its author.[46]

Abraham bar Samuel *alias* Peter Samuel, meanwhile, had left Chamberlen's group, perhaps after having made certain promises to the widow Coveney, but certainly richer than before their acquaintance. In June 1652 he was at Southampton, where Nathaniel Robinson, the Baptist minister, came into contact with him. Robinson was a respected member of the Cromwellian establishment, and no doubt Samuel thought that he could be of some assistance. Robinson, however, was very wary about involving himself and his congregation in a scandal similar to that which broke in Hexham only several months before, and wrote to Henry Jessey for advice. Robinson asked Jessey for his opinion regarding "two Jewes one of wch videlzt. Abraham Bar Samuel hath bene with us in thesse parts". Robinson confessed that he "found little satisfaction" from his own interviews with Samuel and certain inquiries that he made of a friend of his who had travelled much in Germany:

> I could not with confidence comend his condition to others till I had Indeavored to gett fuller sattisfaction concerning them and he oft declaring both himself and brother were well knowne unto you I make bould to desire a few lines from you: if you please to give us any encouragmt myself and others shall doe for them and returne it to you, were they or others reall we humbly concive it were better they abode in London and sett to some employment both in respect of the offenc such a way of life carryes with it and other respects: and truely sir if yourself or other please to impart any such reall occasion you will find a ready people to contribute to ther yearely maintenance

Robinson's chief worry was that, like in Hexham, "we may receive a Jesuitt instead of a Jew".[47]

Henry Jessey passed the letter on to John More, the Overseer of the church at Lothbury Square, with a covering note written on the back, "I feare Abram is to blame", Jessey suggested,

> Eleazar sd. what he got, he gave no part to him, and sd, he was Reed by one in Oxford, and both had a stipend I think half yeerly thence. Speak to Eleazar, and yn write yor thots yt I may sennd back, being yor Friend and Brother Coveting yt they had a holy Coveting

---

[46] Paul Isaiah, *The Messias Of The Christians, and the Jewes* (London, 1655).
[47] Robinson to Jessey, 19 June 1653: Bodl. Lib., MS Rawl. D 828: letter inserted in MS record book as p. 7.

Peter Samuel seems to have absorbed most of the blame for having sought alms in Southampton because it was already becoming clear in Lothbury Square that something was amiss. Samuel's courtship of the widow Coveney seems to have gone sour, and the church resolved to send for her "to the end they may giue an account of her absense from the publik meetings of the Chirch". She seems to have been reconciled despite her financial claims on Peter Samuel, and indeed the last word John More wrote in the church records was the name of "Sister Coveny".[48]

John More's last entry in the church book is dated 26 June 1653; Dr Peter Chamberlen began to keep the records from Christmas Day 1653. The communal events of autumn 1653, the entire period of the sitting of Barebone's Parliament, is thus undocumented. We know little of how the members of Chamberlen's church reacted to Cromwell's millenarian experiment, apart from the fact that Dr Peter Chamberlen himself was summoned by the Lord Mayor and held in custody on 26 December 1653 for having theatened Cromwell's life the previous October: the "3. Witnesses not Agreeing & He denying, was dismissed." John Spittlehouse, meanwhile, was arrested about the same time for writing seditious petitions against Thurloe.[49]

It was during this same period that Paul Isaiah began to set in motion the chain of events which would lead to his expulsion from Chamberlen's gathered church. His wife Rebecca was already pregnant, and Isaiah was toying with the idea of another conversion, "goeing to othr Assemblies under the Notion of selling of Books", presumably including his own. His wife received two payments of charity from the church in July 1653, and Isaiah himself received money twice in September. In November, Isaiah received a substantially larger loan of over three pounds. His intention of having his child baptized at birth, contrary to the very basic tenet of Chamberlen's society, having been made known, Paul Isaiah was excommunicated on 1 January 1653-4: Chamberlen noted the apostate's name in its pre-Christian form, "Eleazar Bar Ishay".[50]

The final break with the apostate Jew and his wife came later. On 17 January, the church paid Rebecca Isaiah five shillings which had been passed on from Brother Willis, another member of the congregation. But on 29 January Chamberlen recorded the church's final decision regarding this sad affair:

> This day the Church had notice that (the Jew) Eleazar Bar-Ishai (who calleth himself Eleazar Paul who for the love of a woeman (as we now discover) hath

---

[48] *Ibid.*, pp. 7, 13, 16.
[49] *Ibid.*, p. 16; *Cal. S.P. Dom., 1653-4*, pp. 277, 294, 446.
[50] Bodl. Lib., MS Rawl. D 828, pp. 7, 17, 41.

made outward profession of ye Faith of Christ by being Baptized, becaus his wife did else refus to be Married unto him) is falne from ye Faith & hath long dissembled with the Church by goeing to othr Assemblies

Chamberlen recorded that the final act of treachery was that Isaiah

hath now carried away his Child to be Sprinckled by the Presbyterians or Others without giving either Notice, or causing any Dispute about the Busines. And threfore having put the Lord Jesus Christ to an open shame Wee do in the name of Iesus Christ pronounce the said Eleazar Bar-Ishai alias Paul to be delivered unto Satan. And do account him as a Heathen & an Infidel for neglecting to hear the Voice of the Church.

Paul Isaiah's wife Rebecca was also held responsible for the public humiliation of Chamerlen's church:

And forasmuch as Rebecca his Wife was conniving to the said Act of her Husband in deineing to come with her Child upon Intreaty of ye Church. Whereby she became partly guilty of ye said Act, and disobedient to the Councel of ye Church Endeavouring also to justifie the said Conniving under ye Notion of a Wife to a Husband ... The Church doth therefore declare that they withdraw the said Rebecca ye wife of ye sd Eleazar untill ye Lord hath fully satisfied them by her Repentance, that she deserveth to bee owned as formerly[51]

These official protests were to no avail, and two days later Isaiah's daughter was baptized in the church of St Peter, Paul's Wharf.[52] Meanwhile, the financial records of the church show that Chamberlen's congregation called itself to account for its ill-advised charity to this insincere Jewish convert. Not only had Paul Isaiah "put ye Gospel to an open shame", but he had managed to receive over £127 from various sources:

To ye Jew Eleasar in all	—	4-11-4
of La: Mayern	—	10
Mr. Blake	—	10
Mr. Roswell's Church	—	6
Mr. Selden	—	10
Sister Anne	—	14
		7-01-4

besides above 120*ll.* testified by Abraham ye Jew and Mr. Foster And what was given by severall of Dr. Chamberlens freinds before he went for Ireland[53]

This financial record is particularly interesting in that it shows how widely known the case of Paul Isaiah must have been. The reference to the Lady

---

[51] *Ibid.*, p. 41.
[52] *Registers of St Peter, Paul's Wharf,* ed. W.A. Littledale (Harl. Soc. Reg., xxxviii, 1909), p. 174. The child is referred to as "Elizabeth d. of Paule Isayah, Jew, and Rebecka his w.".
[53] Bodl. Lib., MS Rawl. D 828, p. 9.

Mayor is not surprising, in view of the fact that Isaiah dedicated his *Vindication* to the Lord Mayor in 1653 "for those many noble and gracious favours received from you".[54] The penultimate reference must surely be to John Selden, the famous jurist and Christian Hebraist.[55] Thomas Roswell was the leader of the "Separated Assembly" which broke away from Chamberlen's church about this time.[56] "Sister Anne" must be Chamberlen's wife, but the identities of Mr Blake and Mr Foster are uncertain.[57]

The financial record also makes mention of someone having gone to Ireland. Dr Peter Chamberlen was in London during this period, so the reference must be to Peter Samuel *alias* "Abraham ye Jew". Paul Isaiah remained in London as well, to his wife Rebecca's continuing shame. On 19 February 1653-4 she wrote a letter to Chamberlen's congregation in which she sought to explain her actions and to protest her exclusion from the church. Rebecca Isaiah argued that "as i have owned you for a church soe yourselves know that i have owned him for a husband soe that as i ow subiection for myself to you as a church soe i also ow subiection to him as a husband in such things as hee ought to have the command". She noted that she never sought to conceal the intended baptism from the congregation; on the contrary, "from time to time as i have had any sight into itt i have speedily discovered it with often desiring that hee might bee spoken to about itt". As for the charge that she dressed the child in fine clothes so as to give honour to the baptism, Rebecca protested that "i uterly deny for i put nothing on the child but what i putt on itt on any day when i put on clean cloths". Rebecca Isaiah begged the church either to explain why they had excluded her, or to permit her to join with them once again, in spite of her husband's excesses. She recalled "the bitterness that i did receiv from some when i had more need of comfort", and hoped that this unwarranted exclusion might be brought to an end. Dr Peter Chamberlen replied in a long and uncompromising letter in which he rebuked her for putting her husband before her church, and in permitting and even aiding in the baptism of her infant child.[58]

Paul Isaiah thus left Chamberlen's church, leaving behind him a trail of discord and unhappiness. During 1654 he published a new edition of his *Vindication* which shows his latest re-conversion. Isaiah thanked "my Saviour who has now established me as a Member of the Church of England" through the good offices of Dr George Wilde, formerly Laud's

[54] Isaiah, *Vindication*, ded.

[55] The entire subject of John Selden and the Jews has been curiously neglected. Meanwhile, see I. Herzog, "John Selden and Jewish Law", *Pub. Soc. Jew. Juris.*, iii (1931).

[56] Bodl. Lib., MS Rawl. D 828, p. 18.

[57] Samuel, "Strayings", p. 84 suggests that Mr Blake "may just conceivably have been the celebrated Admiral, who was ashore at the time."

[58] Bod. Lib., MS Rawl. D 828, pp. 47, 49-56.

chaplain, now deprived, and a future bishop of Derry. In accordance with his new Royalist bent, Isaiah excised the dedication to the Lord Mayor and the Parliament which appeared in the first edition of the previous year, and transformed the crafty and insinuating Jesuit who first converted him into "a Romish Priest, one of the Fathers, a grave man, the Dean of the Mother Church at Antwerp". Indeed, even his newly adopted country underwent a demotion from "this blessed and prosperous Country of England" to "this remote Country of England".[59]

Paul Isaiah published his last book in 1655, the year of the Whitehall Conference called by Cromwell to discuss the readmission of the Jews. The work was simply a translation of Sebastian Muenster's dialogue between a Christian and a Jew which had appeared a century before and was published many times thereafter. This time the dedication was to the Rev. Richard Parr, the Anglican minister now living at Camberwell. Isaiah thanked him for the "many favours which I have received from you, as to the refreshing of body, with the outward things of this life, and to the comforting of my soul", which seems to indicate that he had found a new source for charity. It was also in this work that Isaiah made the unwelcome revelation that "though perhaps there may not be now in *England*, any great numbers of professed Iewes (some to my owne knowledge there are, who have their synagogues, and there exercise Iudaisme)".[60]

Another child was born to Paul and Rebecca Isaiah in December 1655, and he was duly baptized as well in the church of St Peter's, Paul's Wharf.[61] The following year a collection was made on his behalf at Coventry which produced £1 10s, and he received over three pounds from the bursar of Magdalen College, Oxford at about the same time.[62] Paul Isaiah died in March 1656 and was buried at St Chad's church in Shrewsbury.[63] It was here that Elias Ashmole the famous antiquary saw Isaiah's tombstone and thought it of sufficient interest to make a note of it:

> Mr. Paul Isaiah, a
> learned Jew, con
> verted to the

[59] Paul Isajah, *A Vindication of the Christians Messiah* (2nd edn, London, 1654), epistle to the reader.

[60] *Idem, The Messias of the Christians, and the Jewes* (London, 1655), sigs. A2^{r-v}, A7.

[61] *Registers of St Peter, Paul's Wharf*, ed. Littledale, p. 175.

[62] T. Sharp, *Illustrative Papers on the History and Antiquities of the City of Coventry* (2nd edn, Birmingham, 1871), p. 70: the collection was made at St Michael's church and Isaiah's signature appears in the church accounts; *A Register of the Members of St. Mary Magdalen College, Oxford*, ed. W.D. Macray (London, 1894-1915), iv. 11.

[63] *Shropshire Parish Registers* (Diocese of Lichfield, vol. xv), *St. Chad's Shrewsbury*, ed. W.G.D. Fletcher (Shrewsbury, 1913), i. 263; H. Owen & J.B. Blakeway, *A History of Shrewsbury* (London, 1825), ii. 223.

Faith: buried Mar: 21.
1656 זלחח .[64]

We know nothing more of Peter Samuel nor of his journey to Ireland, apart from the fact that he was still alive and in England in 1660 when he joined with another convert named Paul Jacob in petitioning Charles II, newly restored, for "that Charitie & Maintenance, which yo' most noble Progenito:ʳˢ did soe freely giue".[65] Paul Jacob, now a very old man, had tried the same approach years before with Charles's grandfather James I, with as little success.[66]

Several months after Paul Isaiah had left his congregation, Dr Peter Chamberlen noted in the church records a "Querie Whether all oʳ Troubles following imediatly after yᵉ Excomunication of yᵉ Jew, & . . . his wife (being cheifly asked by those who now trouble us) And that Excomunications are not for . . . Yᵉ Soul but yᵉ fflesh." For indeed the affair of Paul Isaiah signalled the disintegration of Chamberlen's church, led chiefly by the other central figures there, John More and Dr Theodore Naudin, who by Chamberlen's testimony had apparently opposed Paul Isaiah as well. As had happened at Hexham, the exposure of the Jewish fraud was the signal for the breaking up of the major part of the church. On Christmas Day 1653, Dr Chamberlen noted that his flock had sadly dwindled, there 'being onely Br Naudin, More, Light, Smith, Chamberlen Sister More, Iones, Sara, Rawlinson Sister Monck went away as not yet reconciled to sister Read".[67]

Among this group that had fallen away was Arise Evans, the Welsh tailor-prophet, who had "wholly forsaken the Faith".[68] Evans is one of the more well-known of the religious radicals of the period, if only because Dr Christopher Hill singled him out especially for study in order to demonstrate that it is possible to obtain an idea of what ordinary people were thinking by examining their published remains, instead of relying on the biased evidence of heresy trials and the accounts of those who applauded their suppression.[69] Evans was a Royalist millenarian, and proclaimed as

---

[64] Bodl. Lib., MS Ashm. 854, p. 201; Elias Ashmole, *Works*, ed. C.H. Josten (London, 1966), iii. 941; J. Le Neve, *Monumenta Anglicana* (London, 1717-19), ii. 49; Owen & Blakeway, *Shrewsbury*, ii. 236. The Hebrew word is an abbreviation for "may his memory be preserved in the life of the world to come".

[65] SP. 29/9, f. 236.

[66] *Cal. S.P. Dom., 1623-5*, p. 517: text reprinted M. Adler, *Jews of Medieval England* (London, 1639), p. 376.

[67] Bodl. Lib., MS Rawl. D 828, pp. 16-18, 88 (entry for 9 Apr. 1654).

[68] *Ibid.*, p. 18.

[69] C. Hill, "Arise Evans: Welshman in London" in his *Change and Continuity in Seventeenth-Century England* (London, 1974), pp. 58-9. See also C. Hill & M. Shepherd, "The case of Arise Evans: a historical-psychiatric study", *Psychological Med.*, vi (1976), 351-8.

early as 1652 that "*Charles*, the Son of *Charles Stuart* by name, comes to the Elect Jewes, to deliver them from the power of darknesse; and to bring them to Jesus Christ and eternall life."[70] Evans even tried to convince Menasseh ben Israel, the Jewish proponent of readmission, that Charles II was the Messiah, and asserted that "he that lives five years to an end, shall see King *Charles Steeward* flourish on his Throne to the amazement of all the world, for God will bring him in without blood-shed."[71] Arise Evans spent only a short time with Chamberlen's congregation; before that he was a communicant at William Gouge's parish church in Blackfriars, and was supported by Gouge when arrested during the 1640s.[72] Of his experience at Lothbury Square, Arise Evans recalled that

> after the King was put to death, seeing no remedy for it, I remained silent a long time, in which God called me aside to look into the clossets of the *Anabaptists*, . . . and by reason of some acquaintance I had with Doctor *Chamberlen*, he brought me into their secret Chambers, where *I* saw no small abomination committed [sic], and now being taken among them as a friend, and pittying them, I often shewed them the necessity of *I*nfants baptisme, and lawfulnes of it, and that there was but one true succession of Ministry, and Ministers, which they had not, and at the last they were so offended at me, that they forbad me to come among them, and I having experience enough now of their wayes, was soon perswaded, being weary to see their corruption, division, malice, and enmity toward one another[73]

Arise Evans, like most of Chamberlen's followers at Lothbury Square, saw little purpose to remaining in a Christian fellowship that had all but collapsed.

The rest of Chamberlen's church book chronicles the sad tale of the disintegration of a gathered congregation. Not only do we find that from the new year 1654 the "busines of Brother Eleazar & Sister Coveny was also taken into Consideration", but other, much more trivial incidents continued to disturb communal peace.[74] At this point, Chamberlen appears to have felt the lack of fellowship, and even took to advertising in the local press: "All Christians", he proclaimed, "may meet at Dr. *Chamberlains* in White Friars every third day called Tuesday".[75] Dr Capp thinks that this is

---

[70] Arise Evans, *A Voice from Heaven* (n.p., 1652), p. 11n.

[71] *Idem, Light For the Iews* (London, 1656), pp. 4-5, 20; *idem, A Rule from Heaven* (London, 1652), sig. Bbb6ʳ; pp. 105-6. See also R.H. Popkin, "Menasseh ben Israel and Isaac la Peyrère II", *Stud. Rosenthaliana*, xliii (1984), 12-20.

[72] See Katz, *Philo-Semitism*, pp. 121-4.

[73] Evans, *An Echo*, pp. 90-2: repr. *Trans. Bap. Hist. Soc.*, ii (1910-11), p. 139n.

[74] Bodl. Lib., MS Rawl. D 828, pp. 19-22. See also the more conventional dispute reprinted in [Anon.], *A Discourse Between Cap. Kiffin, and Dr. Chamberlain, About Imposition of Hands* (London, 1654).

[75] *Perfect Diurnall*, 217 (13-19 Feb. 1653-4), p. 3116 = 3344.

another sign of ecumenism among the Fifth Monarchists as the millennium approached: they were willing to admit that true saints might also be found in rival congregations.[76] But it equally may be that Chamberlen found it increasingly difficult to run a church in which a large part of its small membership opposed him and his views.

It is ironic and even amusing to note that it must have been during this turbulent period that the unfortunate Thomas Tillam visited Peter Chamberlen's church. Both men had been members of Hanserd Knollys's congregation and may have met then. Tillam wrote a long and undated letter from London to his own church in Hexham in which he described Chamberlen's fellowship:

> My dear ones, in the spirit of truth and love, you will not surely be offended, yt the hand of my Father hath drawn me to ye great city, to obey him in those pretious truths, which he pleased to make known unto me, and which he hath filled brimfull of mercy in ye practice of. For after I had enjoyed heavenly communion with my pretious brethren of Coleman St., and had acquainted them with my purpose to obey Xt in ye 4th principle [the laying on of hands], and had received this gratious letter to ye sts. in Chesire, from them, I departed in much love, to ye melting of my hard heart, and having found many congregations in ye practice of the ordinances I wanted, I was, by a blessed hand, guided to my most heavenly Br. Doctor Chamberlen, one of ye most humble, mortified soules, for a man of parts, yt ever I met with, in whose sweet society, I enjoyed ye blessing of my God, by the laying on of their hands, and after a love feast, having washed one another's feet, we did joyfully break bread, and concluded with an hymn: in all wch the singular majesty of Xt shined forth to ye mighty conviction of some choyse spectators.[77]

Chamberlen's church was undoubtedly following the time-honoured principle of not quarrelling before strangers.

The last words in the records of the Lothbury church book was a notation for 23 May 1654 where we find "Sister Smith admonished of miscalling her husband (Dog &c) & humbled, & reconciled."[78] On this basis it has often been assumed that Chamberlen's church broke up finally about this date. But Chamberlen's group supported the Fifth Monarchy manifesto of 2 September 1654, which included the signature of fourteen members "In the name of the whol Church that walks with Dr. Chamberlain". Curiously, Chamberlen himself did not sign the manifesto, but John Light did, apparently reconciled after his departure earlier on. John Spittlehouse also appears there, as do three other original members, John

---

[76] Capp, *Fifth Monarchy*, p. 181.

[77] Hexham church book: repr. *Records of the Churches of Christ . . . at . . . Hexham* (Hanserd Knollys Soc., 1854), p. 323; D. Douglas, *History of the Baptist Churches in the North of England* (London, 1846), p. 57; Thirtle, "Chamberlen", 22-3.

[78] Bod. Lib., MS Rawl. D 828, p. 131.

Davies, Richard Ellis, and Richard Smith. The other nine members do not appear in the records of the church, but might well have been regular congregants who simply had not come to the especial attention of Dr Chamberlen.[79] Louise Fargo Brown, in her pioneering study of the Baptists and the Fifth Monarchy Men, was impressed that the "single Baptist church which signed the Fifth Monarchy manifesto as a unit was that of Dr. Peter Chamberlen, a visionary deeply imbued with Fifth Monarchy ideas."[80] Whether the church by that time had any real existence as a unit remains doubtful.

III

Those who knew Peter Chamberlen best asserted that he first began observing the Saturday-Sabbath about 1651, that is, before the Lothbury Square church was even organized. Nevertheless, despite what is usually claimed, there is no evidence that Chamberlen's congregation ever met and prayed on a Saturday. Like Henry Jessey, Chamberlen was not anxious at that point to make an issue over the complete observance of the Ten Commandments; that might wait until the day when the church was firmly established – as it happened, a day which never came. But Peter Chamberlen was by no means the only member of the church who observed the seventh day as the Sabbath. In 1657, three years after the breakdown of Chamberlen's church, John Spittlehouse, one of its formerly prominent members, published a short pamphlet with William Saller appealing to the chief magistrates of the Commonwealth to transfer the observance of the Sabbath to Saturday as required by biblical law. They thought that in the first stage this could be accomplished "without the least prejudice to the people, if you will but remove the Markets and Fairs, which fall on that Day, to some other day in the week". They noted that the strict provisions for the observance of Sunday also prejudiced the Saturday-Sabbath, for "many not being able to leave their callings two Days in a week; and therefore, albeit convinced of the truth of the Lords Sabbath, yet are by reason thereof, necessitated to break the Lords Sabbath, and to observe that of Mans erecting". The re-education of the parishioners might also be easily achieved "if the Clergy of this Nation would set themselves to preach from *Exod.* 20. 8, 9, 10, 11. [the Ten Commandments] they might in a very short time convince the judgement of their Congregations". Their specific pro-

---

[79] *A Declaration Of several of the Churches of Christ* (London, 1654): repr. *Trans. Bap. Hist. Soc.*, iii (1912-13), 129-53.

[80] L.F. Brown, *The Political Activities of the Baptists and Fifth Monarchy Men in England during the Interregnum* (London, 1911), p. 59.

posal, then, was to permit those who wished to observe the Sabbath on Saturday "to work on their callings on the First-day of the week".[81]

A secondary effect of the alteration of the Sabbath day to Saturday in accordance with the provisions of the Ten Commandments, Saller and Spittlehouse argued, "would be a means to remove a great stumbling-block to the Jews, who make it an Argument (that Christ is not the Messiah) because Christians, who profess themselves to be his followers, are Sabbath-breakers". The conversion of the Jews to Christianity, in turn, "will be a preparative to the accomplishing of those glorious Prophecies, which hold forth the unity which shall be betwixt Jew and Gentile".[82] Saller and Spittlehouse's plea seems also to have become known to the Jewish community in London which in the two years since the Whitehall Conference had begun to establish itself with some security.[83]

It was about this time that Dr Peter Chamberlen joined in with some other Saturday observers to form the Seventh-Day Baptist congregation which would eventually move to Mill Yard and be called by that name. In Chamberlen's day they seem to have met near Whitechapel, not far from Lothbury Square. The time had come for Chamberlen to assert himself as a religious leader in Cromwellian London, and promote the cause of the Saturday-Sabbath based on the word of God as recorded in the Old Testament. How he did this and the extent of his influence may never be known precisely, as the records of the Mill Yard congregation survive only from 1673. An early church book presumably was destroyed in the fire which consumed the meeting house in 1790.[84] Certainly he was the only member of the congregation who had any sort of national standing, and it was therefore only natural that he should have been the one to have represented Mill Yard at the debate with Jeremiah Ives on the question of the Saturday-Sabbath, held in Stone Chapel near St Paul's in January 1658-9.

---

[81] William Saller & John Spittlehouse, *An Appeal To the Consciences . . . touching the Sabbath-day* (n.p., 1657), pp. 12-13.

[82] *Ibid.*, pp. 13-14.

[83] Thomas Tillam, *The Seventh-Day Sabbath* (London, 1657), pp. 50-1: see above, p. 35. Tillam's pamphlet was an answer to William Aspinwall, formerly of Massachusetts: see Capp, *Fifth Monarchy*, p. 240.

[84] The church book has since 1933 been deposited at the Seventh Day Baptist Historical Society in Plainfield, N.J., U.S.A. Before that date it was in the library of Alfred University in New Jersey, where it had been sent by Dr Williams's Library early in this century. When Thirtle used the book in the writing of his article, it was "in the custody of Lieut.-Colonel T.W. Richardson, the present Pastor of the Church." I have used the original MS in Plainfield, but a photocopy exists in Dr Williams's library, shelfmark 533.B.1. On Mill Yard generally, see F.H.A. Micklewright, "A Congregation of Sabbatarian and Unitarian Baptists", *Notes and Queries*, cxci (1946), 95-9, 137-40, 161-3, 185-8; W.T. Whitley, "Seventh Day Baptists in England", *Bap. Qly.*, xii (1946-8), 252-8; *The Last Legacy of Joseph Davis, Senior*, ed. W.H. Black (London, 1869); *Minutes of the General Assembly of the General Baptist Churches in England*, ed. W.T. Whitley (London, 1908-10), I. liii; *Vict. Cnty. Hist., Surrey*, ii (1905), 39.

Chamberlen's fellow Seventh-Day men in this debate were Matthew Coppinger and the unfortunate Thomas Tillam, about to embark on his mission for Sabbatarian colonization.[85]

Finally, Dr Peter Chamberlen no longer feared to make public his views about biblical law. His first proposal, however, was still rather circumspectly framed. "The Truth is," he proclaimed, that "JESUS CHRIST IS THE ONLY ONE LAW-GIVER. To others may be Legislative Powers many". More specifically, he wrote,

> Behold, I *Peter Chamberlen*, Doctor in Physick, do once again bear Witness, That if the Laws of God be set up, in the Name and Title of the Laws of God: And the corrupt Laws of our Heathen and Antichristian Fore-fathers, and of our more corrupt Lawyers and Courtiers be abolished; There shall be more equal Distribution of Justice, even concerning *Meum & Tuum* (besides other Matters) in one year than hath been done these 500 years by Kings, Parliaments, Councils, Armies, or People, by all the Laws of men; and all People shall rest satisfied.

Chamberlen's programme came down to two succinct points: "1. Liberty of Conscince; but not of Sin" and "2. Gods Lawes to be Enthroned; but not the Jewes". Chamberlen may have been a Seventh-Day man, but he was not a Traskite. He asked all supporters to send their names in to Livewell Chapman the bookseller "who hath promised to keep them secret, till by sober and frequent meetings the matter may be digested, fit to be presented to the Parliament and chief Officers of the Army".[86]

Dr Peter Chamberlen, then, like Milton, Harrington, and many others, had definite ideas in 1659 about how to save the Commonwealth. Dr Woolrych in discussing some of these plans rather dismisses him as "that curious figure", but Chamberlen's suggestions are well in line with the biblical programme which was actually adopted in New England in the 1640s with the additional benefit of tackling a number of very pressing immediate problems.[87] Chamberlen's complaint in 1659 was that he had warned England of the consequences at the very beginning of the republican experiment, but his words had been disregarded. "I lost four years Attendance on the Parliament for the Publick Good;" he lamented, "yet I had many Friends amongst them. I lost both Houses, Lands and Goods by

---

[85] Jer.[emiah] Ives, *Saturday No Sabbath* (London, 1659), esp. sig. A6ʳ; pp. 1, 3: ded. to "they who are in the bondage to the *Jewish* Sabbath, and more particularly to those in *Colchester*", where Tillam had worked.

[86] [Peter Chamberlen], *The Declaration and Proclamation of the Army of God* (2nd edn, London, 1659), pp. 4, 7: recd. by Thomason on 9 June; *idem, A Scourge for a Denn of Thieves* (London, 1659), pp. 3, 7; recd. by Thomason on 16 June. Cf. Capp, *Fifth Monarchy*, pp. 123, 148, 150, 164-5, 178.

[87] A. Woolrych, "Last Quests for a Settlement 1657-1660", in *The Interregnum*, ed. G.E. Aylmer (London, 1972), p. 195.

Committees, and Officers of Parliament and Protector: I lost the Rewards
& Wages due to me from the late King''. Despite all of this, Chamberlen
claimed to ''have done service unto all without Recompence. I ask none,
but the fruit of mine own Labours, which is not yet granted.''[88]

Peter Chamberlen's plans for the reorganization of government were
put more fully in another work published the following December when
there seemed to be even less chance of putting them into practice. Chamberlen's advocacy of the Old Testament laws was expressed in an uncompromising fashion. The central question was whether ''it were not better
for Parliaments to accept of the Legislative Power of Jesus the Law, Statutes, and Judgments ready offered them from God. with the whole Plat-
form of Government prepared by the Word of God, practicable within one
Moneth, and easy to be established''. If God's laws were adopted, he
thought, this would ''end all sutes in a day'' for, he asked rhetorically,
''Was there ever sutes for Title of Land heard of in all the worst of Kings
of *Israel*?'' The judicial laws of the Old Testament were still valid, and he
asked ''Whether Time or Place, Nation or Sex alter that Law? or whether
God be altered that made it? so that, What was Idolatry, Blasphemy, Mur-
ther, Adultery, Theft or Fals Witness so long agoe in *Palestine* among the
Jewes; is it not so now in *England* among the Gentiles?'' To those who would
say that modern law should be based on reason and precedent, Chamberlen replied that there could be no one more rational than God, and no
precedent older than the Book of Moses. The lawyer ''enslaves us to the
Norman Tyranny'' and he and his colleagues ''help on the work of the Jesuits''. Although the Sabbath is not especially singled out among the laws
of God in this work, Chamberlen did ask whether 'the ten Commandments spoken by God, and twice Written with the finger of God: Ordinarily taught to Children, and written on most Church Walls and Windows;
and acknowledged so in all Confessions and Cathechismes, are not the
Law of God?''[89]

But the real moment of truth, for Peter Chamberlen as for every other
Cromwellian religious radical, was the return of the king in May 1660. We
have already seen how another well-known Seventh-Day man, Thomas
Tillam, reacted to this catastrophe. Henry Jessey too lapsed into unfo-
cused opposition to the crown and published works which were potentially
seditious. Chamberlen, meanwhile, seems to have dithered for quite some
time, perhaps uneasy in the now uncertain and potentially dangerous role
of radical religious leader. He was by all accounts not the sort of man who

---

[88] Chamberlen, *Scourge*, p. 4.
[89] Peter Chamberlen, *Legislative Povver in Problemes* (London, 1659), dated by Thomason
3 Dec. 1659.

was likely to join the religious underground. A more practical means of self-support needed to be found, even leaving aside the religious question.

It appears that Chamberlen regained the post of royal physician fairly soon after the Restoration, for in February 1660-1 he wrote to Charles for official confirmation of his position. He reminded the new king that he was "the only surviving Physician to their Majesties; before the misrule." He noted that although "your Majestie hath been pleased to take Notice of yor petitioner, and to own him yor Maties Servant" he was unable to perform his duties until Charles would inform the Lord Chamberlain of such. Charles II himself replied on the petition, nothing that "Doctor Peter Chamberlen, Physitian to Our Royall Father & Mother, Ordinarily Attending Our Happy Births, And (therefore) One of Our First Servants: Is Our Servant & Physitian in Ordinary.'[90]

This is how he was described on a pass to Holland which was issued to Chamberlen two months later, but certainly by the end of May he was back in England, wrestling like many radicals with the thorny question of the Oaths of Supremacy and Allegiance.[91] Perhaps for Chamberlen the problem was less difficult than for others, for he had been associated with the Court before the Civil War. He copied out a tract entitled "A Case of Conscience" concerning the words of the oath, and may indeed have been the author of this work which, although printed, is now apparently lost. He seems to have taken the oath in a modified form, accepting Charles as head of the church "under the Lord Jesus Christ".[92] A copy of Chamberlen's signed declaration, sporting a gilt seal and dated 29 May 1661, still survives.[93] At any rate, all of this was clearly sufficient to keep him in the good grace of the king, who was unwilling to penalize a man who after all not only brought him into the world, but also represented something of the happy period before the Civil War.

So within a year of the Restoration of Charles II, Dr Peter Chamberlen was once again a courtier who had sworn allegiance to the crown. The

---

[90] Chamberlen to Charles II, Feb. ? 1660-1: *Cal. S.P. Dom., 1660-1*, p. 519: full text (SP. 29/31, fos. 141-2) repr. Aveling, *Chamberlen*, pp. 88-9. Dr Capp suggests that Chamberlen seems "to have welcomed the king because he offered religious toleration with stable government", but notes that he did not return "to opposition when this was seen to be an empty promise": *Fifth Monarchy*, p. 201.

[91] *Cal. S.P. Dom., 1660-85, Add.*, p. 25.

[92] Bodl. Lib. MS Clar. 74, fos. 418-23: at the head of the text, Chamberlen writes that it was "Published in a Book, Entituled A Collection of so much of the Statutes in force as contain and enjoin the taking of the several Oaths of Supremacy and Allegiance &c.", printed by Robert White, in Warwick Lane, 1661. According to *Cal. Clar. State Papers*, vol. v, ed. F.J. Routledge (Oxford, 1963), p. 101, the tract was written by Chamberlen himself, but this is not clear from the MS.

[93] Bodl. Lib., MS Clar. 74, fos. 419^r-420^v, written on much smaller paper than the tract itself.

cause of the Seventh-Day was now worn very lightly indeed. Chamberlen continued to observe the day privately at home and did so until his death. But the task of transforming a very fragile Civil War sect into a viable Restoration denomination was gradually let from his grasp. Nowhere was this more clearly made apparent to his fellow Sabbatarians than in his failure to take a stand in the first major trial of a Seventh-Day man, from his very own congregation, or to make any sort of protest to his royal patient before the unfortunate worshipper was executed at the end of 1661.

John James, a ribbon weaver, was taken on 19 October 1661 when the congregation was "assembled the day above-mentioned, (being the seventh day of the week) in Bulstake-alley". James had preached from the eighth psalm, "Out of the mouths of babes", which was interpreted by "one Tipler, a pipemaker, journeyman to a neighbour near adjoining" as an incitement to rebellion, and soon no less than four JPs had arrived on the scene to shouts of "Treason! Treason!". The authorities thought James to be a pathetic fellow, and when acquainted with his beliefs, one of them exclaimed, "What you are a Jew. John James said, that in one sense he was a Jew, and in another sense not". James was known to them, and the JPs told him that this time "he should stretch for it"; one of them said that "if he were not hanged he would be hanged for him". But further inquiries were hardly necessary:

> The Lieutenant spake something also about the Fifth Kingdom, and asked him, wehther it was not his principle? who told him he did own the Fifth Kingdom which must come: whereupon they laughed one upon another and said, "Now they had it from his own mouth."

The clinching bit of evidence seems to have been the charge "about his learning to sound a trumpet, in order to a rising with Venner's Party; to which he said, there was a friend of his who lay in his house, minding to go to sea, being to learn to sound, desired he might have liberty to be taught in his house, but he never learned himself". Even more importantly, James denied himself to be one of the Fifth Monarchist rebels, "neither was he one of those in that rising, judging it to be a rash act."[94]

This, of course, was the key to the government's hysteria regarding John James and his innocent preaching. The Venner Uprising had taken place at the beginning of the year, on 6 January 1661, a rebellion of desperation, led by "one Thomas Venner, sometime a wine-cooper, who by the king's indulgence held a conventicle in Coleman-street, where he, and others, used to preach to them out of the Prophecies of Daniel and the Revela-

---

[94] *State Trials*, ed. W. Cobbett, T.B. Howell, *et al.* (London, 1809-28), vi. 67-72.

tions''.[95] John James was completely unconnected with Venner, but immediately after the insurrection was put down, great efforts were made to prove that the actual rebellion was only the London tip of a great nationwide iceberg.[96] When James admitted a certain sympathy with the notion of a Fifth Monarchy which would be brought into being by the saints, he effectively condemned himself to the gallows, a fact which he himself had cause to recall later on in prison.[97]

John James's behaviour at his trial did little to improve his position. When denied a copy of the charge, the usual practice in treason trials, James cited the precedent of John Lilburne the Leveller who was given a copy when on trial for treason at Oxford years before. When the clerk asked how he would be tried, he "answered, By the Law of God. At which the lawyers gave a great hiss." James was sternly admonished that it "was not a place or time to talk of the laws of God." James's speech in his own defense was so full of saints, revelation, and the Lord Jesus Christ, that one of the justices interrupted him, saying, "Hold, Sirrah; Sirrah, you think you are in the conventicle in White Chapel preaching." James's case was sealed by the intervention of Sir Heneage Finch, the solicitor-general, who charged that

> there were a people, that under the pretence of religion had the liberty of conscience allowed by the king for a time, till they were better informed; but this man, and those of his mind, are none of those men: but they endeavour not only to destroy the monarch, but monarchy itself; not only in England, but all the world over.

Finch asked the jury to consider further,

> That the great trouble this nation had undergone for these twenty years last past, spring from pulpits, conventicles, and seditious preaching; and therefore if these causes were taken away, it might prevent such evil effects for the future.[98]

Dr Peter Chamberlen had access to the king but refused to put himself at risk by intervening. John James's wife attempted to influence the king in a last effort to prevent the death sentence from being carried out. She lay in wait for Charles II to pass a paper to him outlining her case. But Charles "held up his finger, and said, 'Oh! Mr. James, he is a sweet gentleman!'" The next day he reiterated his unwillingness to alter the judgement of the court, and denounced "John James, that rogue: he shall be

---

[95] *Ibid.*, p. 67n.
[96] For Venner, see Capp, *Fifth Monarchy*, pp. 199-200.
[97] *State Trials*, ed. Cobbett, p. 92. Cf. *Vict. Cnty. Hist., London*, i (1909), p. 375.
[98] *State Trials*, ed. Cobbett, pp. 74-5, 80-1, 83-4.

hanged, yea he shall be hanged." James himself was visited in prison by
"several persons of quality" including "especially one of eminency in the
city" who unsuccessfully tried to persuade him to petition Charles II for
his life.[99]

John James's speech at Tyburn before his execution on 26 November
1661 was a public and much publicized plea on behalf of the entire
Saturday-Sabbatarian movement. "First of all," he began, "that which I
have to say before I go out of this world, is, to remove that which hath been
thrown upon me by way of aspersion as if I were a Jesuit." James told his
listeners that in the crowd were some who knew him from childhood, and
said proudly that "I am an Englishman, never was out of the nation in
all my life; never had any knowledge of any other tongue but the English
tongue, therefore altogether incapable of such work and employment as
Jesuits are usually put upon". To anyone who remembered the Case of the
False Jew, such an accusation would be natural. James also proclaimed
that

> I do own the Commandments of God, the Ten Commandments as they are
> expressed in the 20th of Exodus. I do here, as before the Lord, testify that
> I durst not, I durst not willingly break the least of those Commandments to
> save my life; I do declare that the rather, before I would inform persons that
> I do own the Lord's holy Sabbath, the seventh day of the week to be the
> Lord's Sabbath; you know the Commandment "Remember that thou keep
> holy the seventh day." I shall forbear to speak any more to that.

James was beheaded, and after a spell on the Tower Bridge, his head was
"put upon a pole in White-Chapel, over against the passage to the
meeting-place, where he and his company were apprehended."[100]

The hanging of John James was the first official government response
to the perceived menace of Saturday-Sabbatarianism, now inextricably
linked with the Fifth Monarchists and other radicals. John James himself
had affirmed this connection in his interrogation. Dr Peter Chamberlen
declined to speak out publicly against this hysterical government response
to the harmless preaching of a member of his own congregation. Instead
he chose to condemn more generally those for whom "Persecution is their
High Priest". Because of such men, he wrote, "Heaps upon Heaps, Heaps
upon Heaps are found among the Dead, which have been Sacrified to their
mistaken Impiety". His own hope was that King Charles II would prove
to be a tolerant ruler of all his loyal subjects. "I wish him not only King
of *England, Scotland, France and Ireland,*" he explained, "but King of Papists
and Protestants, King of Lutherans and Calvenists, King of Brownists and

---

[99] *Ibid.*, pp. 85, 95.
[100] *Ibid.*, pp. 98-9, 104.

Independants, King of Anabaptists and Quakers, King of Jews and Gen-
tils, Turks and Infidels, King of all the World, King of Kings, and King
of Lawyers and Clergy to.'' This would be a difficult task for the new king
to perform, but Chamberlen warned him, in a somewhat confused meta-
phor, that ''LIBERTY of CONSCIENCE is a weapon of many points and one
handle, which when magistrates let go, he that first catches hold of it
Unites all Interests against that *Single One* that is *Upermost* and cuts all *Oaths*
and *Human Obligations* in pieces, like the *Gordian Knot*''.[101]

Peter Chamberlen's persona as a religious leader of the Seventh-Day
Baptists in London, therefore, came to a screeching halt immediately after
the Restoration. He was until that time the only Seventh-Day man with
any kind of national standing and reputation and would have been a
natural leader. Disillusioned with Chamberlen, frightened by the execution of John James, a number of Saturday-Sabbatarians gathered a more
radical Calvinist congregation at Bell Lane, soon led by John Belcher, a
bricklayer of Seventh-Day Baptist persuasions. Mill Yard became more
identified with the non-Calvinist General Baptist approach. Chamberlen
remained a member of Mill Yard but succeeded during the next few years
in alienating all of his supporters, from fellow congregants to the king himself. When he returned guiltily to the religious question in old age, he was
surprised that no one would listen.

IV

For Peter Chamberlen, as for Henry Jessey, Thomas Tillam and many
others, the years around 1665 signalled the end of the Restoration honey-
moon. But unlike the religious radicals, Chamberlen's reaction to intensified persecution was not one of panic or despair. Plans for reform based
on the Seventh-Day Sabbath and the Old Testament were discreetly laid
aside until the troubles would die down. Meanwhile, he occupied himself
with a continued pursuit of economic success. He petitioned the king to
allow his eldest son Hugh to take over some of his father's duties without
any additional salary, so as to afford himself the leisure to develop his economic schemes.[102] The first of these was a secret, as yet untested, invention
for navigating with all winds in a straight line, which he had patented in
the Netherlands.[103] He also asked the king for a special fourteen-year pa-

---

[101] Peter Chamberlen, *A Speech Visibly Spoken* (London, [1662]), esp. pp. 5, 8, 15. Cf. *idem*,
The Sober Mans Vindication (London, 1662), broadsheet; Aveling, *Chamberlen*, pp. 106-8.

[102] Chamberlen to Charles II, n.d.=1665?: *Cal. S.P. Dom., 1665-6*, p. 140.

[103] *Ibid.*; patented at the States-General, Dec. 1663 & Apr. 1667; States of Holland and
West-Friesland, Mar. 1664; Zeeland, June 1666: Doorman, *Patents*, pp. 149, 151, 181, 202;
Cal. S.P. Dom., 1664-5, p. 451: the request for a patent here is said to have been made by

tent for the sole making of horseless coaches, wagons, carts, and ploughs, such as he claimed to have seen at Augsburg fifty years before.[104] Undaunted by the improbability of turning these ideas into a profit-making enterprise, Chamberlen capped off his requests with yet another scheme, perhaps the most interesting. In about August 1672 he wrote to Charles

> praying for a patent for fourteen years for the sole licensing and publishing of all books or writings printed or written according to the new way of writing and printing true English invented by the petitioner, which represents to the eye what the sound does to the ear, an art much wanted, innocent to all, well pleasing to the learned, profitable to the unlearned and to strangers, and not a little to the honour of the nation.

Chamberlen's plea was sent to the solicitor-general on 5 August 1672, and in his report, dated 14 October, he found in favour of the petitioner, noting that Chamberlen "has bestowed much pains and study in amending the orthography of the English tongue, by devising new letters, and confining the use of the known letters to one particular sound, and rejecting such as are useless."[105] A patent was duly issued the following month.[106] Little more came of this scheme than of the previous ones, but it is illuminating that Chamberlen should have sought to join the ranks of John Wilkins, founder of the Royal Society, and others perhaps less distinguished who sought to perfect a "philosophical language" which would help to break down the barriers between words and things, or at the very least to adapt the English language to more precise usage.[107]

Chamberlen's scientific interests seem to have heralded a certain distancing of his supporters. The king was determined to pension him off, and Chamberlen was reduced to pleading for a key, medal, ring or other token to gain him ready access to his royal patient.[108] At the same time,

---

Hugh Chamberlen, not his father; Hugh Chamberlen to Williamson, 25 Aug. 1665: *ibid.*, pp. 531-2; H.C. to P.C., 27 Apr. 1666: *ibid.*, p. 366. A copy of the bill of patent, printed, is in *Cal. S.P. Dom., 1667-8*, p. 308, dated [26 Mar.] 1668. The bill was read on 8 Nov. 1669: *Hist. MSS. Comm., Hastings II*, p. 315: newsletter addressed to the 7th earl of Huntingdon, from Whitehall. A warrant for a patent is recorded in *Cal. S.P. Dom., 1668-9*, p. 108, dated 18 Dec. 1668.

[104] *Cal. S.P. Dom., 1665-6*, p. 140.

[105] P.C. to Charles II, with report of solicitor-general: *Cal. S.P. Dom., 1672*, p. 443.

[106] *Cal. S.P. Dom., 1672-3*, p. 229.

[107] For more on the search for a philosophical language, see Katz, *Philo-Semitism, cap.* 2.

[108] P.C. to Charles II, 7 Nov. 1667: *Cal. S.P. Dom., 1667-8*, p. 11. Chamberlen also travelled abroad to Ireland, Holland and France at this time: *Cal. S.P. Dom., 1665-6*, p. 332; pass, 17 Nov. 1669: Bodl. Lib., MS Rawl. C 172, fos. 139-40; pass to France for six months: *Cal. S.P. Dom., 1670*, p. 44. Even his movements within England were sometimes reported to the authorities: Matthew Anderton from Chester to Williamson, 20 Sept. 1669: *Cal. S.P. Dom., 1668-9*, p. 497. But Charles was not entirely ungrateful and made two royal grants to Chamberlen: warrant to the Treasury Commissioners, 20 Sept. 1669: *Cal. S.P. Dom., 1668-9*, p. 498: grant of £100, deemed insufficient by Chamberlen, to Charles II, n.d.=

his endless demands for monopolies and patents for what were presented as helpful inventions, brought him into sharp conflict with the other members of the Mill Yard Saturday-Sabbatarian church. Certainly Chamberlen's presence among them gave their congregation a certain amount of eccentric dignity, but on the other hand the distinguished doctor was a patentee, one of the stock figures of abuse for both social and religious radicals. Indeed, it could be argued that the entire Chamberlen family traditionally thrived on denying useful and life-saving knowledge to others. There is a reference in the Mill Yard church book dated 18 January 1675-6 regarding "ye Matter of Dr Chamberlain" on the basis of a complaint "made by bro: Smith ... to this purpose ... upon A Letter by bro: Sal:[ler] to ye D^r hee had declared his Intention of being Satisfied in Case bro: Sall would signify in publique w^t he had done in his Letter ye wch bro: Sall: declared his wilingness to doe". No further record is made of a discussion of Chamberlen's case, but we get a glimpse of the issues at stake in a later minute regarding the expulsion of Chamberlen's wife Anne, from that Christian fellowship:

> The matter & grounds for wch Mrs. Ann Chamberlin was wth Drawne frome by ye church:
> i her Disorderly Leaveing the church & that against her owne Judgment & Contience.
> 2ly Secondly for her Justifieing her husband although Cast out for maneffest Sines –
> 3ly Thirdly in Condeming the church in Dealing wth him Contrary to the word of god.
> 4thly Fourthly for maneffest pride & vaine Glory, Glorying in her husbands learning, Agravatted by this Circumstance Shee saying she Could have a thousand such as wee are in Contempt.
> 5ly. for Despising the Church, Recconing her place in it to be no more than a wooden Stoole.
> 6ly. for her absenting her selfe from the Church & worship of god in it upon noe other pretence but her husbands Compulsion of her.
> 7ly in false accuseing ye Church yt they neglected Their Duty in ye [word omitted] of her soule & further in Deniing matters witnessed against her.
> 8ly her great Contempt of ye Churches messengers by scurolus Language in Calling Bro. Lawrance Shallow pate & that he spooke faningly be Cause hee did not use harsh words & afterwards Gloried in it to Mrs. Sarah.

As at Lothbury Square, Chamberlen's very presence could be seen as a disruptive factor.[109]

1670?: *Cal. S.P. Dom.*, *1670*, p. 614. Warrant for payment from the privy seal dormant, 25 Mar. 1670: *ibid.*, p. 133: grant of further £200.

[109] Mill Yard Minutes, p. 11; xvi-xvii (at the end of the volume): repr. Thirtle, "Chamberlen", pp. 185-6.

Peter Chamberlen was thus expelled from Christian fellowship with the small band of Mill Yard Saturday-Sabbatarians. It seems unlikely that this drastic step showed him the error of his ways and convinced him of the evils inherent in patents, but it was at this juncture that he once again enacted a major change in his chequered career. Chamberlen seems to have abandoned his various schemes, even his latest plan for phonetic reform, and to have thrown himself whole-heartedly once again into religious matters. Chamberlen's constant themes during these last years were the necessity for religious unity and millenarian speculation. No doubt the king and his court were relieved that the aging and cantankerous doctor turned his attention elsewhere, but no joy was felt at Lambeth where successive archbishops of Canterbury became the unwelcome recipients of Chamberlen's letters and requests which, as he got older, became increasingly plaintive and very nearly illegible.

Peter Chamberlen's first sally into the field of religious unity began even before his expulsion from Mill Yard. On 2 October 1673 he wrote in characteristically extravagant fashion to Archbishop Gilbert Sheldon, asking him

> In plain English (my Lord) Who more fit, & Capable then Yo[r] Grace (influenced with His Ma[ties] good liking) to invite the Pope Cardinals, & all the Heads of Jesuits, Sorbonists, Jansonists, Augustins, Dominicans, and Franciscans, together with the Chief of the Lutharans, Calvanists, Socinians, Arminians, & whoever els are for Paul Ajpollo or Cephas: to meet in Post Paper: and Conspire. Not how farr they can Differ & Quarrel Each other but How Close they can Unite, and become all of Christ.[110]

Chamberlen returned to this theme in a further letter to Sheldon "to Unite All the Churches of Europe into a Reformation". He also called for a "Return to the Keeping of the Lawes of God", condemning the "Triple Crowned Horn's Change of Times & Lawes", part of his pet theory that it was the Roman Catholic Church that altered the Sabbath day from Saturday to Sunday, proved by identifying Daniel's beast with the papacy. It is most likely that Archbishop Sheldon took even less notice of this letter than the other, for here Chamberlen was too confused even to dip his pen in ink when necessary, and parts of the letter are very nearly blank at regularly spaced intervals.[111]

Towards this same end, Chamberlen wrote to the governor of New England during September 1677 in support of the Seventh-Day Baptists there,

---

[110] P.C. to Sheldon, 2 Oct. 1673: Bodl. Lib., MS Tanner 42, f. 36.
[111] Same to same, n.d.: Bodl. Lib., MS Tanner 36*, f. 147. Cf. *Cal. S.P. Dom., Add., 1674-9*, p. 32: the proposal is undated, and in any case it is unclear whether it came from Peter or Hugh Chamberlen.

commending the American experiment and offering his services. Chamberlen noted that he "always had a love for the intended purity and unspotted doctrine of New England", and recalled that among his contemporaries at Emmanuel College were John Cotton, Thomas Hooker, and others. He chided them for their strict interpretation of church discipline, and reminded them that it "is great wisdom to suppress sin, but not the liberty of a good conscience; and whilst men grant liberty of conscience, not to admit liberty of sin." The case of New England's Seventh-Day men was particularly relevant here, he thought, for they knew that whatsoever "is against the ten commandments is sin . . . and he that sinneth in one point is guilty of all". Chamberlen's faith in the Saturday-Sabbath did not wane even after his expulsion from Mill Yard.[112]

Perhaps it was this very devotion without proper congregational affiliation that sparked rumours of Chamberlen's alleged conversion to Judaism. Indeed, in July 1680 he felt it necessary to write himself to the archbishop to protest "that I have lately been traduced to Yo^r Grace as a Jew." Chamberlen said that his accusers were "a Combination of Alehous Gossips, some Mechanick Church Wardens, with their pettifogging Solicitor". In this moment of high emotion, even that old Royalist code-word "mechanick" flowed from his pen. Chamberlen noted that to "be a Jew as the Apostle writes to the Romans, is a Crown & an Honour to any Christian. Butt as they intended it, in Opposition to the Name, & Faith of Jesus Christ, I abhorr them." Chamberlen was also worried about "the slaunder, & Scandal, & for the Prejudice they do me in my Practice." The doctor begged the archbishop to compel his "dirty-mouth Adversaries" to appear before him to attempt to prove their malicious tales. This seems not to have happened, and indeed the archbishop's endorsement of the letter might just reveal his appreciation of the comedy of the situation: "Dr Chamberlen no Jew", he wrote on the verso.[113]

Such accusations were hardly surprising, not only because of Chamberlen's peculiar Sabbath observance, but also because as part of his crusade for religious unity he sought to renew his contacts with those most ancient Seventh-Day men, the Jews, at their community in London. Indeed, in 1682 he appealed publicly to "the *Synagogue* of the *Jews* in *London*, being a *Remnant* of the numerous People of *Israel*, scattered into all Countries over the Face of the Earth." Chamberlen claimed to "have heard, that some (of the most Worthy amongst You) have made some Enquiry after a few *Christians*, who keep the *Sabbath* of the Lord Your *God*, and Ours." Cham-

---

[112] P.C. to governor of New England, 1 Sept. 1677: repr. Thirtle, "Chamberlen", pp. 27-8 from *Seventh-Day Baptist Memorial*, i (Apr. 1852).
[113] Bodl. Lib., MS Tanner 160, f. 71.

berlen reminded the Jews that he himself had "been the First that endeavoured to rescue that Commandment" and that "having been conversant with several of your Nation in *Italy*, *Germany*, and the *Low Countries*, I think my self the more engaged to salute you in mine own Native Country." Chamberlen then proceeded to recount the most pleasant visit he had in a synagogue abroad, when he was entertained at Genoa by Rabbi Abraham Attias and his congregation. After making a few short remarks in Italian to the assembled Jews, Chamberlen recalled that he was invited to the rabbi's house "where I met with 5 *Rabbies* more; purposely come together to hear what I would say, and to confer thereupon." Chamberlen's discourse to the rabbies was aimed at convincing the Jews that their Messiah had already come in the person of Jesus Christ: "Upon which the Learned *Rabbi* (*Abraham Attias*) lifted up his voice, and professed He never Read more excellent *Rules* of *Righteousness* and of *Holiness*, than in the *New Testament*." The Jews of London, however, declined to follow the reported lead of their Italian brethren and wisely ignored Chamberlen's plea for further co-operation.[114]

It would appear that by this time Dr Peter Chamberlen had already found a new Christian fellowship, for he wrote a will on 4 May 1681 bequeathing his family estate to his wife and youngest son, the only members of his family not yet provided for, which was witnessed by Richard Parnham and John Belcher.[115] Parnham and Belcher were the pastors of the Bell Lane Saturday-Sabbatarian church, formed in the wake of Chamberlen's failure to lead the Seventh-Day men after the execution of John James in 1661. Chamberlen was presumably already a member. Parnham was a London silversmith, sometime quarter-master in Ireton's regiment who joined with Belcher at Bell Lane in 1668. Belcher was a bricklayer who became a Saturday-Sabbatarian after the Restoration and led the Bell Lane church until his death in 1695.[116]

Chamberlen spent the last two years of his life working ineffectively for church unity, trying to understand the millenarian message of the Book of Daniel, and advocating the restoration of the Mosaic law. Chamberlen must have felt the new archbishop of Canterbury to be a kindred spirit, and William Sancroft has even been described by the historian of the Fifth Monarchists to be one of the two "most distinguished Anglican millenarians", along with William Lloyd, bishop of St Asaph.[117] Even in the 1690s

---

[114] Peter Chamberlen, *The Sons of the East* (London, 1682), pp. 1-2: National Library of Scotland, Edinburgh.

[115] Peter Chamberlen's will, dated 4 May 1681, proved 2 Jan. 1683-4: repr. Aveling, *Chamberlen*, pp. 120-2.

[116] Capp, *Fifth Monarchy*, pp. 242, 257.

[117] *Ibid.*, pp. 191, 226.

Sancroft was still praising Joseph Mede and tinkering with various calculations for the Second Coming.[118] Chamberlen wrote to him in October 1681 asking the archbishop to present Charles II with a paper offering his services in the quest for church unity. "Though a Man cannot be a Woman, nor a Woman a Man", he expressed himself clumsily, "Yet Both may be Reasonable Creatures. Both may be Christians." In return, Chamberlen offered Sancroft the services of his pen should he require it at Assembly or Convocation. But even Chamberlen knew when to be realistic: having apparently lost free access to his royal patient, he could hardly hope for his proposal to meet with success. "Be pleased to send it back" if refused, he asked Sancroft in a post-script.[119] Sure enough, three weeks later Chamberlen was found writing to Sancroft with thanks "for presenting my Letter to His Majestie & for returning it to me, upon His Refusal." It appeared now, he lamented, that "Tis my Province, to do His Matie Service, & He not know it".[120]

The following spring Chamberlen tried to extend his campaign beyond the narrow confines of an unresponsive royal court. In April 1682 he wrote again to Sancroft asking for written permission to ask the clergy and the universities to answer what he considered the most fundamental question facing England at that time: "Who is meant by the Little Horn in Daniel (Chapt. 7th)". If he received no answer within a month's time, he promised to set down his own views in print, or alternatively, to annihilate his opponents, "though my Antagonist write from Rome, or St Omer".[121] With or without the archbishop's permission, Chamberlen wrote various letters addressed to the clergy, the chancellor, Lord Privy Seal, Lord Mayor of London, the legal profession and the two universities during May and June, and published them all with his own views annexed.[122]

Chamberlen was now convinced more than ever that the Papists were to blame for changing the Sabbath unlawfully to Sunday, and in this he agreed with "the Learned *Doctor Moor*" who "laid the CHANGE of *Times and Laws* at the Doors of ROME." He called on the secular authorities to restore God's laws as revealed in the Ten Commandments. When he spoke of the fourth one, he reminded his readers that it was the seventh day that was the Sabbath, not the first:

---

[118] John Evelyn, *Diary*, ed. E.S. de Beer (Oxford, 1955), iv. 636; v. 26, 322.

[119] P.C. to W.S., 8 Oct. 1681: Bodl. Lib., MS Tanner 36, f. 130.

[120] Same to same, 29 Oct. 1681: *ibid.*, f. 155.

[121] Same to same, Apr. 1682: Bodl. Lib., MS Tanner 35, f. 2: very sloppily written.

[122] Peter Chamberlen, *Englands Choice* (London, 1682): the letter to the churchmen is dated 29 May 1682; to the universities 19 Jun. 1682; and to the others 12 Jun. 1682. The appeal to the universities was also published as a separate broadsheet: Peter Chamberlen, *To the Two* LIGHTS *of* ENGLAND (n.p., 1682).

But the little *Horn* hath changed that time, giving the *Lie* to the Seventh day; and saith (in plain terms) that the First day is the Sabbath of the Lord: So that here the time is changed every Week. Then, from *Even* to *Even* was the *Sabbath*, (Lev. 23. 32.) Now, from *Morning* to *Evening* is the *Sabbath*. Then, they might not speak their own words, nor do their own works, nor take their own pleasure, (*Isa.* 58. 13) Now, they have all liberty of works, or sports, or words.

This back-handed reference to the controversy over Sabbath sports nearly fifty years before must have reminded his readers how much of a religious dinosaur he really was.[123]

Chamberlen's final and rather pitiful plea for a public debate on these questions appears to have been ignored. He was still willing "to Answer any Argument to the contrary, whether from the Conclave at Rome, or any of the College of Jesuits. Or any other Roman, Lutheran, or Protestant Penne of Learning", and told Sancroft so several months later.[124] By now the archbishop did not even bother to reply, leaving Chamberlen to rant on that when it came to church unity, "Your Grace, or His Majestie, or His most honorable Council, can do nothing (effectively) without me, much less can I perform any thing without you."[125]

According to Thomas Tanner the antiquary, by November 1682, Chamberlen "was alive, but crazy".[126] It seems that this was a condition that had prevailed for some time. The elderly doctor's unpopularity seems to have been infectious as well. In that same month, Robert Brady the historian and physician petitioned the king to have Hugh Chamberlen's place as the royal doctor. He noted that "his Majesty has resolved not to admit the said Dr. Chamberlain to a place so near his person" and asked "for a grant of the said place to himself, during pleasure". Brady was the Regius professor of physic at Cambridge, the master of Caius College, and sat for the University in the Parliament of 1681. He also held the office of keeper of the records in the Tower, and the king had intervened on his behalf only four months after the Restoration. So it must have come as no surprise that Brady was duly appointed in Hugh Chamberlen's place, and in his capacity as physician in ordinary to Charles II and James II he later had the dubious honour of officiating at the birth of the ill-fated prince of Wales in 1688.[127]

This is the sort of thing that drives men mad. But Peter Chamberlen was by now very far gone. His last letter to the archbishop of Canterbury,

---

[123] Chamberlen, *Englands Choice, passim.*
[124] P.C. to W.S., "26" [19] Sept. 1682: Bodl. Lib., MS Tanner 35, f. 95.
[125] Same to same, 9 Oct. 1682: *ibid.*, f. 104.
[126] Munk, *Royal College*, i. 194.
[127] Robert Brady to Charles II, Nov. ? 1682: *Cal. S.P. Dom., 1682*, p. 546; warrant, 17 Nov. 1682: *Cal. S.P. Dom., 1682*, p. 547; *Dict. Nat. Biog., s.v.* "Brady, Robert (d. 1700)".

written a month before his death, is more a cry of despair than a proper letter:

> If there be no Visible Church of Christ in England. Why in the 19th Article? If there be any: Why may not I find it? I have been of 11. Parish Churches, & could not find the 19th Article amongst them all? If Yo^r Grace can find it in all yor Province though all yor Reverend Bishops search every one his Diocess, I thinck it ought to be as the Thrasure found in the Gospel. But if the Little Horn have so worn out the Saints of the Most High, in thincking to Change Times and Lawes, that the Church is driven to be Invisible in the Wilderness. Where it not a Work worthy Yo^r Grace & all yor Reverend Bishops, to invite her again to be more Visible: Or to gather a Church of Christ, & make it Visible to the World? In which Grave work, if yor Wisdom, thinck my long Experience usefull; be pleased to comaund

Needless to say, Sancroft filed away this letter with all the rest.[128]

V

Dr Peter Chamberlen died on 22 December 1683, aged over 82 years. The inscription on his tombstone in the Woodham Mortimer churchyard near the town of Maldon in Essex, provides more detailed information about his family:

> He had two wives, and by ye first Jane Middleton,[129] had 11 sons and 2 daughters, and amongst them 45 grand-children and 8 great-grandchildren (whereof were living at his death 3 sons viz. Hugh, Paul and John and his 2 daughters and 20 grand-children and 6 great-grandchildren) By ye second, Ann Harrison, had 3 sons and 2 daughters, whereof only Hope was living at his death, who hath erected this monument in memory of his father.

"As for his religion", it is recorded on the tombstone, he "was a Christian, keeping ye Commandments of God and faith of Jesus, being baptized about ye year 1648, and keeping ye 7th day for ye Sabbath about 32 years."[130]

In 1813, the mother of the then occupier of Woodham Mortimer Hall discovered a wooden plug on the floor of a small attic room over the porch

---

[128] P.C. to W.S., 19 Nov. 1682: Bodl. Lib., MS Tanner 35, f. 133.

[129] Chamberlen's first wife left little trace in the records. She was the eldest daughter of Sir Hugh Myddelton, the well-known undertaker and projector of the New River, who lived at Bush Hill, Edmonton and had four sons and three daughters. She must still have been alive in 1631, for on 21 Nov. of that year her father bequeathed to the two younger daughters each a share in the New River and £500 and added, "Whereas my daughter Jane hath had her full porcion upon her marriage I give to her husband Doctor Chamberlaine and my said daughter Jane the severall somes of ten poundes to buy each of them a ring": Aveling, *Chamberlen*, p. 122n.

[130] Text of tombstone inscription in *ibid.*, pp. 122-4.

at the front of the house, and then a screw which was one of several that secured a secret trap door. Beneath was a hiding place which concealed a box containing some of the most treasured possessions of Dr Peter Chamberlen and his wife. Apart from letters, trinkets, fans, spectacles, a few coins, a pair of lady's gloves, and a New Testament bearing the manuscript date 1695, was a small packet labelled "my husband's last tooth" and harbouring the relic inside. But most importantly the cache contained three sets of midwifery instruments, each consisting of a pair of forceps, vectis and fillet, and a fourth pair, very crudely made and apparently the first experimental tool made by the first Chamberlen man-midwife. The other sets also exhibited certain changes, demonstrating that Chamberlen and his family constantly sought to improve the tool. A local retired surgeon recognized the instruments for what they were, and thus was the first outsider to have a glimpse at the secret of the Chamberlen family's fortune. The tools themselves were given to the Medical and Chirurgical Society of London, now the Royal Society of Medicine.[131]

One of the curious aspects of this discovery was the fact that Chamberlen's son Hope by his second marriage, who inherited the house, was apparently unaware of the secret vault, since he sold the Hall in 1715 with the box left intact. Chamberlen in any case entrusted the family secret to three of his sons, Hugh, Paul and John.[132] Little is known of John,[133] but we have already heard a great deal from Dr Hugh Chamberlen, who regained his place at Court and almost always attended James II's queen as accoucheur. We have already seen that he arrived too late to attend the birth of the Old Pretender, but in 1713 he wrote to the Electress Sophia of Hanover to assure her that no substitution had been made as had been commonly alleged.[134] Like his father, Hugh Chamberlen also produced a grandiose improving scheme, his land bank which brought finally only ridicule and derision. He retired to Amsterdam, and may even have been driven to sell a model of the family forceps to a fellow practitioner there.[135]

---

[131] H.H. Cansardine, "Brief Notice presented to the Medico-Chirurgical Society with the Original Obstetric Instruments of the Chamberlins", *Medico-Chirurgical Trans.*, ix (1818), 181-4; Radcliffe, *Secret Instrument*, pp. 1, 16-19. A photograph of the trap door and instruments can be seen in *ibid.*, plate II, opp. p. 17; and in idem, *Milestones*, plate II; and in Eccles, *Obstetrics*, opp. p. 67.

[132] Radcliffe, *Secret Instrument*, pp. 18-19.

[133] Aveling, *Chamberlen*, p. 184.

[134] Brit. Lib., MS Birch 4107, f. 150, dated (in a very different handwriting) from The Hague, 4 Oct. 1713; *Dict. Nat. Biog.*, *s.v.* "Chamberlen, Hugh, the elder, M.D. (fl. 1720)"; Aveling, *Chamberlen*, pp. 125-79.

[135] *Dict. Nat. Biog.* Radcliffe, *Milestones*, p. 32 doubts this "since none of the instruments which were claimed to be the Chamberlen secret bore the slightest resemblance to the forceps which by then had been hidden at Woodham Mortimer Hall." For more on Hugh Chamberlen, see Narcissus Luttrell, *A Brief Historical Relation of State Affairs* (Oxford, 1857), i, 33, 128; ii. 424, 425; iv. 348, 496; v. 302.

His brother Paul, on the other hand, not content with the comfortable practice of a rich man-midwife, turned to quack medicine and bogus cures. His most famous fraud was the "Celebrated Anodyne Necklace, recommended to the world by Dr. Chamberlen for children's teeth, women in labour, &c." He offered them at "Five shillings or 48s. a dozen to sell again." The doctor noted in his advertisement that this "Necklace is a proper thing not only for a New Years Gift for God-Fathers, God-Mothers, Relations, Friends, and Acquaintances, to give to Children and Others; but even for a Present for any one to give their Friends at any time of the year."[136] The line of Chamberlen men-midwives by no means ended with the death of Dr Peter Chamberlen III.[137]

Dr Peter Chamberlen's wife Anne remained a member of the Saturday-Sabbatarian congregation at Bell Lane until its disintegration in the first few years of the eighteenth century. Although by then a number of Saturday-Sabbatarian churches did exist in London, the group she chose to join was her old fellowship at Mill Yard which had expelled her husband as a patentee years before. A church minute dated 6 September 1702 records that the pastor,

> Bro Soursbey acquainted the Church with Sister Chamberlains desire of sitting down with this Church, the Church being Broke with whome she Walked. A Letter also being Read signifieing her orderly Walk, which was subscribed by Bro. Brunt, Bro. Garvas, and Bro. Laborour.

Mrs Chamberlen had left a sectarian conventicle which during her absence had transformed itself into a respected and established nonconformist congregation.[138]

We have already seen how this process was begun with the Mother Church around Henry Jessey, both highly regarded as a religious radical during the Interregnum and as the Christian contact in England of Menasseh ben Israel and other Jews who hoped to capitalize on the Puritan sympathy towards the heroes of the Old Testament. Thomas Tillam transformed Jessey's subtle and almost secret Saturday-Sabbath into something approaching a national scandal. Tillam's farcical management of the Case of the False Jew showed how warily one needed to tread when pursuing the Mosaic law. His radical solution to the lack of Saturday-Sabbath observance in England freed moderates like Henry Jessey from this obstreperous

---

[136] *Dict. Nat. Biog.*, *s.v.* "Chamberlen, Paul, M.D. (1635-1717)"; Aveling, *Chamberlen*, pp. 181-2. Cf. J.E. Hodgkin, *Notes & Queries*, 6th ser., ix (1884), 132; & O., *ibid.*, x (1884), 377.

[137] The last of the family who practised the art of midwifery seems to have been Dr Middleton Walker, the youngest son of Peter Chamberlen's daughter Elizabeth: Radcliffe, *Milestones*, p. 32; *idem*, *Secret Instrument*, p. 72.

[138] Thirtle, "Chamberlen", p. 188.

thorn in their sides, for once Tillam left for Germany to establish his Sab-batarian commune he was scarcely heard of again.

Dr Peter Chamberlen had the opportunity and the reckless courage to transform Saturday-Sabbatarianism into an organized sect which could stand alongside other radical religious groups in seventeenth-century England. But as he himself once put it, "Some men can eat their Cake and have their Cake."[139] Chamberlen was unwilling to devote himself to religious issues alone, and while quite sincere in his espousal of the Saturday-Sabbath, his obsession with fame and excessive financial reward dulled the effectiveness of his work. Dr Christopher Hill remarks that it "is noteworthy how often the intellectual spokesmen of the plebian religious radical movements were men with a medical background – from Paracelsus and Servetus to Chamberlen and Culpeper."[140] But in Chamberlen's case it was just this scientific background which prevented him from becoming a really effective spokesman for his radical religious beliefs.

Nevertheless, it was certainly important after the scandalous conduct of Tillam and his followers to put Saturday-Sabbatarianism on a comfortable footing once again, and Chamberlen helped to do this to a great extent. Despite his very numerous and widespread activities on behalf of various schemes and projects, Peter Chamberlen remained identified with Saturday-Sabbatarianism and is still regarded as one of the more weighty founding fathers of the Seventh-Day Baptists.[141] This in itself is right and just, even if Chamberlen lacked the single-minded devotion necessary for a non-conformist religious leader in Restoration England. For Chamberlen was the most widely known founder of the church at Mill Yard, the parent congregation of the Seventh-Day Baptists, and as we shall see, the direct ancestor of more numerous Fundamentalist and millenarian sects, especially the Seventh-Day Adventists. His was another case of a movement's founder leaving the cause for others to develop: like Roger Williams, Chamberlen could not bear the thought of institutionalizing an idea. During the examination of "a poor man and a young man" over the Rye House Plot in 1683, the suspect indignantly denied all wrongdoing, arguing for support that "I owned the Sabbath day and am of Dr. Chamberlaine's religion."[142] It was the doctor's religion indeed, but Saturday-Sabbatarianism required the intervention of Francis Bampfield and the Stennetts, as we shall see, to turn that belief into a viable institution.

---

[139] Chamberlen, *Poore Mans Advocate*, sig. A4ʳ.
[140] Hill, *Origins*, p. 148.
[141] See *Seventh-Day Baptists in Europe and America* (Plainfield, N.J., 1910), i. 72-3.
[142] Examination of Wood, 1 July 1683: *Cal. S.P. Dom., July-Sept. 1683*, pp. 4-5.

CHAPTER FOUR

SABBATARIAN NON-CONFORMITY
IN RESTORATION ENGLAND

The trial and execution of John James in 1661, the first Seventh-Day man
to suffer so publicly for his belief in the Old Testament law and the Sabbath, was a sobering tragedy that brought about a complete reorientation
of the movement for the Saturday-Sabbath. Dr Peter Chamberlen, the
most prominent among the founders of the Mill Yard congregation, was
already back at court, showing himself unwilling to continue championing
openly a cause which could have such fatal effects. The radicals, many of
whom were Fifth Monarchy men or their supporters, withdrew from Mill
Yard and began another Seventh-Day congregation at Bell Lane. But it
was recognized with the departure of Chamberlen that what was lacking
was a leader, a man not only of spiritual qualities but one who had the necessary authority and organizational abilities to weather the difficult years
which all non-conformists knew stretched endlessly ahead of them.

Such a leader was found in Francis Bampfield (1615-1684), who not only
would put the Seventh-Day men on a sure institutional footing, but whose
personal interests would very largely determine the direction that Saturday-Sabbatarianism would take. Most importantly, Bampfield's understanding of the question of the Saturday-Sabbath in the wider context of
the validity of the Old Testament for Christians ensured that this would
be an important theme in the next century and thereby fuel the revival of
the Seventh-Day Sabbath itself by nineteenth-century millenarians who
like him were unhappy about the ambivalent attitude shown by the Established Church and sects towards what had always been presented as an in-
alienable part of Protestant tradition.

Francis Bampfield in any case is one of the most interesting figures in
Restoration non-conformity, a member of a distinguished Devon family,
a graduate of Wadham College, and a Royalist during the Civil War.[1] Indeed, this last fact was still thought to be extraordinary in the eighteenth
century when Thomas Crosby, one of the earliest Baptist biographers, noted that:

---

[1] Generally on Bampfield, see J. Ivimey, *A History of the Baptists* (London, 1811-30), ii.
476-81; *Dict. Nat. Biog.*; A.G. Matthews, *Calamy Revised* (Oxford, 1934), p. 26, who notes that
Bampfield was the son of John Bampfield, Esq. of Poltimore, Devon and Elizabeth, daughter of Thomas Drake of Buckland Monachorum.

> One thing was very remarkable, if not singular in him; that though he joined heartily in the reformation of the church in those times, yet he was zealous against the parliament's war, and Oliver's usurpation; constantly asserting the royal cause under all those changed, and suffering for it.[2]

Indeed, Bampfield testified in his autobiography that he read the prayer book service in his parish longer than any minister in the country until prevented from doing so by the army. After the Restoration, Bampfield suffered as a non-conformist, and was arrested for preaching at Shaftesbury in 1663, remaining a prisoner in Dorchester jail for nearly nine years. It was during this period of imprisonment that Bampfield became a Saturday-Sabbatarian, and managed to gather a church around him in Dorchester jail, preaching to visitors from his cell. After his release, Bampfield founded a Sabbatarian congregation which eventually settled at Pinners' Hall in London.

Francis Bampfield, like Henry Jessey and Peter Chamberlen, exemplifies the essentially respectable quality of extreme Sabbatarianism. His brother Thomas was a speaker of the House of Commons and represented Exeter in three Cromwellian parliaments and in the Convention Parliament of 1660.[3] His eldest brother Sir John Bampfield was created a baronet in 1641, and the latter's son played an active part in promoting the Restoration.[4] Bampfield was succeeded in his ministry by Edward and Joseph Stennett, father and son, who similarly were pillars of respectable nonconformity.[5] Indeed, what is instructive about the Saturday-Sabbatarian movement in the period after the Restoration is the way in which this group adapted to the new and more oppressive conditions. During the Civil War and Interregnum, we saw a disparate group of men united only in their belief that the seventh day ought to be worshipped as the Christian Sabbath, linked with Fifth Monarchist plans for the reform of the law based on the Old Testament in which the divine commandments were first revealed. But after the Restoration, these hopes for change were dashed with astonishing clarity. The Fifth Monarchists were suppressed; the Quakers began to preach pacifism. The Saturday-Sabbatarians tried to make the difficult transition to respectable non-conformity.

---

[2] Thomas Crosby, *The History of the English Baptists* (London, 1738-40), iv. 363-8.
[3] *Dict. Nat. Biog.*
[4] *Ibid., s.v.* "Sir Coplestone Bampfield (1636-1691)".
[5] *Ibid., s.v.* "Joseph Stennett (1663-1713)".

I

Any biographical discussion of Francis Bampfield is inevitably coloured by the fact that the eminent divine wrote the story of his own life and published it as a modern illustration of the life of St Paul. Bampfield recorded his descent from two honourable and ancient Devonshire families, and noted the fact that he was from birth designated for the ministry. In 1631, at the age of about sixteen, he entered Wadham College, Oxford, and remained a student there six or seven years, taking two degrees in the process. Bampfield recalled that during his student days he "was somewhat swoln and prejudiced against the strict Profession of Religion amongst the *Puritan* Party, (the Land being then mostly divided into but Two Parties, *Puritan* and *Prophane*)". Even he could not resist having the occasional "fling at times at the *Non-conformists*", but he was never one of their fiercest persecutors. "During this time", Bampfield testified, "he held on in the Common-Prayer-Book track, even to the exposing of his Life to open danger, when Souldiers came in upon him with Swords and Guns, whilst he was at his superstitious Worship."[6]

In conformity with the seventeenth-century autobiographical convention of seeking to determine the workings of the Holy Spirit and the precise moment of dedication to Christ, Bampfield incidentally provides his readers with interesting psychological details. He confessed that as a child, even before he had reached theological understanding, he was plagued by nightmares: he "lay for many years under a spirit of bondage to Fear, being very often frighted in terrible Dreams, wherein he fell into deep Waters, the Earth sliding away from under him, whilst he endeavoured to climb up to the top of an Hill or Rock for safety, which he was not able to do: falling over Bridges into the Sea, and down from thence into the Gulph and horrible Pit". In these misadventures he was not alone: the "Devil many times seemed to be at hand, running to lay hold on him, though always he escaped, yet so terrfied as awakened him, and left cold sweats upon him: yet this kept him several years in aw, and held him back from many Sins." One minister described Bampfield as his own spiritual Father, and from his own account it would appear that this was not far from the truth.[7]

Francis Bampfield was ordained in 1641, and was presented to the living of Ramparish in Devon by his father, "being patrō of the church". At the

---

[6] [Francis Bampfield], *A Name, an After-one* (London, 1681), p. 2. Bampfield matriculated on 16 May 1634 at the age of 18; B.A. 1635; M.A. 1638: *Alumni Oxonienses*, ed. J. Foster (Oxford, 1891-2), *s.v.* "Bampfylde, Francis". Various Bampfield pedigrees are now Bodl. Lib., MS Rawl. C 409 (II), f. 83; B 73, f. 58ᵛ; Ashm. 1107, fos. 320-1.

[7] [Bampfield], *A Name*, p. 3.

beginning of 1647, Bampfield also received the living of Wraxall in Dorset-shire, in his father's gift as well, with the approval of the County Commit-tee. The inhabitants of Wraxall were especially enjoined to "pay their tyths unto Mr. Francis Bampfield" and to take notice "that the parsonag house and gleab lands, heretofore belonging to the church of Wraxall, shall and may belong to the sayd Frances Bampfield".[8]

Bampfield in his autobiography was careful to justify the legitimacy of his ministry, noting that he was approved by every possible authority. To those who placed authority in the magistrate, he could cite "the Attests, the Hands and Seals of two Kings, and of one Protector; tho as to this last, and one of the other, they were other Men, who voluntarily of themselves procured this for him, without his seeking." To those who championed the episcopate, he might cite "the Hands and Seals of Bishop *Hall* [of Exeter], for Deaconship"; to Presbyterians he could bring forth approbations of such officials, and approval by the Triers in Cromwell's time. If there were those who placed the approval of ministers in the people's hands, Bamp-field could remind them of his "call to one of the most populous Towns in all *Dorsetshire*, by some Thousands of that Town, and by Multitudes of other neighbouring Places thereabouts, as any Minister in *England*, that he knows of, had in that Day."[9]

The hundred pounds that Bampfield received from his parishioners he returned to them, and supported himself out of his own private income. This unexpected generosity notwithstanding, Bampfield soon quarrelled with his flock over doctrinal matters, for although he was a Royalist in his politics, he thought that church practice was in urgent need of reform. Bampfield took his parochial duties seriously, and "at that time he kept up a Meeting most Evenings, for some time, to speak to some practical Case of Conscience, and had written diverse little Books of Diaries of his own Experiences." But having discovered that his parishioners refused "to be governed by the laws of Christ's House", he resolved to leave his parish, and finally accepted in 1657 the less valuable living of Sherborne, where he served until after the Restoration.[10] There, according to Anthony

---

[8] *Ibid.*, p. 6; *The Minute Book of the Dorset Standing Committee*, ed. C.H. Mayo (Exeter, 1902), pp. 138-9.

[9] [Bampfield], *A Name*, p. 6. Anthony Wood claims that he took the Engagement in 1653, but Bampfield protested after the Restoration that not only was this untrue, but that he even "Preached against it, for which I Suffered a short Imprisonment": Anthony Wood, *Athenae Oxonienses*, ed. P. Bliss (Oxford, 1813-20), iv. 126; Francis Bampfield, *A Just Appeal* (London, 1683), p. 8.

[10] [Bampfield], *A Name*, p. 6. Bampfield was also collated to a prebend in Exeter Cathe-dral on 15 May 1641, in which he was reinstated at the Restoration, but finally deprived and succeeded on 31 Oct. 1662: Matthews, *Calamy*, p. 26; *idem, Walker Revised* (Oxford, 1948), p. 7.

Wood, "he continued, carrying on the trade among the factious people, not without great disturbance from quakering witches, as he pretended".[11]

During September 1660, ejected ministers were restored to their livings, and at least fifty clergymen withdrew voluntarily from their posts before being forced out.[12] Francis Bampfield's predecessor William Lyford had died in office so he was in no immediate danger.[13] Nevertheless, as early as 10 September 1660, Bampfield was presented at the Dorset assizes for not using the Elizabethan liturgy.[14] But it was only when the church settlement of the new king became apparent that Bampfield was pushed finally into religious disobedience. He recalled in his autobiography that when the Act of Uniformity was promulgated in 1662, by which all clergymen had to submit completely to episcopacy, the entire religious question suddenly became clear in his mind.[15] Bampfield resolved "not so much as to touch that unclean Constitution of humanely invented Worship, and so he has continued ever since, a total thorow *Nonconformist*, though Afflictions and Persecutions have abidden him from that time."[16] He resigned his living to "a great Church full of weeping eies, and sad hearts" and moved to a hired house in town, leaving Sherborne without any authorized clergyman at all.[17]

The first of these "Afflictions and Persecutions" was his arrest on 19 September 1662 in a raid by the ecclesiastical authorities on worship conducted at his own house. Also taken were several of his parishioners and Humphrey Philips, his assistant at Sherborne.[18] Philips was also a graduate of Wadham College, and when he took his MA in 1656 he became a fellow of Magdalen, where he remained until ousted from his fellowship at the Restoration. Philips had assisted Bampfield in 1658 and had been chaplain and tutor at the Bampfield family seat in Politmore, Devon, so when he was forced to leave Oxford he returned to Sherborne and found himself at Bampfield's side in September 1662.[19] Ironically, according to

---

[11] Wood, *Athenae*, iv. 126.

[12] M.R. Watts, *The Dissenters* (Oxford, 1978), p. 217.

[13] Wood, *Athenae*, iv. 126.

[14] Bod. Lib., MS Clar. 73, fos. 218-19: presentment of the grand inquest for the County of Dorset at Assizes and general Gaol Delivery held at Dorchester.

[15] The Act provided for the ejection of non-conforming ministers by St Bartholomew's Day, 24 Aug. 1662: Watts, *Dissenters*, p. 219.

[16] [Bampfield], *A Name*, pp. 4, 7.

[17] [Anon.], *A Brief Narration of the Imprisonment of M'' Francis Bampfield* (n.p., 1662), pp. 3-4. Bampfield's successor at Sherborne was installed in his new post on 23 Apr. 1663: Matthews, *Calamy*, p. 26.

[18] *Narration*, title p.

[19] Matthews, *Calamy*, p. 388: Matthews also notes that Philips was a native of Somerset and ordained at the age of 24. When Philips took out a licence under the Declaration of Indulgence in 1672 he would describe himself as a Presbyterian: *Cal. S.P. Dom., 1672*, pp.

an anonymous narrative of their arrest, one of the chief reasons that Bampfield was so popular in Sherborne was "his loyalty to the King, (for you must know that this Town has been notorious for their Loyalty) whose Cause he constantly asserted under all the changes to the last".[20]

It was there on Friday evening, 19 September 1662 that "one *Thornton* of this Town, an *Apothecary*" and "one *Sugar* with other Soldiers" surprised Bampfield, Philips and about ten others at worship in their former minister's home. They came equipped with a warrant from the deputy lieutenant and by the time order could be restored, Bampfield's supporters had grown to twenty-five in number, who were all carried away to prison with their minister. Numerous irregularities caught the attention of Bampfield's flock: the women attending the service were allowed to go free, and the rest were kept imprisoned until the following Wednesday without being summoned and without a formal complaint having been lodged. On Sunday there was no public worship in Sherborne as the town's only minister still was confined, and permission for Bampfield to conduct services from his cell was not granted. Bampfield later explained to the deputy lieutenant, with Sir John Stroad of Parham in the chair, that he had been at prayer with his family, and the door being open a number of townspeople came into his home and joined with them. The deputy lieutenant did not doubt that Bampfield's words at that time were godly, but nevertheless declared the meeting as tending to sedition. Bampfield and his assistant Philips were released on Wednesday with the rest of the prisoners, and were compelled to pay costs and to give sureties for their good behaviour and for their appearance at the next assizes. It was said that the prisoners had been very roughly treated by the soldiers and forced to suffer physical hardships; "others that came to visit the Prisoners were violently handled, one tumbled, another kicked down stairs by the Soldiers".[21]

On 23 July 1663, Francis Bampfield was again arrested at Shaftesbury for preaching and "for being at unlawful conventicles".[22] Also taken at the same time were fellow ministers Josiah Banger, Peter Ince, John Sacheverell and Thomas Hallet.[23] At the Dorset winter assizes he was bound in security of £40, his sureties being his brother Thomas and Humphrey Philips, also in jail.[23] Bampfield recalled years later that "when several Justices were requiring me to take an Oath, one of them set a great Bible before me, wherein was the *Common Prayer* bound up with it, who would have me

---

236, 402, 574. Cf. Francis Bampfield, *A Continuation of a Former Just Appeal* (London, 1689), p. 10.

[20] *Narration*, pp. 3-4.

[21] *Ibid.*, *passim*; the pamphlet is dated in the text as of 25 Sept. 1662.

[22] *Cal. S.P. Dom., 1663-4*, p. 612; Matthews, *Calamy*, p. 26.

[23] *Ibid.*; Richard Baxter, *Reliquiae Baxteriana*, ed. M. Sylvester (London, 1696), i. 432.

swear by the Contents of that Book; I suspected the Trap, and opening the Book, found the *Common Prayer* there, and so escaped the Snare.''[24] Bampfield stubbornly refused to pay his fine of forty marks and thereby admit the illegality of non-conformity, and on this account would languish in Dorchester jail for nearly nine years.[25] ''The rest at last were released upon some Bonds given for their good Behaviour,'' writes Richard Baxter, but Francis Bampfield remained imprisoned, ''although he was all along against the Parliament War.'' Indeed, Baxter noted,

> But though he and his Brother were the likest Men I knew in *England* successfully to have perswaded those that are contrary minded, that it is unlawful for a Parliament to take up Arms to defend themselves, or punish Manufactures, against the Will and Word of the King, yet this would not keep either of them out of Prison: And so their endeavours for that work were stopt against their wills ... But since, alas, *Francis* having fall'n into the Opinion for the *Saturday* Sabbath, &c. their Afflicters think themselves justified for afflicting them.[26]

Bampfield himself thought it ironic that a Royalist non-conformist should be treated in exactly the same harsh manner as revolutionary sectarians, and wrote to Charles I telling him exactly that. He reminded the king that he had never participated in the Civil War, abhorred insurrections and seditions, and would never lift a hand against any lawful authority.[27] Bampfield and the others (with the exception of Hallet) seem to have been moved to Windsor Castle for a time the following June, but the king failed to answer his plea.[28]

But it was only when Bampfield became convinced of the validity of the Saturday-Sabbath that he saw himself as ''passing into the Scripture-Path''. About 1665 Bampfield had a letter from a ''near and dear Brother, and Friend of his from the Country'' who asked him in prison whether the last day of the week or the first might be the Sabbath according to God's command. Bampfield admits that ''he was somewhat startled at this new Proposal'', although he himself had had his doubts about the scriptural justification for observing Sunday as the Sabbath at least since replying to the same question posed to him by a lady member of his former congregation in Sherborne about 1658 or 1659. Bampfield thought it strange that ''tho he preached up Sabbath-Duties and Priviledges in that Town'' he could find no solid basis for his arguments in favour of Sunday. Bampfield

---

[24] Bampfield, *Continuation*, p. 7.

[25] Matthews, *Calamy*, p. 26.

[26] Baxter, *Reliquiae*, i. 432.

[27] Bampfield to Charles II, June ? 1664: *Cal. S.P. Dom., 1663-4*, p. 612: Bampfield is described here as a Quaker.

[28] *Ibid.*, various warrants dated 13 June 1664.

set aside his friend's letter for a month's time, but when he received a second request for an immediate answer to this pressing theological question,
he spoke to "*Jehovah Ælohim*, to Father, Son, and Holy Spirit, to Christ
God-Man, in Prayer about it, and then makes Scripture-Testimonies to be
the Men of his Councel". But it was the text of the Scripture itself which
finally convinced Bampfield of the validity of the seventh day: "He was
now in a short space of time, the very same day of entering upon this enquiry, got so far forwards in this way, of the seventh-day Sabbath from that
Light and Truth which *Jehovah Ælohim* sent forth from his word by his Holy
Spirit, that, he forthwith concluded, there was no either going back, or
stepping aside, for him out of this Scripture-Path". Bampfield's reasoning
was very straight-forward: "For, if all the Old Testament were for it, the
New was not against it". Indeed, Bampfield confessed, now "he begins to
be more confirmed, and wondereth how he could so much overlook, so
self-evidencing a Truth and Duty so long". In true Puritan fashion, once
convinced of the meaning of a scriptural passage, the now obvious meaning became for Bampfield the only one, regarding which no compromise
was possible.[29]

Bampfield's discovery of the Sabbath day was most inconvenient, especially for a man who was a prisoner convicted of religious offences. Bampfield immediately found that "a very formidable Sight stares him in the
Face; for he saw such an Army of Opposers, not only profane, but professing, not only Foes, but Friends, all almost as one Man up in Arms against
him". Bampfield recounted that he "privately observed the Seventh-day-
Sabbath for some time, but with great Difficulties, and sore Trials, and
distressing Hardships in the Prison". Eventually he succeeded in winning
over a number of fellow prisoners to his interpretation of the divine commandment. Heartened by this support, Bampfield made a public profession of his intention to observe the Sabbath day on a Saturday,

> which being understood by some Ministers and others, two Ministers came
> to him in the Prison, a little before the end of the sixth day, with vehement
> earnest importunate desirings, beseechings, and entreatings, and other argu-
> ings and charmings, that, he would forbear, tho but one day, the next day,
> which was the seventh day, to consult and consider of so weighty a matter,
> in so great a change for one week, Oh for one week longer! His answer was
> quick, short, full, and resolved, in the Strength of the LORD, No

The very next day, being a Saturday, Francis Bampfield publicly celebrated the Sabbath in Dorchester prison, and recounted later that since then

---

[29] [Bampfield], *A Name*, pp. 12-13.

he "never met with any Objection, that could shake or stagger him, but all wrought for his fuller Confirmation and Establishment."[30]

It was also in prison that Bampfield was honoured by the Lord with what he called "somewhat of a Vision in the Spirit, wherein two of the choicest Revelations were made manifest to him and in him". Bampfield related that

> in a very dark evening, whilst a Prisoner, a little before his going to his Lodging, he bowing his knees in Prayer, was on a sudden taken up in his Spirit as if he had been actually in Heaven ... where he had a clear view of Christ in his Glorified Humanity by an Eye of Faith, He sittle in the sides of the North.

Bampfield recalled that this vision "was as real to him as if he had conversed with Christ personally in the flesh; and it is still so, when he is in a right worshiping Frame: being led to him as to the one Mediator and Advocate to carry on all his Affairs in the Court above." Bampfield's second vision was "A Self-evidencing view of those Glorious Appearances of Father, Son, and holy Spirit, and distinctness of Communion with each of these in their several subsistences, shining forth in the Face of *Jesus.*" These experiences, he thought, "raised him into a higher way of Later-Day-Glory hymnifying, than his former way of singing by Mens Forms read out of a Book".[31]

Bampfield dated these visions at about 1667, and indeed he had plenty of time to draw sustenance from them during his long imprisonment. He saw his confinement as an honour, "for Christ's sake, for the Gospel sake, for Righteousness sake, for the Elect's sake", and even in prison he managed to gather a church and a group of followers, although he warned them that he "did always reserve to himself the liberty of answering of Christ's Call to any other Place or People; for, he was the LORD's, having given up himself unto Him, to be wholy and only at his dispose, and not to be during Life staked down to any particular Place or People."[32] Richard Baxter recounted that Bampfield and the other ministers in prison at Dorchester preached "to the People of the Town who came to them, every day once, and in the Lord's Day twice; till at last the Jaylor was corrected, and an Order made against Jaylors letting in People into the Prisons to hear".[33]

Francis Bampfield was released from prison in May 1672 "as a mark of the King's clemency" without, he proudly recorded, "paying one pen-

---

[30] *Ibid.*, p. 14.
[31] *Ibid.*, p. 4.
[32] *Ibid.*, p. 7.
[33] Baxter, *Reliquiae*, i. 432.

ny of that Fine which was laid upon me'' nine years before.[34] Richard Baxter wrote about that time that Bampfield and his brother Thomas were still ''so much against the Parliament's Cause, that to this day (even while he lay in Jail) he most zealously made his followers renounce it''.[35] Soon after his release from Dorchester prison he was confined again for eighteen weeks at Salisbury.[36] It was there on his release that he took the momentous step of committing himself to believers' baptism in fulfilment of a resolution that he had made while still in prison. Bampfield recounted that his original intention had been to join with two other men and a woman that he had met in London, and to that end ''being thoroughly satisfied in each other, took Boat and rowed down to *Battersey* near *London*, and having discovered a convenient place of passing into the *Thames* River, intended there to submit to this Appointment of their LORD the next Morning''. But before the end of the Sabbath, the little group had some difference of opinion, which ''graciously over-ruled this Affair for Good.'' Later on ''he with one more travelled from *London* to *Salisbury*, where, about the middle of the Day, in the broad River of that City, which runs with living water, he received his being baptized as by the Hand of Christ himself . . . and baptized another: and further also received Imposition, or stretching out by laying on of Hands''.[37]

On his release from prison, Bampfield also found the occasion to marry. He had been helped in prison by a certain Mistress Town, an Irish minister's daughter, who had brought Bampfield and other ministers food and various necessities. After the others were released, she continued to come to him until his own freedom was obtained. When Bampfield resumed his preaching in various places in the area, this woman came with him as well. ''This being envied and maligned by some,'' he wrote, ''to prevent, or remove any occasion of Scandal or offence, he declared unto some of the Church, that he was willing to take . . . a Wife, according to the Word, she being every way the fittest for him, she being a Sister in the same way of Church-fellowship, and a Virgin modest and chast''. The fact that Francis Bampfield was a scion of a distinguished family while this woman was ''a poor Maid without a Portion'', set many to argue that he had married beneath his social station and in this way had behaved dishonourably, to the extent, he discovered, ''that his Ministry was in a great measure rendred much useless and successless in those Parts.'' This was one of the two

---

[34] *Cal. S.P. Dom.*, 1671-2, p. 597; Francis Bampfield, *The Lords Free Prisoner* (London, 1683), p. 1.

[35] Baxter, *Reliquae*, iii. 150.

[36] Bampfield, *Prisoner*, p. 1. Here too Bampfield was released ''without paying one farthing of the Fine''.

[37] [Bampfield], *A Name*, pp. 14, 17.

reasons he gave for quitting the area of Dorchester and coming to live and work in London.[38]

The second reason for coming to London about 1672 was the publication of his first work justifying the Seventh-Day Sabbath, *The Judgement of Mr. Francis Bampfield*, which was printed in that year. By the time his pamphlet and its reply were printed, Bampfield himself was in a position to put into practice the principles which he championed. As early as December 1662, Charles II had promised to use the royal dispensing power to relieve recusants, and in March 1672 he suspended the penal laws against them. Non-conformists were thereafter permitted to take out licences to preach, but only as individuals, not as representatives of entire churches.[39] Francis Bampfield was among the very many that availed themselves of this privilege. On 29 June 1672 a licence was issued in Dorchester "to Fran: Bampfield a Nonconforming Minister to teach in any licensed place." The records also note that the licence was "made in Parchm^t thus by my Ld Cliffords Order".[40] G. Lyon Turner, the Edwardian editor of these documents, points out that Bampfield's licence refers "in an absolutely unique fashion" to Lord Thomas Clifford, a protégé of Lord Arlington, soon to be appointed Lord High Treasurer. Turner prints five documents that bear Clifford's name, and thus link him with the issuing of indulgences, and two of these prove his authority to issue them directly.[41] Secondly, Turner notes that this is the only case in which a licence was made out in parchment: the "practically universal practice" was to make them out on partly printed, partly written forms which were on thick paper. Finally, this document contradicts Richard Baxter's claim that he was the only minister who held a licence which did not specify the sect or "perswasion" to which he belonged. Bampfield's licence, in fact, is made out in precisely the same

---

[38] *Ibid.*, pp. 23-4. Bampfield there writes further that her grandfather Mr Slado sold a considerable estate in England in order to purchase another one in Ireland, where he lived for a time in Limerick. He there supported lecturers, and two of his daughters, including Bampfield's mother-in-law, were married to ministers. Bampfield's wife's father Mr Town was said to be a Doctor of Divinity with an Irish estate worth £200 a year who fled to England during the Irish Rebellion of the 1640s.

[39] On 15 Mar. 1671-2, Charles II, in exercise of his alleged "dispensing power", issued a Declaration of Indulgence to such ministers and others "as do not conform to the Church of England".

[40] *Original Records of Early Nonconformity under Persecution and Indulgence*, ed. G. Lyon Turner (London & Leipsic, 1911-14), i. 523; *Cal. S.P. Dom., 1672*, p. 292. Turner suggests (ii. 1132) that Bampfield is listed as of Dorchester because he was at that time in prison there, and was not released until 1675. Bampfield in fact seems to have been at liberty before the indulgence was issued: Turner apparently relied on the entry in the *Dict. Nat. Biog.* for Bampfield's date of release.

[41] *Ibid.*, iii. 263. Elsewhere (iii. 715), Turner notes that this case is also peculiar in that it is one of the few in which Lord Clifford had been principal, not Arlington.

way, and was issued four months before Baxter's.[42] "It certainly would be interesting," Turner muses, "to trace the ground of Lord Clifford's special interest in Francis Bampfield." In a footnote, Turner suggests that there "was, of course, the general reason that Bampfield was a Devon man, and the special one that he was well connected, one brother being a baronet, and another the Recorder of Exeter."[43]

Another interesting anomaly in Bampfield's career in 1672 is the fact that he did not sign the address of thanks which was sent from grateful non-conforming Dorset ministers to the king on 10 May of that year. These public acknowledgements of the royal clemency are in fact quite rare, and apart from Dorset survive only from Dartmouth, Cornwall, Devon, and Wiltshire. The address from Dorset, however, is somewhat unlike the others in the extreme servility of expression: we "prostrate ourselves att your Maties singular Clemencie therein exp^{r}ssed". Three of the four men who were arrested with Bampfield back in July 1663 signed, namely Josiah Banger, Timothy Sacheverell, and Thomas Hallet. The fourth man, Peter Ince is missing from the list of grateful ministers for some reason, but in any case Ince was not licensed to preach in Dorset.[44] Calamy reckoned that only four ejected Dorset ministers refrained from signing although they were licenced to preach in that county: two of these were Francis Bampfield and Humphrey Philips, his former assistant.[45] G. Lyon Turner thought the language of this document showed "an almost Jacobite devotion to this Stuart Prince"; indeed, "Whoever composed it must have known how such flattery would delight the easy-tempered King."[46] It is unclear why Bampfield, a devoted Royalist even during the Interregnum, would not sign a document which so perfectly agreed with his political sentiments.

II

In any case, Bampfield himself testifies that soon afterwards he left Dorset and came to live in London. Finding there a number of followers who urged him to lead them and to administer the Lord's Supper, Bampfield

---

[42] *Ibid.*, iii. 263. Baxter's license of 27 Oct. 1672 is printed in *ibid.*, i. 575 & *Cal. S.P. Dom.*, *1672-3*, p. 88. On iii. 715, Turner notes further that another applicant before Baxter who secured a licence in which the sect was not designated was Sir Thomas Player, Chamberlain of London.

[43] *Ibid.*, iii. 263. Lord Thomas Clifford was the eldest son of Hugh Clifford, Esq. of central Devon.

[44] *Cal. S.P. Dom., 1671-2*, p. 527; *Records*, ed. Turner, i. 325; cf. iii. 631-7. Sacheverell's Christian name is given differently here.

[45] *Ibid.*, iii. 637. Humphrey Philips was issued a licence to preach as well: *Cal. S.P. Dom.*, *1672*, pp. 236, 402, 574.

[46] *Records*, ed. Turner, iii. 635.

baptized several of them and agreed to stay on at their congregation at
Bethnal Green. Bampfield notes the year of this agreement as 1674, and
records that "this was assented unto and agreed upon by those baptized
Believers, and Seventh-day-Sabbath-Observers." Soon afterwards, however, "some differences in Judgment arising amongst them", the group
split up. In 1675 those who continued to follow Bampfield organized themselves as a gathered church, and soon began to worship at Pinners' Hall,
which he described as "one of the most open noted places in all *London*".[47]
Bampfield scrupulously records that during the months before he organized his own congregation, "the two Sabbath Churches in the City
desired his Labours sometimes with them in the use and exercise of his
Gifts, which he consented to upon their importunity".[48] So Bampfield
seems to have preached both at Mill Yard and at Bell Lane as well. Bampfield's arrival in London and his demonstrated willingness to lead the
Seventh-Day men may also have been the trigger that finally caused the
expulsion of Dr Peter Chamberlen from the congregation that he had
helped to found at Mill Yard. As we have seen, Chamberlen in 1675 was
forced out of Mill Yard as a self-confessed patentee, but found a home in
the more radical congregation at Bell Lane, led by John Belcher.

Indeed, a sharper contrast could hardly be drawn between Bampfield
and Belcher, the two most prominent leaders of the Seventh-Day men during this period. Unlike Bampfield, who was university-educated, Belcher
was a bricklayer by profession; and unlike Bampfield the staunch Royalist,
Belcher was a radical in politics as well as religion. Belcher first appears
in the records as a result of his arrest on 1 April 1658 at Swan Alley along
with Wentworth Day, John Canne and others. Christopher Feake attacked
the arrests and was himself put in the Tower for his troubles. Day (one of
Venner's plotters the previous year) and John Clarke (the Baptist minister
of Newport, Rhode Island and another of those arrested) refused to plead,
denied the legality of the government and argued the case that the magistrates and not they were guilty of treason. Day was also asked to provide
twelve witnesses to prove his claim that Cromwell was a "jugler". Day received a heavy fine and a year's imprisonment; Clarke was fined and imprisoned for six months. Apart from Canne, who was sent to Newgate for

---

[47] [Bampfield], *A Name*, pp. 26-7; *idem, Prisoner*, p. 1.

[48] *Ibid.*, p. 2. Bampfield was then living in Great More-fields but chose Pinners' Hall
as the new place of worship. There was a general unwillingness of the authorities to license
public halls, as opposed to private houses, but Pinners' Hall was an exception. It was used
not only for worship but also for "The Merchants' Lecture" which was given on Tuesday
morning by both Presbyterian and Independent ministers at Pinners' Hall until 1778, and
then elsewhere until this century: *Vict. Cnty. Hist., London*, i (1909), p. 380.

contempt and for handing out copies of the Musselburgh Declaration in court, the rest were released, including John Belcher.[49]

After the Restoration, in September 1661, a government spy named William Pestell reported that the Fifth Monarchy men had sent agents to Yorkshire, Durham, Devon, and Great Yarmouth, including Feake, Canne, John Rogers, and John Belcher who "travell from County to County and are hardly a month in a place". Belcher was described as a dangerous man who would have taken part in Venner's Rising had he not disagreed with the rebels over tactics.[50] Two years later, John Belcher himself was a government agent, informing on the activities of Henry Jessey to Peter Crabb, a royal intelligencer. Crabb wrote to Secretary of State Henry Bennet on 22 September 1663 that "the ffifth monarchy men are now in the same mind, That they were in Veners business And as I am assured by Mr Bellshar who is a very eminent man amongst them, That they are to meete . . . one night this weeke, And so to conclude upon the tyme when to finish the Lords worke as they so call itt".[51]

In July 1671 a meeting of Fifth Monarchy men and Seventh-Day Sabbatarians was discovered in London and raided by Sir John Robinson, the lieutenant of the Tower. Robinson described the group, which included John Belcher, in most uncompromising terms: "These are all desperate persons," he wrote to Joseph Williamson, Lord Arlington's secretary, "I shall take care to destroye their meeting place. A Copy of the informacōn ags^t the preacher I here inclosed". Robinson was exceedingly worried about the good conduct of the prisoners, and went so far as to send a special detachment of soldiers to deal with what turned out to be a false alarm, thereby annoying the Lord Mayor, the sheriffs and several aldermen who thought the liberties of the City thereby invaded.[52] Twenty-six persons were committed to Newgate, and four of the leaders to the Tower, under Robinson's personal supervision.[53] The four were described as "John Bellchar, a most notorious knafe came out of oxfordshire Arthur Squibb[54] Rich: Goodgroome, formerly comitted by my Ld Gen:^{ll} for a

---

[49] Pestell to Nicholas, 26 Sept. 1661: SP. 29/42, f. 69^v; same to same, 28 Nov. 1661: SP. 29/44, f. 267; B.S. Capp, *The Fifth Monarchy Men* (London, 1972), p. 207.

[50] Pestell to Nicholas, 26 Sept. 1661: SP. 29/42, f. 69^v.

[51] Crabb to Bennett, 22 Sept. 1663: SP. 29/80, f. 192.

[52] Robinson to Williamson, 2 July 1671: SP. 29/291, f. 176^{r-v}.

[53] "A list of the ffifth Monarchy men", 2 July 1671: SP. 29/291, f. 179. Probably enclosed in *ibid.*; the descriptions quoted here are from this document.

[54] d. 1680; minister of gathered church; former JP; MP for Middlesex in Barebone's Parliament; prominent Fifth Monarchy man; licensed Baptist preacher, Surrey, 1672: see Capp, *Fifth Monarchy*, p. 263.

dangerous person[55] John Jones, a dangerous person".[56] Furthermore, he noted "ffower apprentices sent to Bridewell that wold not acknowledg their aboade nor Masters names".[57]

Robinson does not in his letter to Williamson specify who the preacher was on the occasion the arrest was made, but he was acting on information that he had received under oath in his capacity of JP for Middlesex from a Captain Thomas Gardner and a certain Richard Pitt. According to the two informants,

> upon Saturday the 24th of June last past they heard a person preach at an unlawfull assembly in Bell Lane neere Spittlefeilds who went by the name of John Bellchar a Bricklayer, a Sabatarian or fifth Monarchy man, and made theire of a Text viz: the first of Solomons Song and the 12th verse, and amongst severall Texts of scripture which he quoted, he named one in Isaiah (as they remember) and the words were to the effect viz: Arise O Jerusalem and shake of thy dust and then sitt downe in peace, which he thus interpreted Arise O Jerusalem, and obey neither prince nor prelate but shake of thy dust till thou sitt downe in peace.[58]

Francis Bampfield himself was then in Newgate Prison, and may have met some of the Bell Lane men detained there.

It was soon clear that Robinson intended to deal with the Sabbatarians most severely. "Sessions began yesterday at Hicks' Hall", he informed Williamson on 18 July 1671,

> This morning I caused to be brought to the Bench the 27 Sabbatarians or Fifth Monarchy men, which I committed to Newgate. The oath of allegiance was there offered and read to them; they all prosecuted to a refused to take it. They were immediately indicted, the grand jury found the bill, and the petty jury found them guilty, so they will be *praemunire*, their goods confiscated, and their bodies imprisoned during his Majesty's pleasure. The four I have in the Tower and the four that are in the Bridewell will be likewise proceeded against[59]

According to the rolls of the Middlesex Sessions, this group was committed "for being dangerous and seditious persons against the Peace, owning themselves to be be [*sic*] of the sect of Sabbatarians or Fifth Monarchy Men and exercising their pretended religion". It is also recorded there that in

---

[55] See *ibid.*, p. 250. The man of this name was apparently not the schoolmaster at Usk, who in the *Bap. Qly.*, n.s., i (1922-3), 228-33 is said to be "the key to the whole Baptist movement" in Wales.

[56] There were two men of that name, and probably both of them signed the Fifth Monarchy declaration of 1654. This John Jones fl. 1668-87: see Capp, *Fifth Monarchy*, p. 253.

[57] SP. 29/291, f. 179.

[58] SP. 29/291, f. 178[r]: probably enclosed with Robinson's letter to Williamson.

[59] *Cal. S.P. Dom., 1671*, pp. 385-6.

addition to refusing the oath of allegiance, the group also refused to promise that they would not take up arms against the king.[60]

The four leaders of the group, including "John Belcher yeoman" were
arraigned at the beginning of October 1671 "for obstinately refusing to
take the Oath of Allegiance". The minutes also show that Jones, Belcher
and Squibb pleaded "Not Guilty" and put their case on the decision of
a jury. Richard Goodgroome, on the other hand, refused to confess the in-
dictment or to plead to it; it is recorded that he "said nothing" at all. Despite the fact that of the thirty-one radicals brought to trial, twenty-seven
were sentenced to imprisonment at the king's pleasure, no further record
is heard of any of these cases. It appears likely that as Charles II was planning to issue his Declaration of Indulgence there was little point in holding
a group which very shortly would be able to conduct prayers publicly and
undisturbed. Indeed, Arthur Squibb was one of those licensed in 1672.[61]

John Belcher's congregation was apparently the most radical of the Saturday-Sabbatarian gathered churches, but other such groups did exist in
England at the time which have left few traces as to whether they inclined
towards Bampfield's Royalist Sabbatarianism or Belcher's political radi-
calism. Anthony Wood recalled that about December 1660 a certain
Banister rented a farm at Cutteslowe, who was "an accounted jew or at
least an anti-sabbatarian".[62] John Cowell, a convert to Saturday-Sabbatarianism who later recanted, testified that it was about 1671 that "the sad
tendency of this Sabbath-keeping more clearly shewed forth it self" even
outside of London.[63]

Indeed, the official records of non-conformity note a number of Sabbatarian groups, although the denominational designations given here are
often suspect. The episcopal returns for Oxfordshire from 1669 record that
"Sabbatarians who observe Saturday" could be found worshipping at a
widow's house in Wathington, and sometimes at a neighbouring
weaver's.[64] In Kingston, about thirty or forty "Presbyterians, Indepen-
dents, Quakers & Sabbatarians mixt" including "Mr Button & one
Belch^r Forein^rs, who under pretence of receiving the rent come hither to
teach"; this must certainly be our John Belcher, later of Bell Lane.[65] A

---

[60] *Middlesex County Records*, iv, ed. J.C. Jeaffreson (Middlesex County Rec. Soc., 1892), pp.
29-30.
[61] *Ibid.*, pp. 30-1; Capp, *Fifth Monarchy*, p. 216.
[62] Anthony Wood, *Life and Times*, ed. A. Clark (Oxford, 1891-1900), i. 353.
[63] John Cowell, *The Snare Broken* (London, 1677), p. 11.
[64] *Original Records*, ed. Turner, iii. 823. These were the episcopal returns made by order
of Archbishop Sheldon in 1669, now in the Lambeth Palace Library, which recorded the
non-conformist conventicles found in each diocese.
[65] *Ibid.*, iii. 824. Turner identifies the first man as Ralph Button, ejected from a canonry
of Christ Church, Oxford and an oratorship to Oxford University. The second he suggests

third group of Oxfordshire "Sabbatarians" met in Worborough.[66] Similarly, in Downham, Cambridgeshire, Samuel Cater ministered to "Some
rich, some meane people", a group of "Quakers, Anabaptists & Sabbatarians".[67] At a house in Bledlow, Bucks, the teacher was "John Sullins –
a maker of Lace – a constant observer of the Jewish Sabbath".[68] Also in
Buckinghamshire, we find the only reference in the episcopal returns for
1669 to "Jewes", who were registered as meeting under the leadership of
"Nicholas Babb a Weaver att y[e] house of Sarah Grimsell", apparently a
widow.[69]

Several other less reliable references show the spread of Saturday-Sabbatarian beliefs to more distant places. At Llangwm in Monmouth, Wales
a certain William Milman was described as "a Sabbatarian Anabaptist"
itinerating in the country, and was licensed for the house of William Rich-
ards there in 1672.[70] Modern-day historians of the Baptist movement have
looked to such isolated references to account for the spread of that denomination in Wales, for "it had a strong Seventh-day tinge which was to be
traced even fifty years later, and we could not account for it."[71]

But perhaps the most well-known provincial observer of the Seventh-
Day Sabbath was John Cowell, who turned renegade in 1677 and published an account of his error. Cowell explained that when he was converted to strict Sabbatarianism he was "understanding but little concerning
the notion sometime before, when by converse with some persons, and
reading some Books, I was corrupted in it, I not seeing the errour of it,
but taking it for a truth". Cowell thought that it was about the beginning
of 1661 that "my foot was taken in this *Snare*" of strict Sabbatarianism. Cowell claims to have been concerned, even at this early stage, with the extre-
mism of the Sabbatarians, but noted that "for many of the persons concerned, they were no small ones neither amongst that People, as *Thomas
Tillam, Christopher Pooly, Edward Skipp, John Fox* &c." Most dangerously, the
Seventh-Day Sabbatarians

> in their Principles, yea, in their Practices too, as with respect to the Worship
> of God were marvelously Corrupted; Pleading, as for the Sabbath, so also for

---

might be William Belcher, a Sabbatarian Baptist, the son of William Belcher, ejected from
Ulcomb, Kent. But it has been suggested that John Belcher was this man's son (Matthews,
Calamy, pp. 45-6). Another possible Belcher was Thomas, the vicar of Sandford, Oxford-
shire during this period (*idem, Walker*, p. 295).

[66] *Ibid.*
[67] *Ibid.*, i. 35: cf. i. 34, 40, 41.
[68] *Ibid.*, i. 78.
[69] *Ibid.*, i. 81: cf. ii. 843; iii. 748.
[70] [Anon.], "Baptist Churches till 1660", *Trans. Bap. Hist. Soc.*, ii (1910-11), 254; [Anon.],
"Wales Under the Indulgence, 1672-5", *Bap. Qly.*, iv (1928-9), 283-4.
[71] *Bap. Qly.*, i (1922-3), 228-33.

Circumcision (which they also practiced), and for the Observation of the whole *Law*: Yea, even to *Offerings* and *Sacrifices*, as may be seen in the Propositions and Queries of *Christopher Pooly*, and *Edward Skipp*, printed 1664.

Cowell printed his own response to Pooly and Skipp, but remained a steadfast Saturday-Sabbatarian even if he eschewed some of their excesses.[72]

"But though I was troubled," Cowell wrote, "yet I kept on in the practice still without much more trouble, till about the year 1668: And then taking notice of the confusion that was amongst Sabbath-keepers in respect of their keeping of their Sabbath, I was again troubled." Cowell overcame his doubts here again, and "thus things stood with me, till about the year 1671, and then the sad tendency of this Sabbath-keeping more clearly shewed forth it self". The issue at question seems to have been

a Sabbath-keeper in the Town where I live, (and she hath more fellows abroad,) a Sabbath-keeper so strict in her Sabbath-keeping, that few others of them (if any at all) do match her for her zeal therein; who is gone so far in her owning of the Sabbath, and the Law whence the rule of it is taken, that she shames not openly to disown the Gospel, and the Lord Jesus Christ the Author and revealer thereof; and in the greatness of her Apostacy and Degeneracy, denies the Lord Jesus Christ to be the Messiah and Saviour of the World; having cast out of her Bible the whole New Testament of our Lord and Saviour Jesus Christ; disowning all those Writings from the beginning of *Matthew* to the end of the Revelation, having in her Bible only those from the beginning of *Genesis* to the end of *Malachi*.

The Saturday-Sabbatarians of his acquaintance tried to put his mind at ease by noting that many people in all ages have fallen away from Christ who were not Sabbath-keepers, and that strict Sabbatarianism does not automatically lead to the wholesale rejection of Christianity. But Cowell was now convinced that the "practice carries it in its womb" and that "many Sabbath-keepers, that are turned (in respect of their Sabbath-keeping) from the Gospel to the Law, and so from Christ to *Moses*, [are] thereby exposing themselves to great danger". Cowell reminded his readers that "indeed the wretched Creature in our Town doth not deny but that Sabbath-keeping was leading to her, as with respect to her denial of the Lord Jesus."[73]

"Another thing that was leading to my leaving off this practice," Cowell testified, was the assertion that he found among many Saturday-Sabbatarians, that "the penalty of death is being in force, for the prophaning the Sabbath (as they phrase it)." Cowell himself had owned this principle

---

[72] Cowell, *Snare*, sig. A3ʳ; pp. 1-2, 6. Edmund Skipp was a preacher in Herefordshire, author of *Worlds Wonder*, answered by R.F., *Antichrists Man of War* (London, 1655).
[73] Cowell, *Snare*, pp. 11-16.

without sufficient thought, but upon more recent reflection, could not "but wonder how any man, having any, even the least entertainment to such a desperate and sanguinary Principle." Among the writers who justified this practice in one form or another, wrote Cowell, were William Saller and Edward Stennett.[74] The first of these writers is well-known to us as the leader of the Mill Yard congregation between about 1670 and 1678. Edward Stennett now requires more detailed consideration.

Edward Stennett was the first in a distinguished line of Baptist divines, who worked mostly in Berkshire, although he may himself have been of Lincolnshire descent. During the Civil War, Stennett may possibly have served as a parliamentary chaplain, and appears to have held a sequestered rectory at Wallingford in Berkshire, where he would work after the Restoration. By 1656 he was a member of a gathered church in Abingdon, and already married to Mary Quelch whose father Richard, a porter at New College, Oxford, was one of the early leaders of the Oxford Baptists.[75] He certainly adopted Saturday-Sabbatarian views by 1658, for in that year he published his *Royal Law*, a short work "serving to prove that the Ten Commandments are yet in full force, and shall so remain till Heaven and Earth pass away; also, The Seventh Day Sabbath proved from the Beginning, from the Law ... to be a Duty yet incumbent upon Saints and Sinners".[76] He amplified these views in a longer work published six years later.[77]

Edward Stennett studied medicine at some point in his life, for after the Restoration it was by its practice that he supported himself and his family at Wallingford. Stennett maintained a Saturday-Sabbatarian congregation at rooms in the ruins of Wallingford Castle where the local magistrates' writ did not run. Legal entry to the castle precincts could be had only by warrant from the Lord Chief Justice, so worshippers there were protected from prosecution. In order to circumvent this legal impasse, the local JP and a neighbourhood clergyman (whose family had been receiving free medical attention from Stennett) bribed a number of people to say that they had been present at an illegal conventicle. Stennett fought the case at the Newbury Assizes, and through a series of accidents and coincidences the case against him was dismissed. First, the magistrate's son ran away with an actress, and in searching for him the father missed the assizes. The clergyman and a key witness died. The second witness broke a

---

[74] *Ibid.*, pp. 18-19.

[75] E.A. Payne, *The Baptists of Berkshire* (London, 1951), pp. 47-8; *Dict. Nat. Biog., s.v.* "Stennett, Joseph". But Stennett does not appear in Anne Laurence, "Parliamentary Army Chaplains 1642-51" (Oxford Univ. D.Phil. 1981).

[76] Edward Stennett, *The Royal Law* (London, 1658), title p.

[77] Edward Stennett, *The Seventh Day is the Sabbath* (n.p., 1664).

leg and could not attend. Finally, although Stennett's gardener was kept drunk for days to persuade him to perjure himself, he steadfastly refused to testify against his employer.[78] In 1672, Edward Stennett took out a proper licence as a Baptist preacher at his house in Wallingford.[79]

It was Edward Stennett, then, who replied to John Cowell's accusations against the Saturday-Sabbatarian movement. Admittedly, Stennett argued, there were a number of notable Saturday-Sabbatarians whose extreme conduct was open to criticism. "I thought you had learned better," he wrote to Cowell, "then to judge of the truth by the miscarriage of its Professors". In any case, Pooley and "some of of those you now cry out against have returned and professed their Repentance". Cowell himself had once held extreme views which he no longer owned, so, Stennett writes, "you should first have answered your own Books, before you meddled with other Mens". As to the woman who denied the divinity of Jesus, this belief was obviously false, was never held by Christopher Pooley as Cowell claimed, and in any case had no demonstrable connection with Saturday-Sabbatarianism: "for you have spent one Section, to shew the Miscarriages of Mr. *Pooley*, and some others, concluding that these Miscarriages were the direct tendency of Sabbath-keeping, which made your beam of Sabbath-light heavy". There was no real reason to connect Sabbath observance as a religious principle with the practices of a handful of extremists, "so we are of a sudden fallen down into the Kennel, To *Thomas Tillam* and *Christopher Pooly*".[80]

III

Thus when Francis Bampfield began to minister to his little group of followers at Pinners' Hall, he joined a fellowship that already included two established congregations, one of which was led by a man with a notoriously radical past, John Belcher, whose followers he almost certainly met at Newgate Prison. Bampfield could also count on the support of Edward Stennett, who with his son Joseph would be the mainstays of Saturday-Sabbatarianism after Bampfield's death in 1684.

The church book of Bampfield's congregation still survives, although

---

[78] Payne, *Baptists*, pp. 48-9.
[79] *Cal. S.P. Dom., 1672*, p. 462.
[80] Edward Stennett, *The Insnared Taken* (London, 1677), pp. 6-7, 8, 11, 94. Stennett mentions Saller on pp. 19, 91; Bampfield on p. 42. The Brit. Lib. copy (1471 de 11) has notes by Joseph Stennett, and a separate title page dated London, 1679. The appendix (p. 150) notes a newly published book entitled *A Confession of Faith* which Joseph Stennett remarks in pencil helps to vindicate his father's views. On p. 162 is a list of books "promoting the seventh-day sabbath, but much out of Print", including works by Brabourne, Ockford, Spittlehouse, Cowell, Bampfield, Saller, Heylin, W.G., and Stennett himself.

the entries for these earliest years were taken "out of a former Church-Book written with Mr. Francis Bampfield's own hand, by me Jos: Sten-nett". These records show that the church was organized under Bampfield on 5 March 1675-6. The eight men who signed the original covenant "Laid their Church-State upon ye only Sure Foundation, & agreed to Form & Regulate it by the only Certain Rule & Measure", which was expressed in the following principle:

> We own the LORD Jesus Christ to be the One & Only LORD & Lawgiver to our Souls & Consciences. And we own the Holy Scriptures of Truth as ye One & only Rule of Faith Worship & Life, According to which we are to Judge of all our Cases

The eight men who signed with Bampfield were Thomas Pierce, William Mercer, William Tovey, James Warner, James Humber, John Belcher Jnr, Andrew Geddes, and Samuel Thompson.[81]

Thus spiritually armed, Francis Bampfield and his little band of followers appealed in 1677 to all Saturday-Sabbath observers to join with him in Christian fellowship. Bampfield noted that there were "divers exceeding great and precious Prophecies and Promises, relating more peculiarly unto the Revivers and Observers of the weekly Seventh-day-Sabbath, which shall go a little before the Coming and Appearing of our LORD Jesus Christ in Glory, when he will gather in the out-casts of *Israel*, and do his other latter-day-Glory-works". Seeing as how the Second Coming of Christ was at hand, Bampfield suggested an annual convention of Satur-day-Sabbatarians at London with representatives from every such church not only in England but in Holland and America as well. Apart from prayer and other spiritual matters, participants at this congress might promote "the training ... in the Knowledg of the Original Tongue, and of other Scripture-Learning, and for the procuring of a more exact literal Translation of the Old-and-New-Testament into our Mother-Tongue". They could also discuss the education of children, the relieving of the poor, and other good works. Most importantly, the members of this Saturday-Sabbatarian congress would be encouraged "to enquire, what may be further a Duty upon us, towards the two, and the ten Tribes of *Judah*, and of

---

[81] Bampfield church book: a vellum-covered foolscap book with the letters F.B., now deposited in the library of the Seventh-Day Baptist Historical Association in Plainfield, New Jersey. The volume was sent there in 1951 by Dr Williams's Library, which retained a photostatic copy, now shelfmark 533.B.2. The earliest entry is for 14 October 1686, but earlier details were copied from the first church book, now lost. The book continued to be used after the amalgamation with the Mill Yard congregation until 1863 when the Seventh-Day Baptists worshipped under the leadership of W.H. Black. Extracts from the book were printed in the *Trans. Bap. Hist. Soc.* iii (1912-13), 8-17 under the title "Bampfield's Plan for an Educated Ministry". This reference, *ibid.*, pp. 8-9.

Israel, to help forward their Conversion, as also what the Spirit has to say more particularly and especially to our Churches, and to other Churches, in this great Providential-day, and such like publick-spirited Inquiries".[82]

At about the same time, in order to promote the Saturday-Sabbath, "whilst others were following of the King with Petition upon Petition, subscribed with multitudes of Hands, from Cities, Towns, and Counties", Bampfield caused another curious document to be "put into the Hands of the King". It was in the form of an appeal from a woman named Elizabeth Hooker, who also signed in Hebrew. This woman, describing herself as "a mean Handmaid", claimed that it was the hand of God himself which prevented the Popish Plot of 1678 from succeeding. In return, Elizabeth Hooker asked Charles to declare at the next session of Parliament his intention "to set up the Laws of Christ in the Scriptures of Truth, as the one, and the only Rule of your Government". After such a declaration, it would be possible to say truthfully that "The Law of God is the Law of the Land". Bampfield reports that a "like Address was made by the same Advice and Hand, to the King to the same Effect, in answer to that loud awakening Call, by that Signal Blazing Star ... And a third, sometime after to the present Mayor of *London*, for the like End."[83]

Yet despite this enthusiasm, some theological thinkers still tried to reason out the problems inherent in any discussion of the Sabbath, even in the restrained days after the Restoration when Bampfield was establishing his new church. It was explained in a Restoration edition of a popular catechism that the Resurrection of Christ was "not appointed to supplant or swallow up" all the principles which had prevailed since Creation. It was simply a question of precedence, "as for some hundreds of years in the ancient Church, the Jewish Sabbath was retained in (a great part, at least, of) the Christian Church together with the Lords-day, and the services proportioned to them both, but the latter preferred before the former".[84] An astrological writer had a simpler explanation: excessive Sabbath observance was due to the influence of Saturn, for in "Ecclesiastical affairs he portends great Superstition, Idolatry, Hypocrisie, Monkery, Jesuitism, and the several Orders of Friers; all manner of Debauchery and Basenesse under Religious pretences, Sects, Schismes, Heresies, Jewish Superstition and Ceremonies."[85]

---

[82] Printed in Bampfield, *Name*, pp. 24-5. Cf. *Cal. S.P. Dom., 1676-7*, p. 543. A similar letter, signed by Bampfield, Pierce, Belcher Jnr, Andrew Geddes and "Wiatt Measer" (William Mercer?) appears in *ibid.*, dated 8 Feb.? 1677, although the text of the letter suggests the more probable date of 8 Apr. 1676.

[83] Bampfield, *Name*, pp. 25-6.

[84] H. Hammond, *A Practical Catechism* (7th edn, London, 1662), p. 195.

[85] Richard Edlin, *Prae-Nuncius Sydereus* (London, 1664), p. 60.

The extreme non-conformity of the Saturday-Sabbatarian stand was what worried many people. Thomas Cleadon, an Essex rector, was certain that Sunday was the Christian Sabbath, "and may be made evident to any one, who can but so far deny himself, as to think that he may err and be mistaken in his opinion, and is resolved to receive the truth". In any case, Cleadon observed that Sunday as the day of Christ's Resurrection had been observed as the Sabbath for so long in all Christian churches throughout the world:

> Now that they all should live and dye in an erroneous & sinful practice, without repentance, so much controverted, and an inconsiderable party of them, much inferior to multitudes of them both in Learning, Parts, Gifts, and Spiritual Grace and Holiness, should yet only be in the right, who hold the *Jewish* Sabbath, the Seventh day from the Creation, to be still in force, and accordingly do observe and keep it, contrary to the declared judgment and practice of all other Christians, cannot be thought but to proceed either from ignorance, or from pride, or from both, one or both of these having been the root and cause of all the Schisms, and Errors, and Heresies, which do, or even have disquieted and disturbed the Churches of Jesus Christ.

The argument from number, needless to say, little impressed Francis Bampfield.[86]

More scholarly appeals to reason were also published at about the same time that Francis Bampfield was gathering his Sabbatarian congregation. James Durham published a very large volume with an introduction by John Owen in which he discussed each of the Ten Commandments in turn. Durham argued that "a Seventh day (whatever it be which is chosen of God) and not the Seventh day in order, is to be sanctified by vertue of the fourth commandment." Indeed, the "Sabbath may be changed from the last or Seventh day to the First day of the week without any derogation to this command". But Durham condemned the Sunday practice of going

> to the fields and visiting of Neighbours to put off a piece of time, that so much time may be saved on other dayes of the Week, wherein many men think they have more to do . . . Mens sitting upon choice in the Church at such a distance that they can scarcely hear, and that they may the more securely confer together on common purposes . . . many also sleep, vary, and wander in their thoughts, and are as stones and statutes [*sic*] in the Church . . . Little ones and boyes going and running up and down playing and making a noise, and servants gadding . . . Much idle loitering over the Sabbath, doing nothing, and much sleeping it over.

---

[86] Thomas Cleadon, *A Serious and Brief Discourse Touching the Sabbath-Day* (London, 1674), pp. 6, 9. The author's name is corrected to "Cleandon" by a previous owner of the copy in the Bodl. Lib. (Pamph. C. 122 [19]), who also thought it "Worth reading".

Durham's picture of the Sabbath in the Restoration church is hardly encouraging: as he himself says, "Idleness is a sin any day, much more on this day."[87]

Gabriel Towerson, formerly a fellow of All Souls and later a Hertfordshire rector, also wrote a moderating analysis of the Ten Commandments which he published the year after Durham's book appeared. Towerson dedicated his study to the archbishop of Canterbury and as expected championed an orthodox Anglican approach. His argument was that "there is no Obligation upon us *Christians*, either from the Law of Nature, or this particular Precept, to observe either a precise Seventh day, or that Seventh day which the *Jews* observ'd." Certainly, that is, the Christians should have a Lord's Day and a day of rest, but in his view there was no justification for observing it in the Jewish fashion, either in respect of the onset of the day itself – "when it began to dawn towards day" – or in regard to prohibiting lawful activities. The entire question of the difference between divine commandment and custom was irrelevant, for both Sunday and Saturday "have the same Worship of God for their End, and the like signal Acts of God for the Occasions of their Institution". There was a social aspect to the Sabbath as well, Towerson reminded his readers, for "take away all Recreation, and you make the Sabbath to afford little Refreshment to Servants, and other such Labouring People, for whose Benefit we find it to have been in a great measure design'd".[88]

Thomas Grantham, one of the ministers ejected by Cromwell's Triers, devoted an entire chapter to the Sabbath question in a long work on proper Christian practice published after his death. Most of his remarks are conventional, but among his numerous cases of conscience he dealt with the question of whether a Jew converted to the Christian faith is still bound to keep the Mosaic law, including circumcision. He claimed that it was commonly argued that the obligation of forsaking the Mosaic law was a great obstacle to the conversion of the Jews. But the more universal issue here in his view was "whether the Gospel do indeed annul the Law of Ceremonies". Grantham's answer was unequivocal: "Where-ever the Gospel is truly received, the Law, as aforesaid, must needs vanish away." The coming of Christ abrogated the Seventh-Day Sabbath, and this Judaising practice must cease "unless a Woman may lawfully have two Husbands at the same time".[89]

A more interesting and more general condemnation of the Saturday-

---

[87] James Durham, *A Practical Exposition of the X. Commandements* (London, 1675), pp. 243, 255-6, 304-5.

[88] Gabriel Towerson, *An Explication of the Decalogue* (London, 1676), pp. 181-2, 188-9, 196.

[89] Thomas Grantham, *Christianismus Primitivus* (London, 1678), 2nd ser., pp. 156-74; 3rd ser., pp. 73-4. On Grantham, see Matthews, *Walker*, p. 250.

Sabbath and its attendant vices was published a few years before Bampfield's death by George Hickes, about to be made royal chaplain, who years later would be a non-juror. Hickes was incensed that "many unsound Judaizing Christians have still dreamed, that the *Mosaick* Code was yet in force, and have thereupon lived in strict religious observance of some or all the Ceremonial Precepts, and vented such opinions, as have perplexed the Consciences of ignorant and unlearned men, and filled the Church of God with unprofitable scruples and doubts." Hickes's list of "pernicious Impostors and Enthusiasts" included not only Mohammed himself, but also "Labbade of late in *Holland*;[90] *Naylor*; *Venner*; *Muggleton*, and some other Enthusiasts of our own Country, not so extravagant, that would take it ill to be mentioned here". But he went on to condemn "*Goodman*, and *Kilby*, and *Knox*'s works . . . and every one knows to what strange, inward extraordinary callings, motions, and directions *Coppinger*[91] and *Hacket*,[92] and their Associates formerly pretended; and I need not tell whom they followed,[93] or what profession they were of." Indeed, he wrote, the "late instance of *Venner* and his company, and the later Insurrections in *Scotland* are also pat examples to this Theam".[94]

But perhaps of all the offences in Hickes's pantheon of sin, pride of place might go to the claim that the laws given by God to the Jews were still valid and incumbent upon Christians. Hickes noted that

> the defence of it was not long since offered to the Press by one Mr. *Bampfield*; and the late *Scottish* Rebels in their new Covenant or Scheme of Reformation, declared that they would be governed by the Civil or Judicial Laws, which God gave to his peculiar people, excepting the Laws of *Slavery*, *Polygamy* and *Divorce*. And the Colony of the *Massachusets* in *New England*, though they have not expresly declared the *Jewish* Laws to be indispensably binding, yet it appears from their Capital Laws, the greater part of which are both for matter and stile *Mosaick*, that they had an unreasonable superstitious veneration for them

These men were "our Modern *Kaeraites*, who make the Scriptures the sole and adequate rule of human actions". Men like Bampfield and his followers were fanatics who "as *Buxtorf* sets for the Modern *Jews*, have an

---

[90] The reference is to Jean de Labadie (1610-74), theologian and founder of the Labadists, pietistic communities that held goods in common: see now T.J. Saxby, "The Life and Ministry of Jean de Labadie" (Oxford Univ. D.Phil. 1985).

[91] Edmund Coppinger championed with Henry Arthington William Hacket who claimed to be the Messiah in a demonstration at Cheapside in 1592. Hacket was soon hanged, Coppinger starved himself to death eight days later, and Arthington repented and was pardoned: *Dict. Nat. Biog.*, *s.v.* "Coppinger, Edmund (d. 1592)".

[92] A sign here points to the note: "Bancrofts dangerous positions, 1 4."

[93] A sign here points to the note: "Cartwright and Travers".

[94] G[eorge] Hickes, *Peculium Dei, A Discourse about the Jews* (London, 1681), pp. 2, 3, 20, 22.

haughty and magnificent opinion of their own Religion, and think that God and Messias belong to few or none but themselves".[95]

Also among those who addressed themselves to the question of the Saturday-Sabbath during the period of Bampfield's imprisonment and death was the famous John Bunyan, who published a little-known work on the subject in 1685. Bunyan advanced numerous arguments to show that with the coming of Christ the Seventh-Day Sabbath was void. Its continued place of reverence among some Christians reminded him of what occurs when a lord or great man dies: "He has now no relation to a wife, to children, virtually; yet his name still abides, and that in that family, to which otherwise he is dead." Despite their obvious invalidity, Bunyan wrote,

> I have observed, that though the Jewish rites have lost their sanction, yet some that are weak in judgment, do bring themselves into bondage by them. Yea, so high have some been carried as to a pretended conscience to these that they have at last proceeded to circumcision, to many wives, and the observation of many bad things besides. Yea, I have talked with some pretending to Christianity, who have said, and affirmed, as well as they could, that the Jewish sacrifices must up again.

Bunyan reminded such Saturday-Sabbatarian observers that he could not put out of his mind the point that "if the seventh day sabbath was by divine authority, and to be kept holy by the churches of the Gentiles, it should not have so remained among the Jews, Christ's deadliest enemies, and have been kept so much hid from the belivers, his best friends." For indeed, since Christ's time the Seventh-Day Sabbath was observed only by "the Jews, and a few Jewish Gentiles". When looking at the entire sad history of Saturday-Sabbath observance in his time, Bunyan wrote, "I will rather conclude, that those Gentile professors that adhere thereto are Jewified, legalized, and so far gone back from the authority of God, who from such bondage has set his churches free." Bunyan also hinted darkly that he had much more to say on the subject, but reserved his final judgement on the Saturday-Sabbatarians for another time, when he would also reveal "some other wild notions of those that so stiffly cleave to this."[96]

The Saturday-Sabbath and Bampfield's practice of it therefore remained a topic of theological discussion, and it was not surprising that Bampfield was called upon to defend himself. It was William Benn who made a formal appeal to Bampfield for a written explanation of his behaviour, and in reply received a short document setting out the scriptural

---

[95] *Ibid.*, pp. 15, 22-3, 25.

[96] John Bunyan, *Questions About The Nature and Perpetuity of the Seventh-Day Sabbath* (London, 1685), repr. in *Works*, ed. G. Offor (London, 1862), ii. 380, 384-5. After its initial publication, this work of Bunyan's did not reappear until 1806, when it was included in a collection of the author's writings.

proofs of Saturday-Sabbatarianism. Benn published Bampfield's "Judgment" as well as his own somewhat longer rebuttal of it, and generally saw the phenomenon as another sign of Restoration decadence. "In times when People are generally debauched in their Intellectuals as well as in their Morals," he wrote,

> and take as great a liberty of opining as they do of practising, it is no wonder if in this Age, when as all Sects seem to have a general resurrection, that the *Jewish* Sect have also their Abettors; but if People would but seriously consider, that the change of the Day hath the same Foundation that the Scriptures themselves have . . . the Controversie would quickly be at an end: It would then be an easie thing to believe, that when the whole *Jewish* Frame of Worship was laid aside, it was fit that the very Time it self should also put on Mourning

Benn's own reply repeats the standard claim "that the Commandment requires only the observation of one day in seven, and doth not institute any particular day, either the last or the first." In any case, Benn's little book must have had the effect of spreading Bampfield's well-documented views even further afield.[97]

IV

His church established at Pinners' Hall, Francis Bampfield devoted much of the rest of his life to intellectual rather than institutional pursuits, and sought to clarify some of the central philosophical and theological problems connected with Saturday-Sabbatarianism, especially the rightful relations between Christians, Jews, and Hebraic culture. In this he would be a forerunner of more widely known religious schools which incorporated such views in the eighteenth and nineteenth centuries. His ideas on these subjects were first aired in a large folio volume published in two parts in 1677. The first section, entitled *All in One*, aimed at demonstrating that "All Useful Sciences and profitable Arts" might be found in the Bible, that "one Book of *Jehovah Aelohim*". Bampfield is drawn in this book to suggest that the Bible itself might be a guide in reconstructing not only the Christian educational framework, but our entire attitude to a wide variety of questions. For example, Bampfield suggests that maps might be "drawn of the Earth, of Countries, of Places, of Distances, and such like, as do exactly agree with the Scriptures", including "the Hebrew signification of those proper Names, both of Persons and of Places" so that we would recreate a sort of "Scripture-Geography". Since the Bible contains only in-

---

[97] [William] Benn, *The Judgment of Mr. Francis Bampfield* (London, 1672), sig. A2ʳ; pp. 3-7 (Bampfield's judgement), 28, 41.

fallible truth, Bampfield appears to be reasoning, then the Scripture might likewise serve as a useful guide to subjects, like geography, which hitherto had been excluded from religious examination. So since we know that Shem travelled eastwards after the Flood, it might be asked whether he "did not possess and people *America*, where divers Names of places are still retained much according to the Scripture-Hebrew":

> and, if so, whether then, the late Globes and Maps be drawn according to the Original Truth, which do place *America* in such a quarter and coast of the Earth, that yet received her first inhabitants from the East-borders of *Asia* (as they now call it) and which do leave such a vast Ocean of so many Leagues between *Sinear* and *Anjan*, between the North-East parts of *Asia*, and the North-West side of *America*, as they commonly describe them? and, whether these be not continent, at most but dis-joyned by some great River or narrow Channel of the Ocean?

Similarly, Bampfield thought that the Scripture could serve as an infallible model for grammatical studies as well. In this regard, Bampfield asked if it might not be necessary and profitable "to compose a Grammar of the Original Language or Languages, wholly according to Scripture, and the Rules found there, and no longer to make Scripture speak according to Philosophick Grammars, and their Rules invented by men". The reason for this attempt was clear: "seeing that these Arts and Sciences are to be fetched out of the Original Language, and not from Humane Authorities, that so, in these later days, we may have a proper remedy against the confusion of Tongues". Bampfield thought this grammar might help us to understand the "Orthographick", etymological and syntactical elements of this original language, which Bampfield identified as Hebrew, and which he knew enough to describe as a language based on an "Analogy of all those words, from the Root to the Branches throughout", including "Points" and "Accents". Furthermore, Bampfield wondered "whether all other Languages are not Hebrew Dialects, having cognation with this Original Tongue". In planning his scriptural grammar, Bampfield pledged to lay aside all "wrong-fancied-Anomalies" that have obscured our understanding of the text and have caused us to see "humanely-pretended Paragoges, Redundancies, Expletives, Pleonasms, Insignificancies, Deficiencies" where none exist.[98]

The study of Hebrew was of paramount importance for Bampfield, and he was angered by the learned authors who "would have Original Hebrew, which is the Mother Tongue, to go to School, and to learn to speak of Daughter-Languages". Certainly, he thought, a "cognation of other Languages to, and a collating of them with the Original Hebrew, hath its great

---

[98] Bampfield, *All in One*, title p., pp. 42-4.

use, and may be put to a more growing and profitable improvement; only special heed must be taken, that they be all drawn to side with the Hebrew, but not to put the Hebrew violently by force to be of their party against its own natural meaning.'' Bampfield thought a search should be made for ''the true Authograph, or the Divine own first Writings of the Original Scriptures'', a work which would suit ''the greatest, holiest Prince''. Then a new translation of the Bible might be achieved, ''an exact literal version of the holy Scripture, word for word, as they are in their order''. Hebrew should be taught to the people, ''especially such of them as have more opportunities and advantages for this'', including ''the young capable Children''. A new Hebrew lexicon could spread this knowledge ''to our common people'' if parts were printed in ''all sorts of little Bibles''. Once accomplished, godly men would be in a position to turn seriously to the question of ''How may the Original Scripture-Language be made the Universal Character, all the inhabited Earth over?''[99]

Francis Bampfield's identification of Hebrew as the language spoken by Adam before the Fall was by no means an original observation: this question had been under discussion for decades and was still a subject of controversy during the years that Bampfield wrote about the Sabbath question.[100] What makes Bampfield's views interesting is that he saw Hebrew study as an almost mystical activity which would yield manifold practical religious benefits. Whereas his contemporaries either emphasized the importance of Hebrew in translation of the Scriptures, or attempted to learn the rudiments of kabbalistic analysis, Bampfield continually stressed the educative religious aspects of the language, even to an absurd degree. Indeed, he even ruminated over the notion that ''a translating of Hebrew Verbs of the self reflexive conjugation, would not promote these self reflecting meditations and acts?''[101]

If larger and more philosophical questions dominated the first part of Bampfield's major work, in the second section he returned to more familiar ground and sought once again to justify Saturday as the true Sabbath. Most of the material would have been familiar to Bampfield's readers: he argued that God himself, by resting on the seventh day, he ''*Ælohim* the Creator himself did Sabbatize''. As for Jesus Christ, ''He was the First-seventh-day-Sabbath-Observer'': the marginal reference was to Genesis ii. 1-3. Bampfield observed that the ''First day Christ all his life through never observed, as the weekly Sabbath. He has left us an example (a Pat-

---

[99] *Ibid.*, pp. 128, 162.

[100] *Ibid.*, p. 167.

[101] See D.S. Katz, *Philo-Semitism and the Readmission of the Jews to England, 1603-1655* (Oxford, 1982), *cap.* 2; *idem*, ''The Language of Adam in Seventeenth-Century England'', in *History and Imagination*, ed. H. Lloyd-Jones, *et al.* (London, 1981), pp. 132-45.

tern, a Copy, such as Writing Masters do leave to their Scholars) that, we should follow his steps.'' Not content with his usual arguments, Bampfield taunted his Puritan opponents with a quotation from the martyred Charles I:

> There is this passage in a Querie of King *Charles* the First concerning *Easter*, propounded to the Parliaments Commissioners at *Holmby, April* 23. 1647. I conceive, saith he, the celebration of this Feast (of *Easter*) was instituted by the same authority, which changed the Jewish Sabbath into the Lords day, or *Sunday*: For, it will not be found in Scripture, where *Saturday* is discharged to be kept, or turned into the *Sunday*: Wherefore it must be the Churches authority that changed the one and instituted the other: Therefore my opinion is, that, those who will not keep this Feast, may as well return to the observation of *Saturday*, and refuse the weekly *Sunday*. When any body can shew me, that herein I am in an error, I shall not be ashamed to confess, and amend it, till when you know my mind, *C.R.*[102]

Bampfield's last major work, published four years later in 1681, is similarly devoted to philosophical matters, this time on an even grander scale. His plea was for the establishment of what he variously called a ''House of Wisdom'', a ''House of the Sons of the Prophets'', or ''An House of Exquisite Enquiry, And of Deep Research'', based on the study of the Hebrew language. Bampfield's arguments were very similar to the ones that he had presented four years previously, but they were now framed in an even more extravagant manner. Bampfield was merciless towards the so-called scholars ''not thorowly understanding one word of the Bible in the original language'' and was mortified that ''scarcely one Christian among the common people of many hundreds doth understand one word of Hebrew all his life long.'' This was the reason why Christians stood little chance in their debates with Jews, who began teaching their children Hebrew from the age of three, and continued studying the Old Testament during their entire lifetime. Hebrew could be a universal language, with great benefit to diplomats, merchants, military men, statesmen and many others: ''What a shame and rebuke is it unto Christians, that the Emperor of *China*, who has so many several Languages of Peoples under his large Dominion, has yet one kind of Character ... Whil'st the many Princes, who outwardly profess the Christian Religion, do not yet agree to own and commend the Hebrew-Letters as the only Universal Character''. Hebrew is itself a language perfectly agreeing with the thing expressed, ''as *Tzippor* is a Sparrow, and so it doth sound in several Languages, which Name they have from the sound they make thus *Tzip Tzip*'':

---

[102] Francis Bampfield, *The Seventh-Day Sabbath the Desireable-Day* (n.p., 1677), pp. 3, 8, 24n.

> And not only the similitude of sound, but also one and the very self-same reason of Origination and Derivation; the primitive proper meaning of that nomenclation, or that name, by which such a Person or thing is called, having its first foundation in the Hebrew word, and in created Being. The King, and God of the Hebrews will have a time to Recrown this Hebrew Language: For there are many both Mysteries in Grace, and Secrets in Nature, which are best opened by Hebrew significancies

Here again, Bampfield's arguments are hardly original, but his mention of a universal language, China, a philosophical language, and a mystical linguistic key to divine secrets, virtually recreates the entire history of thought on the subject.[103]

Bampfield's House of Wisdom was to be based on the careful study of this divine tongue, but in true Baconian fashion other subjects were not to be neglected. Promising students might also be trained in medicine, astronomy, geography, husbandry, seamanship, warfare, and handicrafts. The more prominent fields of study, of course, would be "the works of Creation", the "Scripture-judicial-laws for rewards to the obedient and for punishments upon the disobedient", and "Practical, mysterious, or experimental Christianity". The promotion of such wisdom would be accomplished by a careful diet,

> sufficient but sparing, fitted to a Studious life, of Flesh at the most not above once in a day, and that of pure clean young beasts, cattle, fowls or Fishes, all of good nourishment and easy digestion: much in the use of Herbs for broth, Sallads, & otherwaies, and of the tops of green buddings in the Fall and Spring especially, of both which Herbs and Tops a discreet choice should be made of what is apt and proper for Food, and also for Medicin if the Case call for it ... some sorts of Roots also ... Good Fruits also in their Season, Milk and Honey

Bampfield complained that there was "scarce one man of a thousand, who knows aright how to make one meal in order to health and other good ends." His own source of dietary information, of course, was the Bible itself: "what they translate Locusts," Bampfield corrected, with a host of scriptural citations, "is properly such tops of green buddings ... The tops of Trees and of Herbs, fit food for the Sons of the Prophets." From what we know about the diet of early modern Englishmen, Bampfield's suggestions for a reformation of diet would have provided a very sound corrective.[104]

Bampfield's programme for a House of Wisdom based on the study of

---

[103] [Francis Bampfield], *The House of VVisdom* (London, 1681), pp. 5, 7-8. Cf. Katz, n. 101 above.

[104] [Bampfield], *House*, p. 9.

the Hebrew language and the literal meaning of the Holy Scriptures is well within the Renaissance tradition of "realistic utopias": even the name which Bampfield gave to his short work reminds us of this. "This is an ingenious Age in almost every Art and Science else," he admonished his readers, "which the Virtuosi of the times are set much upon highly to advance, and greatly to promote in their several sorts of Learning, though it doth appear to me, through a God-taughtness, they lay aside, at least the Best, if not the only way of thorow obtaining of a Satisfying Knowledg, which is the Holy Spirits teaching".[105]

V

Bampfield's musings on these important issues, and the effective leadership of his congregation, came to an end with his arrest at Pinners' Hall on 17 February 1682-3.[106] Bampfield was one of the many non-conformists who suffered from the dramatic reversal of royal policy after the Exclusion Crisis of 1679-81. When the Dissenters supported the Exclusion Bill in May 1679 they lost the support of Charles II, who since his Restoration had been pleased to link his own Roman Catholic cause with that of the non-conformists. The persecution of Dissenters began in earnest by the end of 1681, which no doubt drove some of them to participate in genuine acts of insurrection, such as the Rye House Plot in 1683 to murder the king and his Catholic brother James on their way back from the Newmarket races. A number of Dissenters were involved in Monmouth's Rebellion of June 1685 against James II: two grandsons of William Kiffin the Baptist pioneer were executed for their part in the disturbances.[107]

Francis Bampfield's legal troubles began in February 1682-3 and he died in Newgate prison exactly one year later. During this his last imprisonment he published a number of short accounts of the legal action taken against him, which provide a fascinating picture of the persecution of Dissenters during these difficult years between the Exclusion Crisis and the dispensations of James II which took effect from 1686. What must have been particularly galling to Bampfield was that he was initially accused of attempting to bring in Popery, for it was precisely the uproar over the Popish Plot that gave the Exclusionist Whigs a majority in the crucial elections of January 1679. "It's under a pretence of such private Conventicles," stated the magistrate, "that all the Popish-Plots are hatch't and carried on." But the key question of Sabbath observance was soon put to

---

[105] *Ibid.*, p. 25. Cf. M. Eliav-Feldon, *Realistic Utopias* (Oxford, 1983).
[106] Bampfield, *Prisoner*, p. 2.
[107] Watts, *Dissenters*, pp. 252-7.

Bampfield, and he could not deny that he observed Saturday instead of the Sunday and thereby broke the laws of King Charles at the very least, if not of King Jesus. Yet even then, Bampfield recounted, "usually the burden of the Song was, *Have you been at* St. *Omars*, as if we all had been Jesuitically educated, and principles, whereby to insinuate, as if we were bringers in of Popery". Bampfield was released and told to go home.[108]

Bampfield affirms that he steadfastly continued his preaching at Pinners' Hall and at his own house while the authorities prepared the legal means to put an end to his ministry. On 24 February 1682-3 he was arrested yet again and brought to the magistrate and "made a *Gazing-stock*, variously reported, some against me, others for me, one calling me a Christian Jevv". When brought before the magistrates at the Old Bailey, Bampfield was in due course asked to take the Oath of Allegiance, and refused on principle to swear a non-religious oath. But by this time the courts were used to dealing with conscientious recalcitrants, and the recorder knew to ask Bampfield whether he had been at university and had taken a degree. His affirmative answer marked Bampfield as one who at least at some time in the past had no scruples about oaths-taking: "Oh those University-Oaths, so many, and so often multiplyed by inconsiderate Students, how much guilt has been contracted thereby!" he lamented. It seems that his captors wished to be done with the whole tiresome business, and Bampfield recounts that he overheard one of the officials say, "his hand is already upon his own bible, read on". Had the official succeeded in reading out the text of the oath while Bampfield non-committally held his own Bible, it would have sufficed, "but the Lord gave me to see the snare was laid for me". Bampfield was taken away to Newgate Prison to reconsider his position.[109]

Bampfield was well aware that imprisonment was the penalty only for the first refusal to take the Oath of Allegiance. The second refusal brought with it the charge of *praemunire*, imprisonment for life or at the king's pleasure and forfeiture of property.[110] Newgate Prison in the best of circumstances was an extremely nasty place, described by one contemporary Quaker inmate as "being usually stocked from the veriest Rogues and meanest sort of Felons and Pick-Pockets . . . in measure a Type of HELL upon EARTH."[111] Bampfield seems to have been in the confidence of some of those accused in the Rye House Plot and also incarcerated in Newgate.[112] But Bampfield

---

[108] Bampfield, *Prisoner*, pp. 2-3.

[109] *Ibid.*, pp. 3-4; Wood, *Athenae*, iv. 128.

[110] Watts, *Dissenters*, p. 224.

[111] *The History of the Life of Thomas Ellwood*, ed. S. Graveson (London, 1906), pp. 154, 157.

[112] Francis Bampfield, *A Just Appeal* (London, 1683), pp. 1-2, 7-8: dated from Newgate, 17 Oct. 1683.

steadfastly refused to take the Oath, and when called again to the Old Bailey in October 1683, cheekily declined to swear obedience to all the king's laws on the grounds that even lawyers who studied for many years did not know all of the king's laws, so how could he, a humble minister, swear to something he did not know. "Not that in all, or any of this," he reminded his persecutors,

> I have any the least design of raising any Tumults, or making any Insurrections, or carrying on any Malign Plottings at all, . . . And I can with the more Freedom write thus, because I have not been engaged in any of the Wars, I never took the Solemn League and Covenant, but my self and another drew up our Expectations and Reasons against it, which were like to have been Printed; Neither did I take the engagement, but Preached against it, for which I Suffered a short Imprisonment.[113]

Francis Bampfield was summoned to appear again in court on 17 January 1683-4 when the jury was instructed to find him guilty of *praemunire*. Eleven days later, he was given one last chance to take the Oath of Allegiance, and failing do to so was sentenced to forfeit all goods and chattels during life and to remain in jail during life or at the king's pleasure.[114] "I have for these last full Twenty Years and more, been a Nonconformist", declared Bampfield triumphantly, "and for this I have suffered Ten Years (of those Twenty) Imprisonments for that Nonconformity; neither, that I remember, have I had one hours trouble in all those Ten Years, for my suffering in that Cause."[115]

The authorities hoped that Bampfield's sentence would provide a deterrent to others. Henry Crispe, the Common Serjeant of London, wrote to Sir Leoline Jenkins the secretary of state that he hoped Bampfield's punishment "will make others who cannot or will not take the oath of allegiance very careful how they come into the hands of justice".[116] Bampfield himself, meanwhile, was resigned to what looked like a life sentence. He wrote another short work summarizing the views about Hebrew, the Old Testament, and the Ten Commandments that he had expressed before. "It would be a great, high Honor put upon Kings, Princes, Nobles, learned Schollars, and rich Ones, if they did in their several places and capacities, advantages and opportunities, afford their help to promote the Hebrew

---

[113] *Ibid.*

[114] *Idem, A Continuation Of a Former Just Appeal* (London, 1684), pp. 1-2. Matthews, *Calamy*, p. 26, giving the date of sentencing as 16 Jan. from Guildhall Sessions Book: Wood, *Athenae*, iv. 128 prefers 18 Jan. A letter dated 21 Apr. 1683 from Henry Crispe, Common Serjeant of London, to Sir Leoline Jenkins refers to Bampfield as having been convicted of *praemunire* "last sessions": *Cal. S.P. Dom., 1683*, pp. 195-6.

[115] Bampfield, *Continuation*, p. 8.

[116] *Cal. S.P. Dom., 1683*, pp. 195-6.

language". Indeed, Bampfield fervently hoped that they would "commend the Hebrew Character to be the universal Character all the inhabited Earth over: all Embassies unto Forreign Kings and Princes to be in that Hebrew language". Finally, in his last work, Bampfield concluded with a plea

> That the law of the ten words with its annexed judicials, such as are purely judicial, ought to be the one and the only measure of Government in all Nations, and of Distributive Justice as to a rendring of Rewards to the Obedient, and as to the inflicting of Penalties on the Disobedient.[117]

Nearly twenty years before, Bampfield had written to the king with this plan in mind, and with as little effect.[118]

One of Bampfield's eulogists would write that "His Life in Prison as elsewhere did preach, All might learn of him, all of him did teach."[119] We cannot know if Bampfield had any particular plans to make use of his unlimited term of imprisonment. Hanserd Knollys, then aged 84, was also imprisoned in Newgate at this time for six to eight months, but left no account of any discussions with Bampfield.[120] Confinement proved too severe for his health, and Bampfield died in Newgate on the Saturday-Sabbath 16 February 1683-4 and was buried in the Baptists' burial ground in Glass House Yard, Aldersgate Street three days later.[121] One observer thought that Bampfield "had as many followers to his grave as ever he had to his conventicle, the whole rabble of Dissenters being mustered together to show yet their readiness to appear upon the least occasion."[122]

The death of Francis Bampfield left the Saturday-Sabbatarian congregation at Pinners' Hall leaderless and without the means to withstand such virulent and effective attacks on their faith for very long. The only divine who could possibly take his place, Edward Stennett, was still outside the fold, but his son Jehudah, the author of a new Hebrew grammar, was already a member, as was Jehudah's brother Benjamin. On 14 October 1686 the church reorganized during a special day of prayer. Edward

---

[117] Francis Bampfield, *The Holy Scripture* (London, 1684), sig. A2ᵛ: dated from Newgate, 1684.

[118] B. to Charles II, June ? 1664: *Cal. S.P. Dom., 1663-4*, p. 612.

[119] W.T., *An Elegy On . . . Mʳ Francis Bampfield* (London, 1684), broadsheet. The anonymous author was one "who waited upon him in his Sickness": he gives the date of Bampfield's death. Another elegy was published by a fellow prisoner in Newgate, Hercules Collins, *Counsel For the Living* (London, 1684) for Bampfield and Zachery Ralphson, also in the gaol. But neither is mentioned in the text, and at its conclusion Collins notes that it was originally written for Ralphson, but might now equally apply to Bampfield.

[120] *Vict. Cnty. Hist., London*, i (1909), p. 381.

[121] W.T., *Elegy*; Wood, *Athenae*, iv. 128.

[122] Newsletter to the duke of Ormond, 23 Feb. 1683-4, from Whitehall: *Hist. MSS. Comm., Ormonde*, n.s. vii (1912), p. 198.

Stennett, pastor at Wallingford, was officially invited to join them, and on 25 October he administered the Lord's Supper to them as his other son Joseph also joined his brothers in church fellowship. It may have been at this time that Edward Stennett agreed to serve as the spiritual leader of the group, although he never consented to be their pastor, and may not have even been asked. On 6 November 1686, Samuel Thompson and Joseph Stennett were asked to put down in writing a summary of the recent changes that the church had undergone, and on 28 November their record was signed.[123]

One interesting minute of these early days of the reorganized church was a plan to put into action a proviso of Francis Bampfield's will which confirmed that he "had given all his Books, both Written & Printed to them, to be employed & Used (as far as might be) to promote a Design of Training up Young Men in Scripture-Learning, spoken of in a book of his Intituled, the House of Wisdom, &c." With the stipulation that his widow might be adequately compensated, Bampfield ordered that his congregation establish the Hebraic college that he outlined with such fervour in his last important work. His church, now following Edward Stennett, appointed a committee consisting of Jehudah Stennett, William Mercer, Richard Denton, and Samuel Thompson "to go to Mrs Bampfield, & to Enquire further of her about the Matter, & to take Care that all Due means be used to have the aforesaid Will fullfilled." On 12 December 1686, the church was informed that Jehudah Stennett had spoken with Bampfield's widow, who had proved amenable to the execution of her late husband's plan. Stennett also wrote a letter to Francis Bampfield's brother Thomas, who had been M.P. for Exeter in the parliaments of 1654, 1656, and 1658, and speaker of the House of Commons from May 1658 until the parliament's dissolution in April 1659. Thomas Bampfield was also active in the Convention Parliament of 1660, but did not sit afterwards. Jehudah Stennett reminded Thomas Bampfield in his letter of 2 December 1686 that his brother in his will named him among the executors of his programme for a House of Wisdom:

> The Reasons why this work has not been hitherto gone about I shall not now Trouble you with; Only I presume to acquaint you that the Circumstances of Mr Bampfield's Freinds are at this Time in better Order than ever since his Death, & now they do intend (God Willing) not to Leave any thing in their Power, Unattempted, to accomplish the Will of their Late Honored Friend.

All Jehudah Stennett asked was that Thomas Bampfield would lend his

---

[123] Bampfield church book, pp. 9-10.

support to his brother's plan for a House of Wisdom, even if he himself did not take an active part in its execution.[124]

Thomas Bampfield's reply to this first letter is now lost; presumably he was living at his home at Dunkerton near Bath and was reluctant to stir for the establishment of such an institution. The church noted in their record book that it would be necessary "to press him to give his Assistance to Accomplish the Will of his Deceased Brother, & to acquaint him, that they waited only for his Concurrence therein, and that they did think themselves Oblig'd to Endeavour it with Diligence". Jehudah Stennett, this time fortified with the signatures of Thomas Dominel, William Mason, and William Mercer, wrote to Thomas Bampfield once again on 9 January 1686-7. It appears from the text that Thomas Bampfield had enquired why no progress had been made in executing his brother's will, in the three years that had passed since his death in Newgate. The four replied that "the Principal Reason why no more Care has hitherto been taken in that affair, has been because of some Divisions, which are now happily in a Great Measure Composed, & we in a Likelyer way to answer Mr Bampfield's Will, then Ever since his Death". All they required now was his brother's approval, and the plan for a House of Wisdom could be put into effect.[125]

Apparently Bampfield's House of Wisdom lay dormant for a further number of years, despite Jehudah Stennett's confident prediction that the church was now in a position to put the plan into effect. Now, at the dawn of genuine religious toleration for Protestant Dissenters, they found themselves excluded more than ever. The Bampfield-Stennett church was not invited to participate in the Assembly of Particular Baptists which was held in September 1689, after the Glorious Revolution. But at the church meeting on 29 September, the Seventh-Day Sabbatarians praised the efforts which had been made so far at the Assembly to improve the level of the clergy and to tend to their education. They noted that the Assembly had appointed a group of "Managers" to investigate the problem, and that "in the Year Last past several of the Elders of divers Baptized Churches in London had Met to consult about the same things in substance", who soon after "did then send a Letter Directed to this Church, desiring them to Assist in so Good a Work, and for that End to Depute some Person or Persons to meet with them in Order to Concert Measures for the Carrying it on". Such a deputation had been appointed, and indeed met with the Baptist elders several times, who presumably were presented with a version of Francis Bampfield's plan for a House of Wisdom. "But the

---

[124] *Ibid.*, pp. 10-12.
[125] *Ibid.*, pp. 12-13.

Great Distractions of the Nation occasion'd by the Late Great Revolution,'' they wrote, "through the Descent of the then Prince of Orange into England &c. putting a stop to the afores^d proceedings; This Church expected upon the Revival of the same Work again, to have been invited to Joyn their assistance again''. Nevertheless, the Bampfield-Stennett congregation had been excluded from these discussions held within the bosom of the Particular Baptist movement. So at the church meeting on 29 September it was resolved to send Thomas Dominel, John Jones and Joseph Stennett "to go to the Place of Meeting of the afores^d Managers appointed by the Late General Assembly'', in spite of the fact that no invitation had been issued to the congregation to participate in the discussions. On 13 October 1689 the deputation sadly reported that they had been excluded from the meeting despite their good intentions, and had been told that no invitations would be issued to any congregation that observed the Sabbath on the seventh day.[127]

Edward Stennett died at some point during the year 1690. On 4 March 1690-1 his son Joseph was ordained Teaching-Elder by John Belcher, Senior, the old radical pastor of the Saturday-Sabbath congregation that met at Bell Lane. Belcher was described in the Bampfield church book ''as a Publique Messenger to all the Sabbath-Churches''. Perhaps to symbolize some sort of reconciliation with the mainstream of the Baptist movement, at the inauguration of Joseph Stennett the words of exhortation were spoken by Hanserd Knollys, and the sermon preached by Isaac Lamb.[128]

On 25 June 1692 the question of Francis Bampfield's library and his House of Wisdom was brought up once again:

> The Church ... being further Inform'd yt M^{ris} D. Bampfield was Likely to be Necessitated speedily to sell ye s^d books, if not otherwise provided for. And that Mr Tho: Bampfield was willing, y^t these books should rather become ye propriety of this Church, & of that walking wth Mr John Belcher Senr [at Bell Lane] & y^t wth Mr Henry Soursby [at Mill Yard], provided these 3 Sabbath-keeping Churches would allow M^{ris} Bampfield a Competent Annuity during her Life, that the s^d books might be put to ye publique use of promoting Scripture Learning amongst ye s^d Churches. And y^t ye s^d M^{ris} Bampfield approved of this method very well. This Church approv'd also of ye s^d Expedient, & Appointed Jo: Stennett Ben. Stennett & Wm Mason to Confer wth principal men of ye 2 above-nam'd Churches in ye Name of this Church, about ye s^d Matter, & to make ye above-s^d offer to them.

---

126 *Ibid.*, p. 13.
127 *Ibid.*, pp. 13-14.
128 *Ibid.*, pp. 14-15.

Suddenly, after years of neglect, Bampfield's project was dusted off and inspected.[129]

Thomas Bampfield's sudden willingness to cooperate in the establishment of his late brother's House of Wisdom can best be understood as a by-product of the controversy he managed to generate on the subject of the Saturday-Sabbath between himself and John Wallis, the famous Savilian Professor of Geometry at Oxford. Thomas Bampfield believed with complete confidence that Saturday was the actual seventh day that God rested after Creation, a calendrical tradition handed down from father to son since the days of Adam and Eve. More remarkable is his assertion that the Saturday-Sabbath was observed in England until the reign of Edward VI when it was changed to Sunday by an act of Parliament.[130] John Wallis took up the issue soon afterwards, claiming that Thomas Bampfield's book had been sent to him anonymously. Wallis argued that we must surely have lost count in the five thousand years since Creation, and he himself was content in observing one day in seven as the arbitrary Sabbath: "If he say the Jews do at this day keep Saturday as their Seventh day. I confess they do. But they do no more know which is the Seventh day; than we, which is the First Day." Generally speaking, Wallis wrote, common sense need not be abandoned completely even when reading the Holy Scriptures:

> 'This somewhat like the Story of a man who *bought a Horse* for *Five Pounds* to be paid the *next day*. And accordingly on the next day he sent *Five Pounds of Candles*. Perhaps (in the Bargain) it was not said *expressly* (in words at length) *Five Pounds of Lawful Money of* England. But, by common intendment, it must be so understood. (And an *honest English Jury*, upon Tryal, would so *Find* it.)

Thomas Bampfield had apparently cited Richard Verstegan *alias* Rowlands, the eccentric Roman Catholic student of Anglo-Saxon from Christ Church, Oxford at the end of the previous century who had claimed that Adam spoke Dutch in the Garden of Eden. Verstegan had also argued that it was the heathens who worshipped the Sun on Sunday: "It was, I suppose," Wallis wrote, "a Fansy of *Verstegan* Then (as it is of our Author now;) But I do not remember that he cites any Author ancienter than himself." Wallis concludes his reply to Thomas Bampfield with the geographical argument so beloved of opponents of the Saturday-Sabbath:

> Let him take a Voyage round the World, as Sir *Francis Drake* did. Going out of the *Atlantick Ocean* West-ward by the Streights of *Magellan* to the East-Indies; and then, from the East, returning by the *Cape of Good Hope* (the usual way) homeward. And take with him as many as please of those who are of his mind.

---

[129] *Ibid.*, p. 15.

[130] Thomas Bampfield, *An Enquiry Whether the Fourth Commandment be Repealed or Altered* (London, 1692).

And let them keep their *Saturday-Sabbath* all the way. When they come home to *England*, they will find their *Saturday* to fall upon our *Sunday*; and they may thenceforth continue to observe their *Saturday-Sabbath* on the same day with us.[131]

Thomas Bampfield replied to Wallis, and Wallis answered Bampfield in turn, devoting seven pages to explaining the geographical point to the Sabbatarian, who appears not to have grasped the evidence of two hundred years of circumnavigation.[132]

Thomas Bampfield's new-found interest in the Saturday-Sabbath in any case came too late to be of much use to his brother's project. On 18 December 1692, the church was informed that both John Belcher, Senior, of Bell Lane and Henry Soursby of Mill Yard had finally refused to be associated with the Hebraic House of Wisdom. Thomas Bampfield himself died in 1693, and Francis Bampfield's widow passed away on 6 February 1694.[133] The books which Bampfield had left for the House were in any case still in 1697 in the custody of Joseph Davis, one of the executors of the will and the patron of Mill Yard. When Joseph Stennett and William Mason tried to take possession of the founder's books, Davis "refus'd to deliver them, pretending he had ye right of disposing them to ye end propos'd in Mr Bampfield's Will.[134] The church vaguely decided to consult the joint executor with Davis, John Belcher Jr., who meanwhile seems to have gone to Rhode Island, never to return.[135] This apparently was the end of Francis Bampfield's House of Wisdom: the question of Bampfield's books was not revived before January 1703, the last church meeting recorded in the surviving minutes.[136]

Joseph Stennett since the mid-1690s had moonlighted as a Sunday lecturer at the General Baptist congregation at Paul's Alley, Barbican, after the death of Thomas Plant in 1693. In 1704, Joseph Stennett took a leading part in reviving the London Baptist Association, the "Assembly", and was asked to write an official history of Baptism, although he was unable to do more than make some preliminary investigations and died in 1713. Joseph Stennett's hymns are still sung, and indeed he is best known as a

---

[131] John Wallis, *A Defense of the Christian Sabbath* (Oxford & London, 1692), pp. 1, 14, 15, 31, 63, 79. This work is dated 12 June 1692; a second edn was published the following year.

[132] Thomas Bampfield, *A Reply to Dr Wallis* (London, 1693); John Wallis, *A Defense of the Christian Sabbath. Part the Second* (Oxford & London, 1694), pp. 2-9. Wallis also affects to have been confused as to Thomas Bampfield's exact identity (p. 1).

[133] Bampfield church book, p. 15.

[134] *Ibid.*, pp. 15-16.

[135] *Ibid.*; Joseph Stennett, *The Groans of a Saint . . . at the Funeral of Mr. John Belcher . . . April I. 1695* (London, 1695).

[136] Bampfield church book, pp. 16-17.

hymn-writer. In 1688 he had married Susanna, younger daughter of George Guill, a Huguenot refugee, and thus became the brother-in-law of Daniel Williams, who founded the trust which today includes Dr. Williams's Library in London, the centre of Dissenting research. His eldest son Joseph was a Baptist minister in London, as were his grandson Samuel, and his great-grandson Joseph, the fifth and last of the Stennett preachers.[137]

The final fate of Bampfield's books is rather more difficult to determine. If indeed they eventually did pass into the hands of Joseph Stennett's congregation, then they probably were sent along with the rest of the Barbican church's books in 1737 to the Baptist Academy which had been established at Towbridge in Wiltshire by John Davison, and was then under the leadership of Thomas Lucas.[138] This centre for the education of young men for the ministry may not have conducted studies strictly along the Hebraic lines proposed by Francis Bampfield, but to some small extent it fulfilled his hope that when "men will use more faithfulness and diligence to be better skilled in the literal significancy of the Original Language, they will see cause to admire the Wisdom of *Aelohim*, who has so self-evidencingly put things into words, especially in these two parts of Scripture".[139]

VI

When Thomas Lincoln obtained a copy of Francis Bampfield's book *All in One* in 1677, the year of its publication, he wrote a memorandum to himself concerning the author:

> That this Mr Bampfield was M[r] of Arts of Wadha Coll. Oxon, afterwards Episcopally ordain'd, and p'sented to a living in Dorcetshire, and in the beginninge of ye unhappy Rebellion Anno. 1640. a zealous man for loyalty and the Kings party; so that he doubted whether he might sutuâ conscientiâ pay any tax imposed by the Parliament: and consulted Dr Ironside (afterwards Bishop of Bristol) about y[t] Question He publickly read ye Commonprayers longer than any Minister in Dorcetshire Afterwards Mr Baxter turn'd him to ye Parliament party, and he was made Minister of Shereburne; at y[e] Kings returne, beeinge non-Conformist he was put in prison, p'ach'd sedition there, then turn'd Jew; p'each'd and writt for y[e] Saturday sabbath, which doctrine he further prosecuted in this wild and erroneous and fanatique worde. &c.[140]

---

137 *Dict. Nat. Biog.*, *s.v.* "Stennett, Joseph".
138 Bampfield church book, p. 17.
139 Bampfield, *All in One*, p. 52.
140 Bodl. Lib., A.20.16.Th.

As a summary description of Francis Bampfield's career, this notation might serve, even in the seventeenth century.

Francis Bampfield's steadfast Royalism is rightly emphasized in Lincoln's blurb, but many found it difficult to explain the phenomenon of radical religious beliefs in the company of conservative political ideals. Anthony Wood, for example, refused to accept the possibility of such a conglomeration, and concluded that as for Bampfield,

> He was always a person so strangely fickle and unsteady in his judgment, that he was first a church-man, then a presbyterian, afterwards an independent, or at least a sider with them, an anabaptist, and at length, almost a compleat Jew, and what not. He was also so enthusiastical and canting that he did almost craze and distract many of his disciples by his amazing and frightful discourses.[141]

It seemed incredible to Wood and many others that belief in the strict observance of the Saturday-Sabbath could be sufficiently strong to overcome both the political reluctance Bampfield may have had to joining forces with John Belcher and the group at Bell Lane, and any religious scruples about the non-Calvinist Sabbatarian church at Mill Yard. These were congregations which grew out of the radical tradition of the Interregnum, and which included among their members many who had been active in the Fifth Monarchy movement. The same Sabbatarian conviction held together under one roof such disparate figures as Henry Jessey the radical, Dr Peter Chamberlen the perennial fence-sitter, and Francis Bampfield the Royalist. If this confessional fact seemed puzzling to Anthony Wood, it must be even more incomprehensible to those trained in the notion of the inevitable split between radicals and conservatives in the era of the English Civil War.

So too should Francis Bampfield's more intellectual pursuits be taken more seriously. Anthony Wood thought that Bampfield's *All in One* was a ''fantastical and unintelligible book . . . full of bombast great swelling and forc'd language'', and that his plan for a Hebraic House of Wisdom was no better.[142] But John Hutchins the historian of Dorset was probably closer to the mark when he mused that Bampfield ''seems to have anticipated the Hutchinsonian conceit of deriving all sciences and arts from Scripture.''[143] John Hutchinson, the author of *Moses's Principia* (1724-30), Newton's undying antagonist, did indeed attempt to use the text of the Bible and the Hebrew language as tools in scientific explanation. As we shall see, the

---

[141] Wood, *Athenae*, iv. 126-7.
[142] *Ibid.*, iv. 127-8.
[143] John Hutchins, *The History and Antiquities of the County of Dorset*, 3rd edn, ed. W. Shipp & F.W. Hodson (Westminster, 1861-70), iv. 265: first pub. 1774.

"Hutchinsonians" became an influential school of thought, derided by Gibbon and many others, but with a considerable following.[144] Francis Bampfield was certainly a forerunner of a fascinating line of investigation which would later flower in the Adventist and Fundamentalist movements.[145]

Francis Bampfield's church remained independent of the Bell Lane and Mill Yard congregations during his lifetime, despite his continued imprisonment after the Restoration. In any case, after Bampfield's death his church shared Pinners' Hall with the Bell Lane church under John Belcher, the congregations praying in shifts. In 1721, eight years after Edward Stennett's death, the two churches left Pinners' Hall and worshipped for a time with their cousins in Mill Yard.[146] Bampfield's followers called Edmund Townshend of the Natton Saturday-Sabbatarian church in Gloucestershire to minister to them in 1727 and moved to Cripplegate, where they worshipped until 1847, when the church appears to have broken up.[147] Surviving members gravitated back to Mill Yard, where that famous congregation worshipped until early this century, led until the end by their well-known minister W.H. Black.[148]

Towards the end of the seventeenth century, it was decided to put out a second edition of a small book about the fourth commandment by Thomas Chafie, who had been minister in a town called Nutshelling, which seemed to the publishers to be as accurate then as before. "I Believe thou are not ignorant of the many dissensions & contentions that have been among the People of God about the Sabbath-day", Chafie wrote to his readers,

> Some stood for the old Sabbath (so called by some) meaning the *Jews* Sabbath-day. Some for a new Sabbath (so called by some) meaning the day of Christs Resurrection. And some for no Sabbath but what Magistrates do appoint. No small Controversies have been between all these about the Sabbath-day, as I believe thou knowest. But the ground and cause of all such their Controversies; and how for Peace and Agreement sake it may be removed and taken away, I suppose thou dost not know[149]

---

[144] See below, pp. 181-97.

[145] See below, pp. 207-12.

[146] Pinners' Hall was held on lease for 99 years by the Hollis family and sub-let for religious purposes: W.T. Whitley, "The Hollis Family and Pinners' Hall", *Bap. Qly.*, i (1922-3), 78-81.

[147] The Natton church was gathered about 1640, became Saturday-Sabbatarian about 1680, and was led from 1660-1720 by John Purser. The church continued to exist until this century. John Cowell was a member of this church until he wrote his denunciation of the Saturday-Sabbatarian movement.

[148] See below, pp. 200-204.

[149] Thomas Chafie, *A Brief Tract on the Fourth Commandment* (2nd edn, London, 1692), sig. A2. The title page proclaimed its recommendation by Dr Bates and John How.

In the forty years between the appearance of the first and second editions of Chafie's little tract, little progress had been made in solving the theological conundrum of the Sabbath. But by the end of the seventeenth century and the beginning of the eighteenth, it was clear that Saturday-Sabbatarianism as a branch of respectable non-conformity would remain for a long time a part of England's religious landscape.

CHAPTER FIVE

ENGLISH AMERICA:
SABBATARIANS, QUAKERS, FREEMASONS AND JEWS

"Road-Island is a chaos of all Religions and like materia prima susceptive of all formes", Richard Baxter was informed by a Connecticut parson in 1671, "It is the Asylum for all those that are disturbed for Heresy, a hive of hornets, and the Sinke into which all the Rest of the Colonyes empty their Hereticks. So that the body of the people are an Hereogeneous Lump of Familists, Antinomians, Quakers, Seekers, and Anti-sabbatarians."[1] It is this last group which interests us here, for a number of months after this letter was sent to Baxter, a Seventh-Day Baptist church was organized at Newport, in a town which already had two Baptist churches, the only city in America to be so blessed. The staid Dutchmen of New Amsterdam, like many others, looked with horror on the lack of religious restraint in Rhode Island, and informed co-religionists in Holland that it was "the receptacle of all sorts of riff-raff people, and is nothing else than the sewer (latrina) of New England. All the cranks of New England retire thither."[2]

Of course, these same facts could be interpreted in yet another way. Even Baxter's Connecticut informant noted that the men of Rhode Island, "if they agree in any one position, is this, That every Man though of any Hedge religion ought to professe and practice his own tenets without any molestation or disturbance." From the settling of Rhode Island by Roger Williams in 1636, and after its expansion with the group led by Anne Hutchinson in 1638, the colony would remain a magnet for those who could not abide the rigid theocracy of Massachusetts. Rhode Island's religious toleration was confirmed in the Charter of 1663 which in many ways made the colony the first secular state of modern times. "The best Limb in it", Baxter was told, "is a church of Anabaptists led by Mr. Clarke who they say is an Animal Rationale, of Competent Abilityes and Morall principles".[3]

The Seventh-Day Sabbath and concern for the Mosaic law would fan out from John Clarke's First Baptist Church of Newport throughout

---

[1] John Woodbridge, Jr. to Richard Baxter, 31 Mar. 1671: Dr Williams's Lib., MS Baxter II (letters), fos. 233-4: repr. R.P. Stearns, "Correspondence of John Woodbridge, Jr., and Richard Baxter", *New Eng. Qly.*, x (1937), 573.

[2] Letter from New Amsterdam, dated 14 Aug. 1657: *Ecclesiastical Records State of New York*, ed. E.T. Corwin (Albany, 1901), i. 399-400.

[3] See n. 1 above.

Rhode Island, and from there to other parts of the New World. The story of the Seventh-Day men now shifts to English America. This too was one of the results of the increased persecution of Saturday-Sabbatarians and others in the years after the execution of their martyr in 1661. Despite the efforts of Bampfield, Belcher and others, the three Seventh-Day congregations in London found it difficult to expand their numbers significantly in the present hostile climate. Their decision to send Stephen Mumford of Bell Lane as a missionary to the wilds of tolerant Rhode Island was pivotal, and excited even the imagination of old Dr Peter Chamberlen, now keen to remain out of the radical limelight. As we shall see, the spread of the faith across the Atlantic, combined with the endurance of many of Bampfield's Hebraic ideas, ensured the transformation of some Saturday-Sabbatarians into Seventh-Day Adventists in the nineteenth century, laying the foundations for that important sect, as well as contributing to the establishment of the Fundamentalist movement as a whole, whose influence on American culture has been and continues to be immeasurably great.

I

Years before the English arrived in Narragansett Bay, the Dutch from at least the early 1620s had been sailing up Long Island Sound to trade with the Indians in the area, first from their boats, and then from a base they established on a small island there.[4] The settlement at Providence was founded by Roger Williams and his small band, in his own words, when "I was unkindly and unchristianly, as I believe, driven from my house and land and wife and children, (in the midst of a New England winter . . .) at Salem".[5] Other religious exiles soon followed, not only Anne Hutchinson two years later, but many others who, unlike Williams and Hutchinson, travelled the much more convenient sea route around Cape Cod, for as yet no roads led from Massachusetts Bay to Narragansett.[6] Dr Robert Child, an English agricultural expert, wrote home to his friend Samuel Hartlib, that these were "banished men, yet rich". He regretted that "they should suffer more, having suffred twice banishment for consciences sake, first in England, secondly in the [Massachusetts] bay patent".[7]

Roger Williams, then, arrived in New England in 1631, was banished from Salem in 1635 and founded Providence the following year, having

---

[4] C. Bridenbaugh, *Fat Mutton and Liberty of Conscience* (Providence, 1974), p. 10.

[5] E.S. Morgan, *The Puritan Dilemma* (Boston, 1958), p. 129.

[6] Bridenbaugh, *Mutton*, p. 10.

[7] Child to Hartlib, 24 Dec. 1645: in G.H. Turnbull, "Robert Child", *Pub. Col. Soc. Mass.*, xxxviii (1959), 51 (from the Hartlib Papers, Sheffield Univ.).

purchased land from the local Indians. Anne Hutchinson came to Massachusetts Bay in 1634, was banished and excommunicated in 1638, and in
March of that year founded the town of Portsmouth on Aquidneck (the
original "Rhode Island") with another Boston exile, William Codding-
ton, who bought the entire island from the Indians.[8] Coddington left Mrs
Hutchinson in May 1639 and moved to the other end of the island; on 16
May 1639 it was "agreed and ordered, that the Plantation now begun at
this South west end of the Island, shall be called Newport".[9] The two
Rhode Island colonies were joined on 12 March 1640, and a fourth town,
Warwick, was founded by Samuel Gorton in 1643. It was in that year that
Roger Williams returned to England to obtain a charter for his new colony
of Rhode Island, which was granted him on 24 March 1644. Three years
later a general assembly was convened at Portsmouth composed of free-
men from the four towns which proceeded to affirm freedom of conscience
and the separation of church and state.[10] At the Restoration, Rhode Island
was the first to proclaim Charles II as king, and was rewarded with a new
royal charter on 18 July 1663 which proclaimed religious freedom regard-
less of "differences in opinion in matters of religion".[11]

Governor John Winthrop of Massachusetts thought in 1644 that the
population of Aquidneck alone included "above 120 families"; Thomas
Lechford reported 200 families there two years earlier.[12] Between 1636 and
1690 the population of Rhode Island colony increased to about 6,000 persons, of whom about 2600 lived in Newport. Nearly all of these families
arrived there before the Restoration, and even by natural increase the
population doubled about every twenty-five years.[13]

---

[8] William Bradford to John Winthrop, 11 Apr. 1638: *Winthrop Papers* (Mass. Hist. Soc.,
Boston, 1929-), iv. 23-4; *Encyclopedia of American History*, ed. R.B. Morris (rev. edn, New
York, 1965), pp. 33-5, 732, 803-4. On the early history of Rhode Island, see also, apart
from Bridenbaugh, *Mutton*: S.G. Arnold, *History of the State of Rhode Island and Providence Plantations* (New York, 1859); *Documentary History of Rhode Island*, ed. H.M. Chapin (Providence,
1916); *The Early Records of the Town of Portsmouth*, ed. C.S. Brigham (Providence, 1901); *Early
Records of the Town of Providence*, ed. W.C. Pelky (Providence, 1892-1915); *Records of the Colony
of Rhode Island and Providence Plantations*, ed. J.R. Bartlett (Providence, 1856-65).
[9] *Doc. Hist. R.I.*, ed. Chapin, ii. 71; Coddington to Winthrop, 9 Dec. 1639: *Winthrop
Papers*, iv. 160-1; *Rec. R.I.*, ed. Bartlett, i. 88; Bridenbaugh, *Mutton*, pp. 11n-12n.
[10] William Coddington opposed the union and left for England in October 1649, where
he managed to obtain a separate charter for Aquidneck in March 1651. Williams convinced
the Council of State to revoke this upstart charter in October 1652, and by March 1656
Coddington had finally accepted the authority of Providence Plantation: *Encyclopedia*, ed.
Morris, p. 35.
[11] *Ibid.*, p. 37.
[12] *Winthrop's Journal: "History of New England," 1630-1649*, ed. J.K. Hosmer, in *Original Nar-
ratives of Early American History*, ed. J.F. Jameson (New York, 1908), ii. 175; Thomas Lechford,
Plain Dealing: or, Nevves from New-England (London, 1642): repr. *Coll. Mass. Hist. Soc.*, 3rd ser.,
iii (1833), p. 96; Bridenbaugh, *Mutton*, p. 8 and n.
[13] *Ibid.*, p. 13, but on p. 8n., Bridenbaugh makes clear that he reckons that there were

Among these men was Dr John Clarke, who in the early 1640s organized in Newport one of the two oldest churches of the Baptist denomination in the New World.[14] The initial group was very small, but steadily
grew in number. When Samuel Hubbard and his wife of Fairfield, Connecticut were enlightened by God "but mostly my wife, into his holy ordinance of baptizing only of visible believers, & being very zealous for it",
and because of this belief

> sore threatened with imprisonment to Hartford jail, if not to renounce it or
> to remove; that scripture came into our minds, if they persecute you in one
> place flee to another: and so we did. 2 day October 1648 we went for Rhode
> Island, & arrived there 12 day. I and my wife upon our manifestation of our
> faith were baptized by broth[r] John Clarke 3 day Nov. 1648.[15]

Samuel Hubbard's wife Tacey seems to have been waiting over twenty
years for the moment to make a public profession of her Baptist principles,
but only recently had convinced her husband of the truth of her cause.[16]
So too, years later, would she bring around her husband to Saturday-
Sabbatarianism and support him as one of the most influential founders
of the first Seventh-Day church in the New World.

---

8 persons to a family, exactly double the multiplier favoured by most demographers.

[14] A controversy raged for years between the Baptist churches of Newport and Providence as to which church was the oldest: see Arnold, *Rhode Island*, i. 107-8; Peterson, *Rhode
Island*, pp. 330-9.

[15] Seventh-Day Baptist Hist. Soc., Plainfield, N.J., U.S.A.: "Mss. relating to Samuel
Hubbard of Newport". This is a 195 pp. handwritten collection of over 100 of Hubbard's
letters, and letters sent to him, some complete texts, some summaries of contents. Hubbard's correspondence covers the period 1641 to 1688, the year of his death. The quotations
above come from Hubbard's brief family history, pp. 10-11: pp. 42-3 are almost identical.
The original journal in Hubbard's own hand is lost, although it may have been in existence as late as 1831 (see remarks in *Seventh-Day Baptist Memorial*, i [1852], 24, 149n.). Hubbard's original was copied out by Isaac Backus at the end of the eighteenth century when
he was working on his *A History of New-England, With particular Reference to the Denomination of
. . . Baptists* (Boston, 1777-96). The Angus Lib., Regent's Park Coll., Oxford preserves
"Extracts of letters which were wrote from England to Newport on Rhode Island, and
from thence to England; taken from a collection . . . preserved by Mr. Samuel Hubbard."
The MS note also testifies that "These extracts were taken by Isaac Backus. Nov. 1. 1792
. . . for Dr. John Rippon in London." Backus himself noted that "Many more of his letters
are in another book No 5 in quarto", and indeed prints in his *History* a number of letters
which are not found in the Plainfield journal. Perhaps this is the meaning of the reference
on p. 3 of the copy at Plainfield that "Several hundred of his letters were carefully copied
into a journal", although only about 100 appear in the existing MS. This further collection
of Hubbard's letters has not been found.
R.G. Huling made a copy in 1880 from Backus's notebook, and noted on 11 Dec. 1900
that he made the copy now in Plainfield for the Rev. W.C. Whitford on the understanding
that the MSS would never be published. Nevertheless, extracts from Hubbard's journal
were published by Huling himself in the *Mag. New Eng. Hist.*, i (1891) and ii (1892). The
Plainfield copy was previously in the library of Milton College, Wisconsin.

[16] Hubbard to John Thornton, Providence, 19 Dec. 1686: Hubbard MSS, p. 191.

The outline of Samuel Hubbard's life can be gleaned from his own journal. Hubbard was born in 1610 in Mendolsham, Suffolk, the seventh child (and fourth son) of James Hubbard and Naomi Cocke of Ipswich. His grandfather Thomas Hubbard, also of Mendolsham, is mentioned in Foxe's Book of Martyrs, and he still had "a Testament of my grandfather Cocke's printed 1549, which he hid in his bed-straw lest it should be found & burnt in queen Mary's days." Samuel Hubbard left England at the time of the great migration and came to Salem in October 1633. The following year he removed to Watertown, where in 1635 he joined the church "by giving account of my faith". Mistress Tacey Cooper came to Dorchester on 9 June 1634, and herself joined the church there seven weeks later. Samuel Hubbard and Tacey Cooper both went to Windsor in 1635, and from there went on to Wethersfield. The Hubbards remained there until 10 May 1639, when they took residence in Springfield, where a church was soon gathered. "I gave acct. of my faith," Hubbard says once again, and joined with five other men in church fellowship. Several children were born to him there, and when on 10 May 1647 he moved once again to Fairfield, he was accompanied by his wife, and his daughters Ruth, Rachel and Bethiah. It was there that his wife, and later Samuel Hubbard himself, were convinced of the validity of adult baptism alone, and threatened with imprisonment, fled to Rhode Island in October 1648 and joined the Baptist church there, still unaware of the entire question of the Saturday-Sabbath.[17]

These bare bones of Hubbard's life story gloss over the political and religious controversy which raged throughout the colonies during this period and which in large measure prompted him to pitch camp so many times in succession. We see from his journal that he remained at Wethersfield, on the Connecticut river near Hartford, during the entire period of the Pequot War, that revengeful expedition by the colonists against the local Indians in reprisal for the murder of a trader named John Oldham on 20 July 1636. John Endecott of Massachusetts and Captain John Mason of Connecticut launched attacks all up and down the area between the Pequot (Thames) River and the present western border of Rhode Island, finally destroying the main Pequot centre near the present town of Stonington, Connecticut, and slaughtering the Indians who had managed to escape at New Haven in July 1637, with a force of men from Plymouth, Massachusetts, and Connecticut. The population of Wethersfield suffered along with the other towns, and colonists left their homes even to go to the fields at their peril.[18]

---

[17] *Ibid.*, pp. 7-11, 39-43.

[18] [Anon.], "Samuel Hubbard", *Seventh-Day Bap. Memorial*, i (1852), 147. For more on

The elimination of the threat from the Pequots led to a further reorganization of the colonists, and those of Connecticut adopted on 24 January 1639 a new frame of government which they called the Fundamental Orders. Hartford, Windsor, and Wethersfield agreed to the new constitution, but Springfield refused to join, and continued under the independent authority of William Pynchon until they began to send deputies to sit regularly in the Massachusetts General Court by 1649. The church at Wethersfield in 1639 consisted of seven members alone, and divided three against four in favour of rejecting the Fundamental Orders. But the three in favour consisted of the church officers, and as no pastor had yet been found, it was they who carried the decision. Samuel Hubbard was one of the four dissenters, so he removed to dissident Springfield and formed a new gathered church which initially consisted of five men.[19]

Throughout this period, it was clear to all of the colonists that what was needed was some form of government which would provide them with adequate protection against any future Indian threat, as well as a system which would leave the liberties of the various colonies intact. Massachusetts was by far the most powerful of the colonies, and took the lead in December 1641 with the adoption by the General Court of Nathaniel Ward's Body of Liberties, a code of practice which was approved over John Cotton's "Moses his Judicialls". Both documents were based on the Mosaic law, and Ward used the Pentateuch as a model for his criminal code. Two years later, on 19 May 1643, representatives from Massachusetts, Plymouth, Connecticut, and New Haven met at Boston and drew up twelve articles of confederation and formed the United Colonies of New England. The territorial integrity of each colony was to remain intact, but both Massachusetts and Connecticut claimed Springfield and Westfield, and in the final determination of the boundary between them, Hubbard's town of Springfield was ceded to Massachusetts. The religious conformity of Massachusetts was famous in New England, and Samuel Hubbard and his wife thought it best to remove to a town that was unquestionably Connecticut's, and so in May 1647 they settled in Fairfield. But this adoption of Baptist principles offended even the magistrates of more tolerant Connecticut, and he was finally forced to flee to Rhode Island, the final station on the radical non-conformists' trail.[20]

"Such was the pleasure of JEHOVAH towards me", Samuel Hubbard re-

---

the colonists' policy towards the Indians and the Pequot War see: A.T. Vaughan, "Pequots and Puritans: The Causes of the War of 1637", *Will. & Mary. Qly.*, 3rd ser., xxi (1964), 256-69; *idem, New England Frontier: Puritans and Indians, 1620-1675* (Boston, 1965); F. Jennings, *The Invasion of America: Indians, Colonialism and the Cant of Conquest* (Chapel Hill, 1975).

[19] [Anon.], "Hubbard", pp. 147-8.

[20] *Ibid.*, p. 148; *Encyclopedia*, ed. Morris, p. 36.

flected years later, "I was born of good parents, my mother brought me up in the fear of the Lord in Mendelsham, in catechising me, & in hearing choice ministers I was brought by the good hand of my heavenly Father to see myself a lost one". Eventually "I was comforted, & did believe that there was no help but only in the Lord Jesus Christ for life and salvation".[21] This hopeful view seems to have been communicated to others in his extended family as well, and characterized Samuel Hubbard's first thirty years in New England, before the question of the Saturday-Sabbath had yet arisen.[22]

Rhode Island was unquestionably a haven for religious radicals of all persuasions, but their emigration to that colony did not free them from religious controversy, particularly when they tried to spread the tolerationist gospel to other areas of New England as well. On 19 July 1651, three Baptists from the Newport church arrived in Lynn, Massachusetts to visit William Witter, a blind and old Baptist, and perhaps to evangelize as well. The three men from Newport were Dr John Clarke the minister, John Crandall (who would later adopt the Saturday-Sabbath), and Obadiah Holmes, who since 1648 had been a freeman of Rehoboth near Providence. The day after their arrival they were arrested and later fined. Obadiah Holmes, having refused to pay, was whipped instead.[23] The man sent to deal with the problem was Samuel Hubbard: "I was sent by the church to visit the brethren who was in prison in Boston," he writes, "for witnessing the truth of baptizing believers only ... the 7 day of August, 1651."[24] Hubbard and his Baptist friends had been well aware that reprisals against their co-religionists were bound to come soon. John Hazel wrote to Hubbard from Rehoboth, part of Plymouth Colony, even in March of that year that "Not only losses and wants but persecutions & death itself for Ch[ts] sake, will be a great advantage."[25] The opportunity had presented itself in June when the Plymouth Colony Court ordered compulsory attendance at their meetings or the payment of a 10s. fine.[26] Having failed to attend or to pay the fine, Hazel was imprisoned at Boston and died soon afterwards.[27] Clarke's mission to Lynn, therefore, was in

---

[21] Hubbard MSS, pp. 11-12, 45.

[22] Robert Cooper, Yarmouth to Samuel and Tacey Hubbard, 11 Apr. 1644: *ibid.*, pp. 21-2.

[23] E.S. Gaustad, *Baptist Piety: The Last Will & Testimony of Obadiah Holmes* (Grand Rapids, Michigan, 1978), p. 22. Holmes was born near Manchester about 1607, came to Boston in 1638, and moved to Salem the following year and joined the church there, whose pastor was the famous Hugh Peter. Holmes later moved to Rehoboth, and in 1651 came to Newport.

[24] Hubbard MSS, p. 11.

[25] John Hazel, Rehoboth, to Hubbard, 24 Mar. 1651: *ibid.*, pp. 24-5.

[26] Same to same, 23 June 1651: *ibid.*, pp. 25-6.

[27] Backus's note: *ibid.*, p. 26; Backus, *History*, i. 215.

some sense a provocation, an answer to the persecution of the Baptist faith in Plymouth.

One important result of the imprisonment of the Newport Baptists was that John Clarke decided to accompany Roger Williams to England in the autumn of 1651 when the Founder of Rhode Island sought support to revoke the independent status that William Coddington had obtained for Aquidneck. John Clarke published in London a full report of the persecution of the New England Baptists for an English audience which saw that sect as one of the mainstays of Puritanism, and looked very unkindly on the recent action taken in Massachusetts.[28] Roger Williams himself published one of his more famous works during that visit, and in October 1652 persuaded the Council of State to revoke Coddington's charter.[29] The Baptist controversy in New England, and Samuel Hubbard's part in it, thus soon became common knowledge in the mother country. Hubbard's brother Benjamin hastened to write to him from their home in Suffolk, explaining that they did not "look at y^r opinion in point of baptism so dangerous in itself as the consequences & effects of it; which usually are very ill; for the most fall into dangerous and many into damnable opinions." As for the present situation in England, Hubbard was informed, "Here is liberty enough of conscience now, some think too much: but I think it is the abuse makes it bad."[30]

Roger Williams returned to Rhode Island, having accomplished his mission, and served for three terms as president of the colony between 1654 and 1657. John Clarke decided to remain in England for the time being and in the end did not return to Rhode Island until 1667, when the persecution of non-conformists became intense after the Restoration. During this time the ministerial responsibility was devolved on Obadiah Holmes, assisted by Mark Luker, John Crandall and Joseph Torrey. All were unpaid, of course, because a hireling ministry was none of Christ's. It was during Holmes's stewardship that the Baptist church split apart, over the issue of the laying on of hands and the six principles of Hebrews

---

[28] John Clarke, *Ill Newes from New England* (London, 1652) took its title from the well-known work by Edward Winslow, *Good News from New England* (London, 1624).

[29] Roger Williams, *The Bloody Tenent Yet More Bloody* (London, 1652) was a reply to John Cotton's *The Bloudy Tenent Washed* (London, 1647), which itself was a reply to Williams's *The Bloudy Tenent, of Persecution* (London, 1644).

[30] Benjamin & Katherine Hubbard, Copdocke, Suffolk to Samuel & Tacey Hubbard, 12 Apr. 1652: Hubbard MSS, pp. 178-9. Benjamin Hubbard wrote to his brother again on 8 Mar. 1654 apparently from New England; his son Thomas wrote to Hubbard from Boston on 31 July 1662 informing him of his father's death nearly two years before, on 28 Oct. 1660, leaving five children born in New England, including himself, "and I being now come over about the land at Seekouk [Rhode Island], having been there to demand my right." Thomas Hubbard informed his uncle from Boston on 29 July 1663 that he had brought over his sisters and was returning to England: Hubbard MSS, pp. 33-4.

vi. 1, 2. Holmes, Luker, Torrey and Crandall withdrew to form their own church, which would be based on more strictly Calvinist principles associated with Particular Baptism. Newport's First Baptist Church pulled back to the tenets of General Baptism (Arminianism), the notion that Christ died for all mankind, not only for an elect. Samuel Hubbard followed the Calvinist Baptists and joined with them in their newly gathered congregation, although no record of his decision remains in the parts of his letter book which have survived. In any case, Hubbard accompanied Obadiah Holmes in 1657 on a mission to Long Island to preach to the Calvinist Dutch. They also counselled their brethren in Boston to found a Baptist church in spite of its explicit prohibition. Thomas Goold, John Farnum, Thomas Osborne and others joined together in Boston for this purpose to found its First Baptist Church. Goold and Holmes also became friendly with John Winthrop, Jr., the governor of Connecticut between 1657 and 1675, which no doubt helped them in their struggle against the continued persecution of Baptists (and Quakers) in Boston during this period.[31]

II

At some point during the first two months of 1665, Stephen Mumford arrived in Newport from the Bell Lane Seventh-Day Baptist Church in London and began to persuade others in the Baptist community that Saturday was the Sabbath of the Lord. Once again, it was Samuel Hubbard's wife Tacey who was first won over on 11 March 1664-5; her husband was convinced three weeks later, and was followed by one daughter in 1666, two other daughters and a son-in-law early in 1667. Ironically, the son-in-law was Joseph Clarke, the son of John Clarke the leader of the Newport Baptists. Young Clarke had married Hubbard's daughter Bethiah in 1664 and lived in Westerley, Rhode Island with Ruth Hubbard Burdick and her husband Robert. Obadiah Holmes's reaction to this further break-up of the community under his temporary charge seems to have bordered on violence, and he was so sternly rebuked by John Clarke when the minister returned from London in 1667 that Holmes withdrew from church leadership for four years. The Hubbards and the other Saturday-Sabbatarians continued their communion with the Particular Baptist church at Newport, however, and took an active part in the congregation's affairs.[32]

---

[31] Gaustad, *Baptist Piety*, pp. 42-9.

[32] *Ibid.*, pp. 50-2. Apart from those noted above, Roger Baster began observing the Saturday-Sabbath on 15 Apr. 1666; William Hiscox on 28 Apr. 1666; Rachel Langworthy on 15 Jan. 1665-6: [Anon.], "A brief and faithful relation of the difference between those of this Church and those who withdrew their communion from it", in the record book of

Samuel Hubbard's non-separating policy during the first years of Saturday-Sabbatarianism in Newport may have initially nurtured the hope that some sort of compromise might be found. John Salmon, a Seventh-Day man in Boston, wrote to Hubbard in June 1667 warning him that outside of Rhode Island, life for a Saturday-Sabbatarian in Boston was not easy. "The six days I am as comfortable as I think I could be elsewhere", Salmon wrote, "but the seventh day I find the want of your: yet thro' mercy I sometimes meet with some inward sweet refreshing on that day". Fortunately for Salmon, "my friend y^t I am wth doth use all tenderness as possibly may be with respect to that day: he will not burden me with anything."[33] Such tolerant attitudes were wholly uncharacteristic of the Massachusetts Bay Colony, and patience even in Rhode Island was strained when confronted with Judaising Baptists.

Clear disagreement concerning such a central point as the day upon which the Sabbath was to be observed was bound to lead to further dispute and acrimony between Hubbard's people and those who worshipped with John Clarke and Obadiah Holmes. The strained relations between the Saturday- and the Sunday-Sabbatarians comes out very clearly in the letter which Thomas Trenicke sent to Samuel Hubbard from Plymouth in July 1668: "I hoped I should never have seen the day in wch such fruit sho^d be found among y^o," he wrote, "so full of gall & wormwood as your letter seems, in one part of it, to intimate in a difference betwixt you and my dear brother Holmes, whose faithfulness for Christ & his truth hath been so long aproved among you many ways." Trenicke and others in Plymouth had not as yet had a full report of the Sabbatarian dispute and prayed that the accounts which they had received regarding the ill-feeling among the Newport Baptists were exaggerated.[34]

By this time, news of the success of the American Saturday-Sabbath had reached England[35], and Edward Stennett hastened to write from Abingdon to his co-religionists in Rhode Island. Stennett wrote that he was pleased that the Saturday-Sabbath had found root in the New World, for

---

First Baptist Church, Newport, pp. 137-53, probably copied by John Comer, pastor there c. 1720, now Newport Hist. Soc., Vault A, Box 50, Folder 5. Backus's copy now Rhode Island Hist. Soc., Backus Papers, Vol. ii, Folder 21, p. 1. The "Relation" is repr. *Seventh-Day Bap. Mem.*, i (1852), 28-39. The original was sent by John Clarke, Mark Luker, and Joseph Torrey, all elders of the new church: Hubbard MSS, pp. 143-8.

[33] Salmon, from Boston, to Hubbard, 18 June 1667: Hubbard MSS, pp. 35-7.

[34] Trenicke to Hubbard, 13 July 1668: *ibid.*, pp. 37-8. Trenicke's earlier letter of 9 Oct. 1677 from Plum Island to Hubbard makes no mention of the dispute: *ibid.*, pp. 34-5.

[35] According to the records of the First Baptist Church, Newport, "they had sent a letter before respecting themselves, dated the 6th October, 1665, which was the first they sent, to several churches in the observation of the seventh day, for advice; who, as soon as they could, sent it". This letter has since been lost: "Relation", p. 29.

"with us we can scarcely find a man that is really willing to know whether the Sabbath be a truth or not". Nevertheless, generally speaking "at present the opposition seems to be declining away", no doubt because the truth of the Seventh-Day Sabbath was so obvious, witnessed by thousands on Mount Sinai and recorded in the tables of stone by God's own finger. "The churches here have generally their liberty", Stennett informed his American brethren, "but strong bands, we hear, are making". Stennett also recorded that there "are, in England, about nine or ten churches that keep the Sabbath, besides many scattered disciples, who have been eminently preserved in this tottering day, when many once eminent churches have been shattered in pieces." Stennett hoped to continue correspondence with the congregation in Newport, but meanwhile was writing this first letter "at a venture, not knowing how they will come to your hand". He promised to write "more largely" if his letter arrived at its destination and if he received a reply from them.[36]

It would appear that the Sabbatarians of Rhode Island were already in contact with the older churches in England, for the month after Stennett sent his letter, Mumford's congregation at Bell Lane sent a more official reply "to a remnant of the Lord's Sabbath-keepers, in or about Newport, New England". They confessed that they were moved and "affected by hearing from you, by our beloved brother John Cowel, and the more, when we perceived the grace of God that is in you, by those choice and savory letters you sent him, which, with his desire, hath encouraged us to write unto you at this time". The believers of Bell Lane told the men of Newport not to give up hope, for one day "great will be the blessing of Sabbath-keepers, when they shall be exalted to ride upon the high places of the earth, and have dignity and prosperity, temporal and spiritual." On that glorious day, they predicted, how "acceptable will it be – even as the rain upon the mown grass – after all our troubles, and frowns of friends, and persecution of enemies, for the truth's sake!" The time of the fourth monarchy was coming to an end, they said, and "the nearer we come to the promised glory, the more will the mysteries of God be opened to us. Then, without doubt, the fallacy of those vain objections (no Sabbath, or a seventh part of time), will appear." At that time, we "shall then see that the ark, wherein were the table laws, only will be there. The Lord will then make manifest that principles and precepts will stand together in a gospel church state."[37]

---

[36] Edward Stennett, Abingdon, to Rhode Island, 2 Feb. 1668: repr. *Seventh Day Bap. Mem.*, i (1852), 26-7.

[37] Bell Lane Church to Newport Sabbatarians, 26 Mar. 1668: repr. *ibid.*, 24-6 & *Bap. Qly.*, xiv (1951-2), 162-4.

The millenarian tone of the letter is obviously quite striking, which is hardly surprising when one considers the names of the signatories. All but one of the eleven men who signed the letter would be arrested in the raid in 1671 on the congregation at Bell Lane and charged as Fifth Monarchists and Seventh-Day Sabbatarians: John Belcher, Arthur Squibb (here listed as Aaron), John Jones, John Labory (here Laborn), Edmond Fox (here Edward), William Gibson, Robert Woodward (here Woods), Robert Hopkins (here Hopkin), Samuel Clarke, and Richard Parnham.[38] The name of Christian Williams is more difficult to identify, but it has been suggested that he is William Christian, who appears in a manuscript written in 1669.[39]

In spite of the difficulties which must have attended the continued membership of Samuel Hubbard and his group in the Particular Baptist church at Newport, in a letter which he wrote from Boston to his cousin in London in the summer of 1668 he shows himself to be comparatively cheerful. He explains that he was recently in Boston ''upon account of a dispute made shew of the Govenor and magistrates with and against some of God's ways & ours'', in regard to the presence and behaviour of a group of Quakers in that city. He praised God for providing him with a ''good house . . . & 25 acres of ground fenced in, & 4 cows which give milk, one young heifer and 3 calves, & a very good mare; a trade, a carpenter, & health to follow it, & my wife very dilligent and painful; praised be God!'' He informed his cousin in England that ''my son Clarke, and my three daughters, with my wife & about 14 walk in the observation of Gods holy sanctified 7 day Sabbath''.[40]

Hubbard's tone was altogether different a year later when he wrote to the Bell Lane congregation in London about the loss of some of their most valued believers in the Saturday-Sabbath, who had now turned back to observing Sunday. Hubbard bemoaned the loss of brother Wyld and his wife, and of John Salmon and his wife, who ''have forsaken the truth & us, & turned back to full communion with this church''. Wyld even wrote a pamphlet against Saturday-Sabbatarianism, which added insult to injury. ''It is a very hard exercise to us, poor weak ones'', Hubbard wrote, ''to loose four so suddenly out of 11 of us here.'' Hubbard complained that since falling off, these four former brethren had made it their business to

---

[38] See above, pp. 103-105. All of these men appear in the biographical appx in B.S. Capp, *The Fifth Monarchy Men* (London, 1972).

[39] By E.A. Payne, ''More About the Sabbatarian Baptists'', *Bap. Qly.*, xiv (1951-2), 162: citing Lambeth Palace Lib., MS Tenison 639 from *Minutes of the General Assembly of the General Baptist Churches in England*, ed. W.T. Whitley (London, 1909-10), i. XLIII.

[40] Hubbard to John Smith, London, 6 July 1668: Hubbard MSS, pp. 50-2. The words after ''Sabbath'' have been obliterated by an accidental ink spill on the MS.

preach against Saturday-Sabbatarianism and to attack the remaining believers at every opportunity. "I sometimes indeed object in a weak measure and bear a testimony against them", Hubbard explained, but his re-
vulsion and disappointment against them was so strong that he could not
communicate with them, let alone debate with them. "Oh methinks I
could for many resons leave them quite," he confessed, "only owning such
as have not nor dare speak against Gods law; but others do not so judge
as yet: its very hard to me & to them." Hubbard wrote to Bell Lane that
one of the fallen even dared to call "those good books of the bretherin
Stennett, Cowell & B. Sellers a rabble of lyes."[41]

Edward Stennett hastened to reply to Samuel Hubbard from Abingdon
and to encourage him and his flock during this trying period. Stennett
comforted those "that keep the commandments of God and the faith of
Jesus in Rhode Island" by reminding them that in England the Saturday-
Sabbatarians suffered no less. He advised them "to bear up and hold out
against the same spirit of antichrist and opposition against the truth which
we have met with here". Stennett testified that "I have seen the spirit of
antichrist as really act in churches as ever I saw it in the parish, since they
have set themselves against the Lord's Sabbath". Those who refused to
recognize the validity of the Ten Commandments were in any case acting
without any reference whatsoever to principles, "for those who will not
keep the Sabbath at God's command, would all keep it if men did command the keeping of it, as I could make manifest by their own principles
and practice." Stennett's advice was to separate finally from the Baptist
churches of Newport, to "withdraw yourselves from them, as sinful & dis-
orderly persons; and if the church will hold communion with those *apostates*
from the truth, you ought then to desire to be fairly dismissed from the
church; which if the church refuse, you ought to withdraw yourselves, and
not be pertakers of other men's sins, but keep yourselves pure; but with
all humility, meekness, and brokenness of heart."[42]

The Saturday-Sabbatarians of Newport also wrote to Joseph Davis on
4 September 1669 for advice along the same lines, as well, and he answered
them from Oxford Castle about the same time that Stennett wrote to
Rhode Island. Davis described his present imprisonment for his beliefs as
tolerable though "my lodgings dangerous, being *in a cold high tower*". He

---

[41] Hubbard to Bell Lane, 3 July 1669: *ibid.*, pp. 54-6. The Newport First Baptist Church
records note that "they concluded not to bring the case to the church to judge of the fact
... therefore those five sent to England, (to a church in Bell Lane, July the 3d, 1669,)":
"Relation", p. 29.

[42] Stennett to Newport Seventh-Day Baptist group, 6 Mar. 1669-70: Regent's Park
Coll., Oxford, Backus Transcripts, fos. 1ʳ-3ʳ. Also repr. in *Mag. N.E. Hist.*, i (1891), letter
xxiii.

confessed that he himself, ''with all the non-conformists, have been greatly disappointed in our expectations''. Unlike the ancient people of Israel, the Saturday-Sabbatarians lacked a prophet who could tell them how long God intended to keep them in the wilderness. ''And of late the eminent leaders of Baptist and Congregational churches have taken upon them to preach down and write against God's holy seventh-day Sabbath'', Davis reported, ''but it prognosticates to me that the breaking of it is near.'' Davis advised the group in Newport to ''be not discouraged by what opposition you have or may meet with.'' Regarding the question of separation from the other Baptist churches of Newport, Davis somewhat vaguely noted that as ''to the churches of Christ, they generally keep from a sinful compliance with the false worshippers.''[43]

Apart from the more personal letters from Davis and Stennett, the church at Bell Lane sent a somewhat official response to Hubbard's information and inquiry concerning the proper behaviour which should be followed after the defection of the apostates. ''We find that doth greatly add to yr trouble'', wrote the Sabbatarians of Bell Lane, ''because those y^t have done this were none of the meanest among you in helping of you in the work of the Lord.'' They went on to give much the same advice that had been given by Stennett and Davis, but noting that the Newport Sabbatarians would be wise to avoid unnecessary arguments with non-believers, ''unless it be those y^o have the particular offence against.''[44]

William Hiscox, Stephen Mumford and Samuel Hubbard replied to Edward Stennett on 4 September 1670. ''Your good counsel we have ponder^d well, & have taken some steps in,'' they wrote,

> but we have no hopes of help from them, but they are encouraging them y^t are drawn back from ye Lords holy sabbath, and he is become a speaker more than ever before. And dear brother, y^r desire is to know our standing (we that is) we of this ch^h are very loth to leave all for some; we being very few here, but 5, & weaklings also, beside brother Stephen Mumford & his wife. This is the very trouble to many of us, & having declared by one for all that we cannot have such full freedom of spirit wth those y^t are fallen back

---

[43] Davis to Newport, 26 Mar. 1670: repr. *Seventh-Day Bap. Mem.*, i (1852), 74-6. In the Hubbard MSS, p. 78 is a brief reference to a letter from Davis to Newport dated 7 Feb. 1669-70 in which he ''informed 'em of his haveing embraced their sentem^{ts} about the sabbath for two years.'' Such information is not imparted in the letter of March, but the reference in the Hubbard MSS may be to the same letter nevertheless. The letter from Newport to Davis has not been found, but Hiscox, Mumford, and Hubbard did send a letter to Stennett in London on 4 Sept. 1670 (Hubbard MSS, pp. 79-81). If this is the letter Davis is answering, then his own letter quoted here must be from 26 Mar. 1671. This is more than likely as the first day of the new year was 25th March, and Davis may simply have made that most common error of forgetting to bring forward the year during its first days.

[44] Bell Lane to Newport, 27 Feb. 1669-70: Hubbard MSS, pp. 78-9.

from ye truth once professed, most do hold yet full communion in breaking of bread & the rest of the ordinances w^th 'em.

The three Saturday-Sabbatarians were nevertheless at pains to emphasize that communion with non-believers did not in any way imply a weakening of their own convictions:

But this grace we are helped to do, we in our measure endeavour to sanctify God's holy sabbath by assembling ourselves, 7 of us to pray & edify each other, and no man disturbs us in any kind

The three prayed, "Oh rich mercy! oh that we might find ye same effect as of old!" and hoped "that the Lord would stir up some to come and help us poor ones!". They also informed Stennett that apart from themselves at Newport were Hubbard's two daughters and their husbands Joseph Clarke and Robert Burdick, all Saturday-Sabbatarians, "and sister Maxon".[45]

The description which Hubbard, Mumford and Hiscox presented of the progress of the Saturday-Sabbath in the New World must have been very saddening for those in the mother church at Bell Lane. Samuel Hubbard himself hastened to write a more private letter to Edward Stennett, explaining that he could not agree with him more about the necessity of withdrawing from communion with the others, but that he himself was as yet alone in this view. Hubbard also discussed a business proposition in the same letter, replying to Stennett's earlier suggestion that the two begin a trade in medicines since Stennett himself was a physician by profession. Hubbard now replied that he had proposed the arrangement to John Clarke, not only a religious opponent and the father of his son-in-law, but also a physician himself. "I spoke also to a friend of mine who, by God's help, saved my life; a man of greatest fame in all our colony & most improved, one mr. John Cranston, doctor of physik, & captain of the town train band." Even in the depths of religious depression, the question of business and trade was not forgotten.[46]

By early 1671, the split between the Saturday-Sabbatarians and the rest had reached crisis proportions. Thomas Goold of the First Baptist Church in Boston was sent to Newport to urge Hubbard and his group to stay within the confines of the official church "and get along as well as they could".[47] The Boston church itself more officially wrote to Hiscox and his brethren urging the avoidance of a "censorious spirit", suggesting that

---

[45] Hiscox, Mumford, & Hubbard to Stennett, from Newport, 4 Sept. 1670: *ibid.*, pp. 79-81.

[46] Hubbard to Stennett, 12 Nov. 1670: *ibid.*, pp. 81-2.

[47] Newport Hist. Soc., Vault A, Box 50, Folder 3: Gaustad, *Piety*, p. 53; "Relation", p. 29.

"may we not say we are all in the dark, and see and know but in part?"[48]
Samuel Hubbard's daughter Bethiah and her husband Joseph in Westerley expressed their view as well, writing to him in August 1671: "to hold
com^n wth those apostates is very unsafe," they argued, "& truly to hold
com^n with those y^t strike at the whole law of God, I must confess I am not
able to maintain". Nevertheless, they suggested, "I think there might be
a waiting some time", and when that time came, Hubbard and his group
must be absolutely sure that "ye moving cause is only and purely in love
unto the law of God" and that "y^o manage it with all humility, patience
& meekness & with faithfulness". Apparently without any intended irony,
Joseph Clarke and his wife asked Hubbard to "present our dutiful respects
unto father Clarke".[49]

The decision to break with the rest of the Baptists in Newport seems to
have come in the early autumn of 1671. On 10 September 1671 Hiscox,
Mumford and Hubbard wrote to the church at Bell Lane in London and
informed them "y^t they had follow^d their advice in with drawing from
table com^n tho' they still met with the ch^h but did not propose to long".[50]
The Sabbatarians themselves seem to have been willing to have continued
to worship, although not to take communion, with the rest of the Newport
Baptists. "And thus, for several months, they walked, with little or no of-
fense from the church; after which the leading or ministering brethren
began to declare themselves concerning the ten precepts, Ex. 20." It was
the Seventh-Day Baptists who were offensive to the rest, and the preachers
could not resist dealing with the most touchy questions concerning the
validity of the Mosaic law, even at the expense of alienating their Sabbatarian brethren, those who in the preachers' eyes "were gone to Mount
Sinai, among the briars and thorns there, and would bring in a yoke of
bondage neither they nor their fathers were able to bear." Finally, after enduring months of indirect abuse,

> Mr. Hiscox, with a grieved heart, and with tears, stood up and said, (being
> no longer able to contain,) that "he desired leave to speak;" to "declare in
> faithfulness, if he or any of those five were such persons as he had been hint-
> ing, both as to the church, or to the world, in his sermons, that he would with
> plainness declare it, and not to take such methods from day to day, in the au-
> dience of the whole assembly, causing the people to imagine they pleaded for
> circumcision and the whole law.

Hiscox called upon the elders to turn to other subjects in their preaching,

[48] N.E. Wood, *The History of the First Baptist Church of Boston, 1665-1899* (Philadelphia, 1899), pp. 108-9.

[49] J. & B. Clarke, Westerley to Hubbard, 8 Aug. 1671: Hubbard MSS, pp. 82-3.

[50] *Ibid.*, p. 84: the quotation above is from a summary in the letter book and not a verba-
tim record of the letter itself.

or the Saturday-Sabbatarians would be driven out of the church. "Here-upon", according to the official report of the dispute, "for a few weeks there was a forbearance".[51]

But soon afterwards Obadiah Holmes returned to the pastoral position he had held in the church until 1667, when he resigned in protest at a re-buke that he had received from John Clarke after an excessively enthusias-tic denunciation of the principles of Saturday-Sabbatarianism. Clarke probably now realized that Holmes had been right to warn of the dangers of tolerating such a sect within the bosom of the church. Clarke and Holmes both preached on the same day, and Holmes took the occasion of his return to lash out against those who "leave Christ and are going to Moses in the observation of days, seasons, and such like". Holmes thought "that it is better that a millstone were hanged about the neck of such, and they to be cast into the sea". Hiscox cornered Holmes later in the after-noon, and even though the prodigal preacher refused to admit that he had been referring to Hiscox and his group earlier in the day, Hiscox retorted

> that the only difference between you and us is, *we* plead for the ten command-ments to be a rule of good living, and to be obeyed in Gospel times; *you* deny them, and say they were never given to be a rule to the Gentiles before or after faith[52]

Several days later, Hiscox was called before the church to explain why he would not join them in communion. Hiscox laid the blame on the four hostile apostates from his Sabbatarian way, "but farther," he added, "my trouble is much hightened by brother Holmes' preaching, for if we be such persons as that, better a millstone were hanged about our necks, &c." Clarke tried to reconcile the two by reminding Hiscox that he and his group had never been mentioned specifically, but Holmes broke him off to say that to "be plain, I did intend brother Hiscox, and such as he is." Hiscox retorted that if it be true that Holmes had said "that we have no more conscience than dogs, it ain't likely that our fellowship should be any way to your comfort and God's glory." This acrimonious debate con-tinued for some time, and inspired Mr Luker "with grief" to observe "that the ringing of the nose causes blood."[53]

The discussion was adjourned until the following week, when the church tried to prod others of Hiscox's group to air their views as well. Samuel Hubbard, when called upon to speak, refused, "desiring Mr.

---

[51] "Relation", pp. 29-31.
[52] *Ibid.*, pp. 32, 34. Holmes's sermon was printed afterwards at Westerley: Hubbard MSS, p. 154.
[53] "Relation", pp. 32-3.

Hiscox might speak for all at once; 'for,' said he, 'our grounds are all one, and it is the quickest way.'" But Hubbard's wife Tacey did agree to speak, and outlined the main grounds of their refusal to join in communion, being the apostasy of four former Sabbatarians, Brother Holmes's recent remarks, and the refusal of the church to observe all of the Ten Commandments. A learned theological debate ensued, until Hiscox lost his patience and shouted "What! do you think to juggle me out of my conscience?" Several other meetings followed, and "there was much discourse, and sometimes too hot words on both sides".[54]

At one of the last meetings between the two sides, the Saturday-Sabbatarians were especially accused of having left off Sunday observance without having consulted sufficiently with the pastors. John Clarke reminded Hiscox that he had often told him "that he stole into the practice." By this time it was clear that no compromise could be reached, and many members of the church "being weary of the contest", began to accommodate themselves to Hiscox's suggestion at this meeting that the two groups separate. Holmes said he would never agree to a separation as long as he lived, and others held his view. At a final session, further accusations flew between the two sides, including a mutual claim between Hiscox and Holmes that the other dared to work at secular business before coming to church. Hiscox reported having seen Holmes come to a meeting on Sunday with his leather apron on, which led him to believe that he had just left his place of work and was hastening to make a belated entrance into the sacred tasks of the day. "By the time he had so far proceeded", it was reported, "there was so much disorder in the meeting, that the other things were not spoke to." One of the members of the church noted "that he thought they had spent time enough with Mr. Hiscox", and the withdrawal of the five Sabbatarians from the congregation was officially confirmed, 7 December 1671.[55]

III

As we have seen, religious toleration in Rhode Island did not prevent theological disputes, and probably contributed to making the colony famous throughout Europe as "a chaos of all Religions".[56] But despite the three-way split among the Newport Baptists, what seemed most astonishing to a world reared on the ultimate impossibility of complete religious tolera-

---

[54] *Ibid.*, pp. 33-6.

[55] *Ibid.*, pp. 37-9. The date of the organization of the Saturday-Sabbatarian congregation is alternatively given as 23 Dec. 1671 or 3 Jan. 1671-2. William Hiscox was pastor of the church until he died on 24 May 1704, aged 66: Backus, *History*, ii. 233-4.

[56] See n. 1, above.

tion was the fact that the colony seemed to manage its affairs without the need for religious persecution.[57] Sir Henry Vane, who had been active in New England if not entirely successful, asked a prominent figure in Rhode Island how political peace among religious division was possible. He received the simple reply that unlike in Old England, in Rhode Island they had "sitten quiet and drie from the streams of blood split by the warr in our native country . . . nor (in this colonie) have we been consumed with the over-zealous fire of the Godly and Christian magistrates."[58] Dr John Clarke summed it up when he wrote that "notwithstanding the different understandings and consciences amongst us, without interruption we agree to maintain civil Justice and judgement, neither are there such outrages committed mongst us as in other parts of the Country are frequently seen."[59]

With such a reputation for religious pluralism, it should surely come as no surprise that Rhode Island became a magnet for religious groups of all persuasions, most of which arrived in the colony before the Sabbatarian split of 1671. As we have seen, Samuel Hubbard and others were themselves drawn to Newport because of the unacceptability of their religious views in other parts of New England. The precise nature of the intermingling of views among these religious outcasts of course can not be determined, but Newport was above all else a very small place. Even in 1690 the population of the city could not have been more than 2000 persons, while the population of Rhode Island as a whole might have reached 6000; in 1650, only about 300 people lived in Newport.[60] Certainly in a town like Newport which championed freedom of religious expression, a good deal of mutual discussion and debate must have gone on, not only between Saturday- and Sunday-Baptists, but between Saturday-Sabbatarians and many others as well, and by looking at some of the other sects connected with the Seventh-Day men we might explain the rapidity with which the new idea spread.

The most well-known and influential of these radical religious groups was undoubtedly the Quakers, who arrived at Newport on 3 August 1657 aboard the ship *Woodhouse*, which had sailed from London to Newport with a brief stop at New Amsterdam, where five Quakers disembarked, having "had movings".[61] A year previously, in July 1656, two Quaker women

---

[57] See, e.g., C. Russell, "Arguments for Religious Unity in England, 1530-1650", *Jnl. Eccl. Hist.*, xviii (1967), 201-26; B. Worden, "Toleration and Cromwellian Protectorate", *Stud. Ch. Hist.*, xxi (1984), 199-233.

[58] Bridenbaugh, *Fat Mutton*, p. 5.

[59] Clarke, *Ill Newes*, sig. b2ᵛ.

[60] R.L. Bowen, *Early Rehoboth* (Rehoboth, 1945), i. 9, 11, 17; Bridenbaugh, *Fat Mutton*, pp. 13, 73.

[61] The voyage of the *Woodhouse* is recounted in a ship's log "by me Robert Fowler, with

who had sailed into Boston from Barbados were arrested, imprisoned, searched for tokens of witchcraft on their bodies, and deprived of one hundred books containing "corrupt, heretical, and blasphemous doctrines" which were burned in the market-place by the common hangman. They were deported at the beginning of August, but two days later another group of Quakers arrived in Boston and were submitted to the same treatment, ending in their forcible return to England three months later.[62]

Barbados for Quakers in the 1660s was "the nursery of the truth" from which their missionary groups proceeded in the New World.[63] The island had first been occupied by the English in 1605, and had submitted to the authority of the Commonwealth in 1652. The principal industry was sugar-making, which was carried on by black slaves brought directly from Africa. In the 1650s, the population of Barbados stood at about 25,000 inhabitants, and about 10,000 slaves.[64] Clarendon thought that the colonists of Barbados were mainly men "who had retired thither only to be quiet and to be free from noise and oppressions in England."[65] The Quakers began their work on the island by 1655, and during the later seventeenth century, Barbados was normally the first stop for Quaker missionaries bound for other parts in America.[66] George Fox himself took a keen interest in the activities of these early American missionaries and their special problems, and as early as 1657 addressed an epistle "to Friends beyond sea that have Blacks and Indian slaves".[67]

The response of the commissioners of the United Colonies of New England was predictable and immediate. On 12 September 1657, "being informed that divers Quakers are arrived this summer at Rode Island, and entertained there, which may prove dangerous to the Collonies," they thought it "meet to manifest theire minds to the Governor there" that they "thinke noe care too great to preserve us from such a pest, the contagion whereof (if received) within youer Collonie were dangerous" and might be "defused to the other by meanes of the intercourse especially to the place of trade amongst us." They also threatened the Rhode Islanders that "it will bee our duty seriously to consider what further provision God

---

my small vessel called the *Woodhouse, but performed by the Lord*, like as He did Noah's Ark, wherein He shut up a few righteous persons and landed them safe": Friends' House Lib., London, MS A.R.B. i, endorsed by George Fox: see also Bridenbaugh, *Fat Mutton*, p. 62; R.I. Coll. Recs., i. 374-8; R. Jones, *The Quakers in the American Colonies* (2nd edn, New York, 1966), pp. 45-52.

[62] *Ibid.*, pp. 26-38.
[63] George Rofe, an important Quaker traveller, in a letter of 1661: *ibid.*, p. 41.
[64] *Ibid.*, pp. 26-7.
[65] *Ibid.*, p. 26.
[66] *Ibid.*
[67] Fox, epistle no. 133: *ibid.*, p. 44.

may call us to make to prevent the aforesaid mischiefe." The simple instruction of the commissioners was that the leaders of Rhode Island would "remove those Quakers that have been receaved, and for the future prohibite theire cominge amongst you".[68]

The commissioners also demanded in their letter a written agreement to their "request" to reach them by the time of the meeting of the General Court of Massachusetts on 14 October 1657. The Rhode Island General Assembly seems to have waited deliberately until 13 October before approving their reply, in order to appear to be fulfilling the "request" without actually doing so, for the document could hardly have reached its destination by the next day, especially considering that it was addressed to the commissioners and not to the General Court. The document itself, signed by Governor Benedict Arnold, is a masterpiece of careful irony:

> And as concerning these quakers (so called), which are now among us, we have no law among us, whereby to punish any for only declaring by words, &c., theire mindes and understandings concerning the things and ways of God, as to salvation and an eternal condition. And we, moreover, finde, that in those places where these people aforesaid, in this coloney, are most of all suffered to declare themselves freely, and are only opposed by arguments in discourse, there they least of all desire to come, and we are informed that they begin to loath this place, for that they are not opposed by the civill authority, but with all patience and meekness are suffered to say over their pretended revelations and admonitions, nor are they like or able to gain many here to their way

Arnold closed his letter with a humble promise "to commend the consideration of their extravagant outgoinges" to the meeting of the General Assembly scheduled for March 1657-8.[69]

Needless to say, Governor Arnold was well aware that the Quakers had come to Rhode Island to stay, but the principle of religious toleration was one that could not be compromised. Indeed, even at the risk of antagonizing the United Colonies, the General Assembly reminded them the following March that "freedom of different consciences, to be protected from inforcements was the principle ground of our Charter".[70] In any case, it appears that members of some of the leading families in Rhode Island went over to the Quaker message upon first hearing, including William Coddington, Joshua Coggeshall, Nicholas Easton, Walker Clarke, and many others. Especially between the years 1672 and 1677 the Quakers controlled the government of Rhode Island, and on many occasions thereafter

---

[68] R.I. Coll. Recs., i. 374-6; Bridenbaugh, *Fat Mutton*, p. 62; Jones, *Quakers*, pp. 54-5.

[69] R.I. Coll. Recs., i. 376-8; Bridenbaugh, *Fat Mutton*, p. 63; Jones, *Quakers*, p. 55.

[70] R.I. Coll. Recs., i. 378; Bridenbaugh, *Fat Mutton*, p. 63.

a Friend was chosen as the colony's governor. By 1690, perhaps one-half of the population of Newport and of Rhode Island itself described themselves as Quakers.[71]

The Quakers were not the only new religious group which established itself in Newport during the first years of Saturday-Sabbatarianism there. During the spring of 1658, shortly after the arrival of the Quakers, perhaps fifteen Sephardic Jewish families seem to have come to Newport as well. After the reconquest of Recife by the Portuguese, a number of Jews emigrated from Brazil to New Amsterdam in 1654, founding the first enduring Jewish community of the New World. Some of these Jews may have travelled further on to Newport, worried that not only had official permission from the Dutch authorities not been received, but a local decree had been issued actually encouraging them to leave.[72] But the nucleus of the Jewish group may have come from an entirely different source, for indeed both the date of settlement and the place of provenance of Newport's first Jews remains shrouded in mystery, and in such a way as to suggest various connections with other radical religious groups there at that time.

Despite some suggestions that Newport's first Jews originated in places as various as New York[73], Amsterdam[74], and Brazil[75], the historian of the Jews of Newport has instead insisted that they came from Barbados, which as we have seen, was the Quaker stronghold in the New World during this period. This claim is supported in large measure by the names of the principal Jewish families who lived in Newport during the first years, compared with the names of known Barbadian Jews in the middle of the seventeenth century. Some individual Newport Jews are indeed sufficiently well-known for their paths to be traced between New England and Barbados.[76] Ezra Stiles noted in his diary in the eighteenth century that the Rev.

---

[71] *Ibid.*, p. 65; Jones, *Quakers*, pp. xv, 24-5, 53.

[72] M.A. Gutstein, *The Story of the Jews of Newport* (New York, 1936), pp. 25-8. Northern Brazil was under Dutch rule between 1630 and 1654. The Portuguese after their conquest of the area gave the Jews three months in which to leave: all left, the majority returning to Holland, others to the Caribbean and North America.

[73] *Ibid.*, p. 27.

[74] E. Peterson, *History of Rhode Island and Newport* (New York, 1853), p. 101. Cf. Gutstein, *Newport*, p. 340.

[75] M.J. Kohler, "The Jews in Newport", *Pub. Am. Jew. Hist. Soc.*, vi (1897), 61-8.

[76] Gutstein, *Newport*, pp. 340-2. For more on the Jews of Barbados, see W.S. Samuel, "A Review of the Jewish Colonists in Barbados in the Year 1680", *Trans. Jew. Hist. Soc. Eng.*, xiii (1932), 1-111; E.H. Shilstone, *Monumental Inscriptions in the Burial Ground of the Jewish Synagogue at Bridgetown, Barbados* (New York, 1956); J.R. Marcus, *The Colonial American Jew, 1492-1776* (Detroit, 1970), pp. 85-211; R. Cohen, "Early Caribbean Jewry: A Demograhic Perspective", *Jew. Soc. Stud.*, xlv (1982-3), 123-34; H. Friedenwald, "Material for the History of the Jews in the British West Indies", *Pub. Amer. Jew. Hist. Soc.*, v (1897), 45-101; N.D. Davis, "Notes on the History of the Jews in Barbados", *Pub. Amer. Jew. Hist. Soc.*, xviii (1909), 129-48; J. Poyer, *The History of Barbados* (London, 1808), which is also useful.

Isaac Touro of Newport showed him a Torah scroll over two hundred years old at the time, which was said to have been brought with the Jews when they arrived in New England.[77]

It seems likely, therefore, that the decision of a group of Barbadian Jews to emigrate to Newport may not have been based on that town's reputation for religious toleration alone, but rather on the news which they had had of the successful Quaker penetration into Puritan New England. For the connection between Jews and Quakers in the late 1650s was not grounded solely on their joint residence in Barbados. In these years following the Whitehall Conference of December 1655, called to discuss the question of Jewish readmission to England, contacts between Quakers and Jews in England and on the Continent had been increasing both in frequency and in importance, so that their common presence in Newport in the late 1650s and in the years before missionary Stephen Mumford's arrival there in 1665 must have sharpened an awareness of the validity of the Mosaic message.

The two or three years before the arrival of Quakers and Jews in Newport was in fact a period of intense contact between the two religions. The English Jews were only in the spring of 1656 making first tentative excursions into English life as they left their self-imposed Spanish and Portuguese Roman Catholic disguises, and the Quakers were anxious to make their acquaintance. As is well-known, Margaret Fell wrote two pamphlets addressed to the Jews during this time[78], and her husband George Fox wrote works persuading them to convert somewhat later.[79] Margaret Fell

---

[77] Ezra Stiles, *The Literary Diary*, ed. F.B. Dexter (New York, 1901), i. 11; G.A. Kohut, *Ezra Stiles and the Jews* (New York, 1922), p. 61. Gutstein writes that a particular scroll in his synagogue is usually identified with the one that Stiles saw: *Newport*, p. 343, with a picture of the scroll opp. p. 30.

[78] [Margaret Fell], *For Manasseth Ben Israel. The Call Of The Jewes out of Babylon* (London, 1656): dated 1655 by Thomason; *idem, A Loving Salutation To The . . . Jewes* (London, 1656): dated 1657 by Thomason. Her later works to the Jews are: *A Call to the Universal Seed of God* (London, 1664); *A Call unto the Seed of Israel* (London, 1668); and *The Daughter of Sion Awakened* (London, 1677). According to D. Carrington, "Quakers and Jews", *Jewish Chron. Spec. Supp.: Tercentenary of the Settlement of the Jews in the Brit. Isles 1656-1956* (27 Jan. 1956), p. 46, "One manuscript – extant in 1938 – entitled 'A Second Call unto the Seed of Israel and the Righteous Law of God justified' is apparently unpublished." There may be a reference to this MS in a letter of 7 Sept. 1657 from John Stubbs to Fell: "Thy book called the Second Call to the Seed of Israel was a while ago finished": Friends' House Lib., London, MS Abraham III, case 17. When Carrington writes that the pamphlet was extant in 1938 he probably refers to a citation in W.I. Hull, *The Rise of Quakerism in Amsterdam 1655-1665* (Swarthmore, 1938), p. 69. But more recently L.H. Hall, "Radical Puritans and Jews in England, 1648-1672" (Yale Univ. Ph.D. thesis 1979), pp. 101-3 has argued that Stubbs in his letter is probably referring either to Fell's *Loving Salutation* or to her *Call unto the Seed of Israel*.

[79] George Fox, *A Declaration to the Iews For them to Read Over* (London, 1661); *idem, An Epistle . . . To the Jews and Turks* (London, 1673); *idem, A Looking-Glass for the Jews* (Philadelphia, 1784).

was especially anxious to have her work translated into Hebrew, and corresponded with fellow Quakers Samuel Fisher and John Stubbs on this important matter.[80] William Caton wrote to Margaret Fell from Amsterdam in October 1656, reporting that the Jews there "are hungering for" her book, warning that "in one of their houses wee had three or four houres discourse with some of them, and a good principle in ye Conscience they owned in wordes, but they could scarce endure to here Christ mentioned". Generally speaking, from his experience "they are a high, lofty proud and Conceited people, farre from ye truth; yet there is A seed Among them, which god in the fullnesse of time will gather into his Garner."[81]

Caton wrote to Margaret Fell from Amsterdam again and reported that her book to the Jews had been translated, presumably into Dutch, in preparation for its translation into Hebrew.[82] That Dutch translation was done by William Ames, who himself wrote to Fell in April 1657 regarding the prospective translator of her work into Hebrew:

> theare is a Jew at amsterdam that by the Jews is cast out (as he himselfe and others sayeth) because he owneth no other teacher but the light and he sent for me and J spoke toe him and he was pretty tender and doth owne all that is spoken; and he sayde tow read of moses and the prophets without was nothing tow him except he Came toe know it within: and soe the name of Christ it is like he doth owne: J gave order that one of the duch Copyes of thy book should be giuen toe him and he sent me word he would Come toe oure meeting but in the mean time J was Imprisoned.[83]

Caton confirmed "that there are some Among them that would willingly become Christians, but that they fear intollerable persecution, and that especially from their brethren".[84] Pending the translation of Fell's pamphlet

---

[80] Fell to Samuel Fisher, Mar. 1656: Frs. Hse. Lib., MS Spence III, p. 37, asking him to have her book to Menasseh translated into Hebrew. See also Fell to John Stubbs, undated (1656?): Frs. Hse. Lib., MS Spence III, pp. 38-40, but note that the dating of this letter is problematic: see (and generally) Hall, "Radical Puritans", pp. 91, 105n. See also I. Ross, *Margaret Fell: Mother of Quakerism* (London, 1949), pp. 90-1.

[81] Caton to Fell, 29 Oct. 1656: Frs. Hse. Lib., MS Caton III, 25. Cf. Ross, *Fell*, p. 91 and Hull, *Rise*, pp. 117-18. The Caton MSS are a collection of over 160 letters written to Margaret Fell, copied out by Caton in 1659. The collection was lost for many years and only found once again in 1935, and is now in the Friends' House Library, London: Ross, *Fell*, p. 91.

[82] Caton to Fell, undated: Frs. Hse. Lib., MS Caton III, p. 13 [Hall gives this ref. as vol. S 81, p. 84]. Cf. Ross, *Fell*, pp. 91-2. Presumably the pamphlet under discussion was Fell's address to Menasseh, which was translated into Dutch by William Ames, according to William Sewel, *The History of the . . . Quakers* (London, 1722), ii. 624. The book appeared as *en Manasse ben Israël, Den roep der Joden uyt Babylonien* (n.p., 1657), 4°, 16 pp.: Hull, *Rise*, p. 205.

[83] Ames to Fell, 17 Apr. 1657, from Utrecht: Frs. Hse. Lib., MS Swarthmore 4/28^r (Transcr. i. 71-4); cf. Hull, *Rise*, p. 205.

[84] Caton to Fell, 5 June 1657: Frs. Hse. Lib., MS Caton III, p. 35; cf. Hull, *Rise*, p. 118; Ross, *Fell*, pp. 95-6.

into Hebrew, Caton also had "seuen or eight score of them deliuered to them at their synagouge, some to the Rabbyes, and some to the Doctors".[85] In November, Caton could write to Fell reporting "that J haue bene with A Jew and have shewed him thy booke, & haue asked him what Languadge would bee the fittest for them hee told mee porteegees or Hebrew, for if it were in Hebrew they might understand it at Jerusalem or in almost any other place of the world". Most importantly, "he hath undertaken to translate it for us, he being expert in seuerall Languadges."[86]

At some point during this period a decision seems to have been made not only to have the Jew translate Fell's *Loving Salutation*, but also to have him relieve Samuel Fisher, whose attempt to translate her book to Menasseh ben Israel into Hebrew seems to have failed. "Some moueinges there is in him towardes the jewes," it was reported of Fisher from his home in Kent, "which will bee fulfilled in the Lordes time".[87] Clearly the translation of Fell's pamphlet could not be delayed that long. It may also be that Menasseh's death in September 1657 gave that book an untimely association. By March 1658, Caton was writing to Margaret Fell as if the Jew had taken on both translations:

> As touching thy booke (titulated A Loving Salutation), I have gotten it once translated in Duch, because the Jew that is to translate it into Hebrew, could not translate it out of English; He hath it now, and is translating of it, like he hath done the other, which Samuel Fisher and John Stubbs have taken along with them: the Jews that translates it, remaines very friendly in his way

Caton also reported that

> Sam. Fisher was in their Synagogue at Amsterdam and among them at Roterdam; they were pretty moderate towards him: (I meane they did not abuse him) but assented to much of that which he spoke: he had some discourse with two or three of their Doctors in private at Amsterdam, and they seemed to owne in words the substance of that which he declared: but they were in bondage as people of other formes are.[88]

---

[85] Same to same, 26 June 1657: Frs. Hse. Lib., MS Caton III, p. 38: cf. Hull, *Rise*, p. 118.

[86] Same to same, 18 Nov. 1657, from Amsterdam: Frs. Hse. Lib., MS Caton III, p. 48: cf. Hull, *Rise*, p. 118; Ross, *Fell*, p. 94.

[87] Stubbs to Fell, 7 Sept. 1657: Frs. Hse. Lib., MS Abraham III, case 17: Stubbs reported that her books to the Jews had already been translated into Latin. As for Fisher, he was very excited about his forthcoming voyage to Amsterdam where he felt he had a mission to seek out the Jews: see also Ross, *Fell*, p. 91; & Hall, "Radical Puritans", pp. 101-3, which deals with some of the intricacies of the letter. See also William Dewsbury to Fell, 2 July 1657, from West Brabing, Kent: Frs. Hse. Lib., MS Caton vol S 81, p. 492: cf. Hall, "Radical Puritans", p. 101.

[88] Caton to Fell, 15 Mar. 1657-8, from Leiden: Frs. Hse. Lib., MS Caton III, p. 507: cf. Ross, *Fell*, p. 94.

The translation of Fell's *Loving Salutation* was completed within two months, for in May 1658 William Caton wrote that he "gott them from the presse and the same day that J came from thence J gott about 170 of them dispersed Among the Jewes who willingly & greedyly receiued them, (they being in the Hebrew tongue) J purpossed to haue brought halfe A hundred of them with mee to England but J disposed of them in Zealand their being seuerall Jewes."[89] In October, Ames would be writing to George Fox reporting that he had gotten his book translated into Dutch as well, "because he who is toe translate it into Hebrew cannot understand english, and I have spoke with one who hath been a Jew toe translate it intoe Hebrew". Ames was writing to Fox to suggest that he consider having the book translated into Yiddish instead, "since I have understood that the Common people of the Jewes cannot speak Hebrew".[90]

There has been much speculation over the years as to the identity of the anonymous Jewish translator of Margaret Fell's work.[91] As of April 1657,

---

[89] Caton to Fell, 21 May 1658: Frs. Hse. Lib., MS Caton, p. 50 (rev. num.): cf. Ross, *Fell*, pp. 94-5 and Hull, *Rise*, p. 119. A copy of Fell's *Loving Salutation* in Hebrew, *Sha'alat Shalom B'Ahavah*, is in the Frs. Hse. Lib., Tracts vol. 133, 38. The translation is followed by a letter in Hebrew by Samuel Fisher "to all the House of Jacob at all corners of the earth", Tract 38a. See also Tracts 53, 22.

[90] Ames to Fox, 14 Oct. 1658: Frs. Hse. Lib., MS Barclay. In about 1660, John Stubbs would suggest to Fox that Margaret Fell's book to the Jews be "printed againe with another Character by a Great Teacher Among the jewes wh[ch] is come forth of Poland. he comes to meetings he writes himself, Samuel, Levi ben Asshur, a Jewish rabbi etc. he wants Employment, and is very poore, he is very perfect in the Hebrew he reads the Syriack Testament without pricks, as readily I thinke as I doe English.": Frs. Hse. Lib., MS Crosfield 7: cf. Carrington, "Quakers", p. 46; Ross, *Fell*, p. 96; Hall, "Radical Jews", p. 147. This was done: a 3rd edn of the *Loving Salutation* appeared in London in 1660, with parallel Hebrew and English columns, printed back to front. In the same letter, Stubbs writes concerning Fox's recently published *Battle-Door* (London, 1660), and notes that

> I have felt something of getting thy Book to the jewes printed in Hebrew if Samuel has as much time, I believe it will ly upon him, Ben Furley if he could doe it as well as any I knowe There is an ould man talkes of foure pounds for doing it

A later hand has added the date 1664 on the back of this letter, but H.J. Cadbury, "Hebraica and the Jews in Early Quaker Interest" in *Children of Light*, ed. H.H. Brinton (New York, 1938), pp. 135-63 has argued for 1660-61.

[91] That this translator was Spinoza was asserted by H.G. Crosfield, *Margaret Fox of Swarthmoor* (London, 1913), p. 50n.; Hull, *Rise*, p. 205; Ross, *Fell*, p. 94; Carrington, "Quakers", p. 46; H.J. Cadbury, "Spinoza and a Quaker Document of 1657", *Med. & Ren. Stud.*, (1943), 130-3; idem, ed., *The Swarthmore Documents in America* (London, 1940), p. 7; L. Feuer, *Spinoza and the Rise of Liberalism* (Boston, 1958), p. 49; L. Roth, "Hebraists and Non-Hebraists of the Seventeenth Century", *Jnl. Sem. Stud.*, vi (1961), 211; J. Van Den Berg, "Quaker and Chiliast: The Contrary Thoughts of William Ames and Petrus Serrarius", in *Reformation, Conformity and Dissent: Essays in Honour of Geoffrey Nuttall*, ed. R. Buick Knox (London, 1977), pp. 182-3. Most recently, Prof. R.H. Popkin has re-examined all of the available evidence concerning Spinoza's Quaker connections and has placed it in the con-

when Ames wrote his letter to Fell, there were four Jews who had been excommunicated from the synagogue in Amsterdam, or accused of heretical
beliefs. Of these four, only the famous philosopher Benedict Spinoza, excommunicated on 27 July 1656, could have been Ames's "Jew at amsterdam that by the Jews is cast out".[92] Spinoza seems to have been introduced
to William Ames by Peter Serrarius, that professional millenarian and
tireless intermediary.[93] That Spinoza was in contact and in sympathy with
the Quakers during this period seems fairly certain, and it may be that his
claim that there is "no other teacher but the light" may have led him to
recognize similar beliefs among the English Quakers in Amsterdam. The
attraction was strong enough for Spinoza himself to have sent for Ames,
as was reported in the Quaker's letter of April 1657.[94] Spinoza continued
his contacts with Englishmen, even after his Quaker period ended about
1658. In 1661, Henry Oldenburg, later secretary of the Royal Society,
sought him out in his village of Rynsburg.[95] Four years later, Oldenburg
would wrote to Spinoza asking for more information regarding the activities of Shabtai Sevi, the Jewish false messiah whose appearance threw
European Jewry into a turmoil of indecision.[96]

The Quaker connection with the Jews in the years before the settlement
of both Jews and Quakers in Newport was thus far deeper than mere casu-
al co-residence on a small Caribbean island under English control. Not
only were the Quakers actively courting the Jews in England and on the
Continent, but they actually engaged as translator a man who might de-

---

text of the work of Serrarius and other millenarians of the period: see his "Spinoza, the
Quakers and the Millenarians, 1656-1658", *Manuscrito*, vi (1982), 113-33; *idem*, "Spinoza's
Relations with the Quakers in Amsterdam", *Quaker History*, lxxiii (1984), 14-28; *idem*,
"Spinoza and Samuel Fisher", *Philosophia*, xv (1985), 219-36; *idem*, & M.A. Singer, eds., *Spi-
noza's Earliest Publication?* (Assen, 1987).

[92] The other three were Uriel da Costa (d. 1640), Juan de Prado (excom. 4 Feb. 1658,
although expelled the previous May); and Daniel Ribera (who was still employed by the
Jewish community on 14 Feb. 1657, and was still making contributions on 21 Sept. 1657):
I.S. Revah, *Spinoza et Juan Prado* (The Hague, 1959), pp. 23-5, 28, 29-30; *idem*, "Aux
Origines de la rupture spinozienne: Nouveaux documents sur l'incroyance dans la com-
munauté Judeo-Portugaise d'Amsterdam à l'époque de l'excommunication de Spinoza",
Rev. Etud. Juives, 4th ser., cxxiii (1964), 359-431, esp. pp. 371-3.

[93] According to Van Den Berg, p. 183. See E.G.E. Van der Wall, *De mystieke Chiliast Petrus
Serrarius (1600-1669) en zijn wereld* (Leiden, 1987). An English translation of this work is in
preparation.

[94] See text of letter above, p. 157.

[95] Oldenburg to Spinoza, 16 Aug. 1661: *Correspondence of Henry Oldenburg*, ed. A.R. & M.B.
Hall (Madison, etc., 1965-   ), 414-15; this is the first letter from Oldenburg to Spinoza,
which begins, "So reluctantly did I tear myself away from your side recently when I was
with you in your retreat at Rhynsburg".

[96] Same to same, 8 Dec. 1665: *ibid.*, ii. 633-7; *Correspondence of Spinoza*, ed. A. Wolf (London, 1928), pp. 214-17. Spinoza's reply to this letter of Oldenburg's, if there was one, is
now lost.

servedly be called one of the greatest Jews who ever lived. The Quakers arrived in Newport from Barbados at the height of the negotiations with Spinoza over the translation of Margaret Fell's book, in precisely the period that the Quakers were anxious to spread their message among the Jews. The Jews came to Newport from Barbados the following year.

Or so it would appear. But the determination of the exact arrival of Jews in Newport is fraught with difficulties even greater than comprehending their relations with the Quakers during this period. We know without question that by 1677 the Jews in Newport had organized a formal community, for in that year two of their number purchased a plot of land about thirty feet in length for use as a cemetery.[97] Certainly they must have been resident in the town long before this. And indeed a further document exists which may demonstrate the presence of Jews in Newport twenty years earlier:

> Th^s y^e [day and month obliterated] 165[6 or 8, not certain which, as the place was stained and broken; the first three figures were plain] W^{ee} mett att y House off Mordecai Campunall and affter Synagog W^{ee} gave Ab^m Moses the degrees of Maconrie

The original document itself now appears to be lost, or at least hidden. N.H. Gould of Newport, sometime Master of St John's Lodge, Newport and then member of the Grand Lodge of Rhode Island, holder of the 33rd Masonic degree, found the document in 1839 (when he was not yet a Mason) among some old papers in a chest which had belonged to a deceased relative, who was a great-great-grand-daughter of John Wanton, the governor of Rhode Island, 1734-40. When the Grand Lodge of Massachusetts requested in 1870 to see the document, Gould refused to show it, but gave the text which was printed in the Lodge's *Proceedings* for that year.[98] Two years later, however, the Rev. Jacques Judah Lyons seems to have been allowed to see the document, although the text as he copied it is somewhat different, while retaining the essential information and the date 1658.[99]

---

[97] Cemetery deed printed in Gutstein, *Newport*, pp. 37-8; facsimile copy in *Pubs. Amer. Jew. Hist. Soc.*, xxvii (1920), betw. pp. 174-5. The original deed is now lost: the existing copy was made in 1767 by the town clerk of Newport, William Coddington. The volume recording land evidences in Newport during the seventeenth century is also lost, so the copy is the only remaining proof of the establishment of a Jewish burial ground there.

[98] Gutstein, *Newport*, pp. 31, 343-4; S. Oppenheim, "The Jews and Masonry in the United States before 1810", *Pubs. Amer. Jew. Hist. Soc.*, xix (1910), 3-17.

[99] Gutstein, *Newport*, pp. 343-4; J.J. Lyons, "Items Relating to Masonry in Newport", *Pubs. Amer. Jew. Hist. Soc.*, xxvii (1920), 416. Lyons quoted the document as follows:

A good claim for the authenticity of this document can easily be made. Samuel Oppenheim, in his article on the early connections between Jews and Masons in the United States, suggested that the author of the text was Moses Pacheco, one of the grantees in the cemetery deed. Oppenheim notes that the administration on the estate of Moses Pacheco was granted in 1688 to Caleb Carr, whose son's widow was the sister-in-law of John Wanton, the eighteenth-century governor of Rhode Island who seems to be the link between Gould and the seventeenth-century Jews and Masons of Newport.[100] Caleb Carr was himself a governor of Rhode Island in the seventeenth century, and Pacheco is mentioned in his will.[101] Indeed, the cemetery deed itself was found in the same group of papers by N.H. Gould, whose son, at the suggestion of Samuel Oppenheim, presented the document to the American Jewish Historical Society at the beginning of this century.[102]

As might be expected, this Masonic document has placed both historians of Freemasonry and of American Jewry in an unenviable position. The early period of Freemasonry is still shrouded in mystery, as guilds of "operative" masons evolved into clubs of "speculative" ones made up of men unassociated with the building trade.[103] Between Sir Robert Moray's admission to a lodge in Edinburgh in the 1630s, or even since Elias Ashmole's joining of a lodge at Warrington, Lancashire in 1646, and the formal establishment of the Grand Lodge of London in 1717, we find a very badly documented era of Masonic history.[104] Yet instead of jumping at a credible piece of evidence of the existence of speculative Freemasonry in the New World as early as 1656 or 1658, long before the formal establish-

---

On ye 5th day of ye 9th month 1658, ye 2nd Tisri A.M. 5518, we assembled at ye house of Mordecaiah Campanall and gave a degree to Abraham Moses'.

Lyons noted that it was unlikely that such a ceremony would take place on the second day of the Jewish New Year, and if it did take place in the evening it would have already been the 3rd of Tisri. It might also have been objected that the year 5518 in Christian usage is 1758, and in that year no one named Mordecai Campanall lived in Newport, and by then the Masons were well-developed and met in the lodge, not in private houses.

[100] Oppenheim, "Jews and Masonry", pp. 17-18, noting that a copy of the record is on file at the Amer. Jew. Hist. Soc., a transcript from the Superior Court of Rhode Island, Book A, p. 97.

[101] Ibid., pp. 17-18.

[102] Ibid., p. 14.

[103] See M.C. Jacob, The Radical Enlightenment: Pantheists, Freemasons and Republicans (London, 1981), who writes on p. 109 that there "is simply no adequate account, in English, of the origins of European Freemasonry."

[104] Elias Ashmole, ed. C.H. Josten (Oxford, 1966), ii. 395-6: entry for 16 Oct. 1646; D.C. Martin, "Sir Robert Moray", in The Royal Society, ed. H. Hartley (London, 1960), p. 246; The Lodges of Edinburgh (Mary's Chapel), No. 1, 1599-1949 (Edinburgh, 1949), p. 8. When Moray became a Mason he was general quartermaster to the Scottish army and in the service of Charles I. Both Moray and Ashmole, then, were dedicated Royalists.

ment of Masonic lodges there, Masonic historians have instead chosen to ignore the possibility, no doubt reluctant to claim Jews as the first known Masons in America. Such early connections between Jews and Masons would hardly be surprising, given the strong kabbalistical, magical, and Hermetical associations of the movement in the seventeenth century, and the many later Jews who became Freemasons.[105]

So too do Jewish historians shy away from accepting this Masonic document, no doubt because of an unwillingness to confirm that the first Jews in English America were Freemasons. On the other hand, the temptation of finding such early evidence of Jewish residence in New England has been too strong to resist, and one finds Morris Gutstein, the historian of Newport's Jews, falling back on the argument that ''all authorities on the subject agree that 1658 is the date the Jews first came to the shores of Rhode Island as a group''.[106] Even Samuel Oppenheim, who believed that the document was genuine, ultimately relies on the fact that ''families long resident in that town, whose ancestors were in the colony from almost its foundation, and in a position to give them correct information regarding the date of the first arrival of the Jews there, fix the date as 1657 or 1658.'' Oppenheim goes on to say that the ''general trend of knowledge on the subject of the early settlement of the Jews in the United States goes to confirm that date'' even though Oppenheim admits that ''contemporary record proof is lacking aside from the document quoted by Gould and the information derived from the cemetery deed just referred to, and also the date in Gould's possession, upon which he based his statements regarding the early arrivals.''[107] In Oppenheim's view, this ''lack of contemporary proof arises from the loss of many of the records of Newport and the colony prior to 1700.''[108]

---

[105] Jacob, *Enlightenment*, cap. 4, ''The Origins of European Freemasonry''; I. Finestein, ''The Jews in Regular English Freemasonry'', *Trans. Jew. Hist. Soc. Soc. Eng.*, xxv (1977), 150-209.

[106] Gutstein, *Newport*, p. 344.

[107] *Ibid*. See also C.S. Brigham, ''Report on the Archives of Rhode Island'', *Annual Report of the Amer. Hist. Assoc., 1903*, i (1904), 605-6, where he notes that the records from the pre-revolutionary period are in a bad state because the British carried them away in 1779 in a boat which later sank. The records remained under water for several days until the governor complained to General Washington, who had them recovered and placed in a store in New York, where they were lost for a time and finally returned at the request of Newport town council in 1782.

[108] Oppenheim, ''Jews and Masonry'', p. 15. Others who accept 1658 as the date of the first Jewish arrivals in Newport include C. Bridenbaugh, *Cities in the Wilderness* (2nd edn, New York, 1960), pp. 94, 104; *idem, Fat Mutton*, p. 63n.; Kohler, ''Newport'', pp. 61-80; S.F. Chyet, ''A Synagogue in Newport'', *Amer. Jew. Arch.*, xvi (1964), 41-50. See also L. Hühner, ''The Jews of New England (Other than Rhode Island) Prior to 1800'', *Pub. Amer. Jew. Hist. Soc.*, xi (1903), 75-99; J.R. Marcus, ''Light on Early Connecticut Jewry'', *Amer. Jew. Arch.*, i (1948-9), 3-52.

Unquestionably, then, with such a menagerie of heterodox religious faiths, Rhode Island in general, and Newport in particular, deserved its reputation as being "like materia prima susceptive of all formes."[109] But like *materia prima* what was required was a significant amount of shaping and moulding to give the final result some recognizable form. It appears, then, that the Quakers came to Newport from Barbados as part of their plan for general expansion in New England, and that the Jews of that island followed because they had heard from their Quaker admirers of the possibility of religious freedom there. Once in Newport, the Jews may have made some formal compact with Freemasonry, which in essence was not a Christian movement like Quakerism, but was a mystical and even kabbalistical club with similar interests and fields of inquiry. In any case, what is undoubtedly clear is that by the time Stephen Mumford came to Newport in 1665, the religious atmosphere of the town was far more eccentric than would appear from the staid correspondence of Samuel Hubbard. The Quakers, Jews, and Freemasons of that small community provided at least passive support for the establishment of a Saturday-Sabbatarian strand of worship, not only by their very heterodox existence, but also by their common emphasis on the Mosaic law, the Hebrew language, and the mystical tradition.

Other connections between these groups in the later years also deserve investigation. The split between the Saturday- and Sunday-Baptists in 1671 was followed shortly thereafter by a visit from George Fox himself to Rhode Island between the end of May and July 1672. Carl Bridenbaugh notes that "this dynamic leader left the Quakers of New England not just a tightly knit organization for divine worship and charitable enterprise but one in close communication with the Friends of Barbados, Ireland, and England."[110] It may be that Fox was encouraged to make his pilgrimage to Newport by the possibility of winning over Jews and Saturday-Sabbatarians to the Quaker message. In any case, the government of the colony between 1672 and 1677, as we have seen, was controlled by the Quakers, and in that final year the Jews obtained permission to establish a burial ground, surely an enduring and public symbol of their acceptance into the community. "Most of the people had never heard Friends before;" George Fox wrote in his journal, "but they were mightily affected with the meeting, and there is a great desire amongst them after the Truth."[111]

---

[109] See above, n. 1.

[110] Bridenbaugh, *Fat Mutton*, p. 68. See also Jones, *Quakers*, pp. 111-15: Fox sailed from England on 12 Aug. 1671 and landed at Barbados on 3 Oct. He later went to Jamaica, then Maryland, and finally from there made his way overland to Newport, arriving on 30 May 1672.

[111] Bodl. Lib., Add. MS A 95: MS journal of Fox's American travels. The quotation

IV

The years after the separation of the Seventh-Day Baptists in Newport were difficult ones for men of that persuasion on both sides of the Atlantic. On 9 April 1671, even before Hubbard and the others left the church, Edward Stennett wrote to them from Wallingford. "Things look here with a bad face," he lamented, "thick clouds & darkness is upon us in many places; the saints are much spoiled in their estates for meeting together to worship the Lord & we are in jeopardy every hour: pray earnestly y^t we may hold out thro' this storm."[112] The church at Bell Lane wrote in a similarly pessimistic tone to Newport the following year, reporting that "we have been under some exercises more than ordinary from the hands of men; most of the brotherhood of the congregation having been put in prison for some time; and tho' not now in hold, yet stand prisoners, & we know not what the issue will be."[113] But Hubbard had little to offer them in his reply: "Dear breth^n", he wrote, "pray for us, a poor weak band in a wilderness beset round with opposites, from the com^n adversary, & from quakers, generals & prophane persons & most of all from such as have been our familiar acquaintance; but our battles are only in words; praised be God."[114] It would appear from Hubbard's remarks that George Fox's recent mission had been only too successful.

It was about this time that Roger Williams himself decided to make a somewhat official response to the great events in Newport. At some point in the autumn of 1672 he wrote directly to Samuel Hubbard, ostensibly a letter of condolence for the death of Hubbard's son at the end of the previous year. "You are now unwilling, I judge, that I deal plainly and friendly with you", he wrote, but

> After all that I have seen and read and compared about the seventh day (and I have earnestly and carefully read and weighed all I could come at in God's holy presence) I cannot be removed from Calvin's mind, and indeed Paul's mind, Col. ii. that all those sabbaths of seven days were figures, types and shadows, and forerunners of the Son of God, and that the change is made from the remembrance of the first creation, and that (figurative) rest on the seventh day, to the remembrance of the second creation on the first, on which our Lord arose conqueror from the dead. Accordingly, I have read many, but see no satisfying answer to those three Scriptures, chiefly Acts 20, I Cor. 16, Rev. 1, in conscience to which I make some poor conscience to God as to the rest day.

---

above is from his *Journal*, ed. N. Penney (Cambridge, 1911), ii. 171, and Jones, *Quakers*, p. 114. The particular meeting referred to above took place on 13 July 1672.

[112] Stennett to Newport, 9 Apr. 1671: Hubbard MSS, p. 89.
[113] Bell Lane to Newport, 24 Mar. 1672: *ibid.*
[114] Hubbard to Bell Lane, 6 Oct. 1672: *ibid.*, pp. 89-90.

Williams then passed on to other topics, noting his famous "four days' agitation between the Quakers and myself" which opened on 9 August 1672. He also asked Hubbard to send his regards to Obadiah Holmes, John Clarke, William Hiscox, Stephen Mumford and others.[115] Such a personal appeal from the colony's founder must have made a profound impression on Hubbard and his fellow Seventh-Day men, but they had searched the Scriptures and had come to radically different views.

So too was Hubbard and his group put under pressure from the Baptist church in Boston, where word had reached them that the Sabbatarian backsliders had been accused by Hubbard and others of apostasy. Thomas Goold, William Turner, and John Williams in the name of the church wrote to William Hiscox, now apparently serving as pastor of the Sabbatarian congregation, noting that they "cannot but be grieved to see how busy the adversary hath been, and how easily he hath prevailed upon the corruptions of our nature, to make breaches and divisions among them whom we dare not but judge, are united into one head, even Christ Jesus." The church in Boston asked Hiscox and the others to withdraw their extreme accusation of apostasy as being conducive to further dispute. "And we, as brethren," they wrote, "made portakers of the same grace of God through the influence of his holy spirit, not being enlightened in the observation of the seventh day as a sabbath to the Lord, shall humbly beseech you all, to put on bowels of mercy, and not be so strait in your spirits towards others". Nevertheless, this their letter should not be misunderstood as a gesture of support: "Now brethren," they wrote, "we dare not justify your action, nor the manner of the actions that have been between you and the church", but they would have preferred to see the debate carried on in a different spirit. Indeed, they asked, "may we not say, we are all in the dark, and see and know but in part?" Their deepest hope was that "it may be the good pleasure of God, that this breach may be healed between you and the church."[116]

But even in Boston it must have been clear that the breach between the Saturday- and Sunday-Sabbatarians was permanent. In England, meanwhile, the lot of the Seventh-Day men was much improved since the dark days of the mass arrests. In 1672, on the eve of the Third Dutch War, Charles II suspended the penal laws against non-conformists and recusants, and Edward Stennett wrote from Wallingford on 15 July 1674 that the "little flock over wch I watch thro' the grace of God are generally well

---

[115] Williams to Hubbard, n.d.: *Letters of Roger Williams, 1632-1682*, ed. J.R. Bartlett (Pubs. Narragansett Club, 1st ser., vi, 1874), pp. 361-2. For more on Williams's debate with the Quakers, see Jones, *Quakers*, pp. 116-18.

[116] Gould, Turner, & Williams, "Church assembled", Noddle's Island, 1 Sept. 1672: Backus, *History*, i. 411-13.

& our number hath increased. Since I last writ to you, nine have been added and more baptized; the Lord is at worke here, I hope upon many more so that instead of fathers we shall have children".[117] A similarly encouraging letter arrived in Newport from Bell Lane the following month, also cautioning them about a certain Isaac Wills who had been an officer with Tillam at Colchester years before, of whom they had had bad reports, as yet unconfirmed. The Seventh-Day men always had to be wary of any association with the scandal of the False Jew which haunted them unceasingly. In Newport as well as in London, they wrote, it "concerns y° to be careful for there are many eyes upon you as upon us, & we have been reproach[d] by some men of bad practices, & truth have suffered much thereby".[118]

Joseph Davis, now in London, also wrote to Newport at the same time, expressing a similar note of optimism. "I cant but let y° know in w[t] manner I was released out of my long captivity", he wrote,

> When all lawful means was used by many of my friends & to no purpose, & I was quite taken off looking unto men, or means y[t] hath depend[ance] thereupon, the king sent & loosed us all generally in the several prisons, & the ruler of the people let us go free without any engagement. I can say it was a wonderful and seasonable mercy to me

Davis related that "the churches in London have as much liberty without opposition as can be desired in their public meetings & there is no hinderance in the professing holiness". In England generally, what was apparent was that "by reason of sin, in many desolating judgments, plague, fire, storm & unseasonable weather, & likewise what the men caterpillars have devoured, y[t] poverty is generally coming upon people like an armed man." In foreign affairs, the "Island hath been lifted up against Holland in the late wars between us, & yet is continued by the French against them." Most interestingly, Davis like Bell Lane also thought it cautionary to inform Newport of Thomas Tillam's activities on the Continent:

> I shall acquaint y° w[t] is come of mr. Tillam. I hear he died in Germany; a very great blemish to the truth he was, I fear he went out as a snuff. The holy sabbath hath been the more slighted by such that have lived out of the power; but I comfortably hope that the Lord will bring forth a sanctified remnant, y[t] shall be his praise in the nations, by being men & women of other spirits, following him fully[119]

---

[117] Stennett to Newport, 15 July 1674: Hubbard MSS, pp. 95-6.
[118] Clie Willyams, John Jones, Hugh Heslepp, Rob. Woodward, Francis Walter, Richard Farnham, Rob. Hopkins, John Laboure to Newport, 17 Aug. 1674: *ibid.*, pp. 96-7.
[119] Davis to Newport, 5 Aug. 1674: *ibid.*, pp. 97-100.

Perhaps it was this radical change in religious climate that inspired Stephen Mumford to visit his mother country at the beginning of 1675. After a difficult journey, Mumford arrived safely in London, to the homecoming of an extraordinarily successful missionary,

> where I was rec^d of ye brethren in wth much joy in some of them who had a great desire to hear of our place & people. Some of them talk of coming with me. The first sabbath I was wth them I heard mr. Bamfield a Dorsetshire man, who now lives in London, who for his holiness of conversation and soundness of doctrine is renowned throughout the city. The last sabth I was at mr. Sellers [Mill Yard] meeting, who are a thriving hopeful people. Br. Davis lives in London & walks wth them

On balance, Mumford could report that the "br^n here are generally well: the meetings of all separates very great and numerous, but daily expecting another scourge". Mumford was concerned that "they have begun to disturb some meetings already: several imprisoned at Bristol."[120] At any rate, Mumford's prediction of Sabbatarian emigration to Newport came to pass, for several months later the congregation at Bell Lane sent a letter of reference to Newport on behalf of William Gibson and his wife, who were "in full com^n wth us & so walked wth us many years".[121]

The Gibsons must have arrived in Newport just in time to witness that catastrophic clash between the colonists and the Indians of New England which became known as King Philip's War, named after the leader of the Indian side. Philip, the son of a *sachem* friendly to the colonists, became chief of the Wampanoag tribe which had been pushed back from Rhode Island. When charges were brought against him for revengeful conspiracy against the colonists, the accuser himself was killed, and three Indians were tried and executed on 8 June 1675. Twelve days later, Philip attacked the frontier town of Swansea, over the border in Plymouth Colony, and on 28 June troops from Plymouth and Boston retaliated by attempting to destroy the Indian stronghold on Mount Hope. The result was a full-scale Indian war, of much greater proportions than the Pequot rising forty years before. King Philip's War continued until August 1676 when Philip himself was captured and killed, and his wife and young son sold into captivity in the West Indies. When the reckoning was made, it was found that one out of every sixteen men of military age was killed, and twelve towns were completely destroyed, with about half of the towns in New England suffering some damage.[122]

---

[120] Mumford to Newport, 14 Mar. 1674-5: *ibid.*, pp. 102-3.

[121] Bell Lane to Newport, 29 May 1675: *ibid.*, p. 107. Gibson also brought two children with him: *ibid.*, pp. 106-7. William Gibson was the second pastor, who took office after the death of William Hiscox in 1704 and continued until his own death on 12 Mar. 1717, aged 79: Backus, *History*, ii. 234.

[122] See generally, D.E. Leach, *Flintlock and Tomahawk: New England in King Philip's War* (New York, 1966).

The Saturday-Sabbath had meanwhile spread to some of the more distant villages which felt themselves to be particularly vulnerable to the Indian threat. As we shall see, the fanning out of the Seventh-Day gospel from Newport made possible the growth of Adventism a century and a half later. One of these towns was New London, Connecticut. Samuel Hubbard's daughter Ruth Burdick had informed him as early as 12 February 1674-5 from Westerley that their minister, John Crandall, and the Lord "hath been at work, as we believe, in ye hearts of some of the inhabitants of New London, & bowing their hearts to be obedient to the Ld Jesus". She gave the names of the new Saturday-Sabbatarians as John Rogers, James Rogers his brother, "& ye 3^d an Indian whose name is Japeth; who gave a very satisfactory acct of ye work of grace whrought upon his heart." When the news reached him, "Mr. Bradstreet the minister of the place being inraged threatened them warning 'em not to speak to any of his church, railing ag^t us all".[123] Samuel Hubbard, William Hiscox, and Joseph Clarke themselves came out to New London in March to receive the new believers into the fold.[124] John Rogers in less than two months found himself in Hartford prison for his views, where he was accused of "many criminal things" by his wife and his father-in-law. He seems to have been freed by the end of the year, for on 22 December 1675 John Rogers wrote to Samuel Hubbard from New London, reporting that we

> do not forbear work on the first day of the week, y^t it sho^d come to a trial the 7th day sabbath may be pleaded for in the audience of the people for ye com^n people are afraid to talk wth us for fear of being tainted wth heresy. The times are so troublesome that there is no passing: we should be glad to see you: but the times being so bad we tho^t it not safe ventring.[125]

Samuel Hubbard followed the events at New London with keen interest and encouraged them to remember that it was "not strange if we or you sho^d meet wth fiery trials as others have." He recounted some more recent trials such as in Westerley, and concluded with a request to "remember my true love to brother Japheth, the first of N.E. Indians: encourage him in the Lord."[126] Hubbard still had hope for the christianizing of the Indians, even at a time when the New England tribes had united in a war of destruction against the Europeans.

But by this time matters had moved forward in New London, and the entire Rogers family was already imprisoned. They were charged with vio-

[123] Ruth Burdick to Hubbard, 23 Feb. 1674-5: Hubbard MSS, pp. 91-5.
[124] Hubbard to his cousin Brooks at Boston, 7 May 1675: *ibid.*, pp. 101-2; Hubbard to Henry Reeve, 1 Nov. 1675: *ibid.*, pp. 105-6.
[125] Rogers to Hubbard, 22 Dec. 1675: *ibid.*, pp. 107-9.
[126] Hubbard to New London, 16 Jan. 1675-6: *ibid.*, pp. 109-11.

lating the Sabbath by labouring on Sunday; their defence was that the law of the colony merely prohibited Sabbath labour but did not specify which day of the week was intended. James, John, Jonathan and James Rogers, Jr., wrote to the town court at New London explaining their point of view, reminding them that "the first table doth teach us our duty to God" and on those Commandments their conduct was based, "Jesus Christ being the chief corner stone." They also demanded to see the warrant of imprisonment against them, and finding it defective, while observing that "the prison door hung open we went out, seeing they had neither warrant nor mitinus; and so we went about our occasions the next day wch was ye 1st day of ye week."[127]

Despite the disruptions of the Indian wars, the connection with the Seventh-Day churches in England was not forgotten. William Saller wrote to Samuel Hubbard in May 1676, as did the entire church at Bell Lane the same month, followed by another letter from Fenchurch Street the following year.[128] Samuel Hubbard's letter to Edward Stennett in England, sent in November 1676, describes the travails of the colonists during King Philip's War, in part, he thought, due to their own poor behaviour towards the Indians in previous years. At the beginning of the troubles, he wrote, he and Joseph Torrey of John Clarke's Baptist church jointly sent over a boat to Westerley and brought back their families, including Hubbard's two daughters and their children: "all came, and Bro. John Crandall and his family, with as many others as could possibly come. My son[-in-law] Clarke came afterwards, before winter, and my other daughter's husband came in the spring, and they all have been at my house to this day."[129]

After the end of King Philip's War, the Rogers family became active again with their aggressive challenge to the religious establishment of New London, Connecticut. By May 1678 they were in prison yet again, although Jonathan Rogers had by then left their society. The cause, Joseph Clarke understood, "is because he doth not retain their judgm^t of the unlawfulness of using medicens, & not accusing himself before ye authority for working on ye first day". Thus it appears that the refusal to seek medical help outside the Lord's goodness was already a tenet of Rogers and his group, the principle that would make the sect, which would later

---

[127] John Rogers to Hiscox and his church at Newport, 21 Sept. 1676. The letter to the court at New London is dated the following day: *ibid.*, pp. 111-15. Backus writes that Hiscox and Hubbard came out again to New London at this time: *History,* i. 474.

[128] Saller to Hubbard, from London, 29 May 1676; Bell Lane to Newport, 31 May 1676; Fenchurch Street to Newport, 1 Mar. 1677: of these last two letters, notices only are given in the Hubbard MSS, pp. 116-17.

[129] Hubbard to Stennett, 29 Nov. 1676: *Seventh Day Bap. Mem.*, i (1852), 84-5; Backus, *History,* i. 433-5.

became known as the Rogerenes, despised throughout New England.[130]

The Rogers family was out of jail the following month: "they was called in court," Samuel Hubbard reported to Edward Stennett in England, "they was fined, bro. James for reading so loud in prison as their public meeting was disturb^d & not going to it". John Rogers was fined "for not going to their meeting on the first day, & for beating his lether for his work for shoes on the first day". When the case of the Rogers family came to trial, the "court rising, as 'tis reported, the deputy gov^r said it appears to me to be for conscience sake, & I^ll have no hand against them, or to that purpose". An important principle was thus established here even in the extreme case of the Rogers family, which not only observed the Seventh-Day Sabbath but also held even more objectionable beliefs regarding medical help. Hubbard also told Stennett that recently a new practice had sprung up in New England whereby "most professors pray in their families mornings and nights, afore meals & after, as in a customary way, therefore to forbear prayer in their families or at meals publickly except some led forth upon some special occasion". This was "a practice started up out of conscience," Hubbard explained, "because [of] the world".[131]

The Rogerenes were thus becoming a sect within a sect, and the Saturday-Sabbatarians of New England continually tried to restrain their excesses, some of which seemed to contradict the very principles of Saturday observance. On 16 July 1678 a letter of reproof was sent to John Rogers for carrying a burden on the Sabbath, signed on behalf of the church by William Hiscox, William Gibson, Samuel Hubbard, Stephen Mumford, John Maxon, John Read, Roger Baster and John Thornton. A similar letter was sent to Japeth the praying Indian "for growing cold & vain".[132]

By this time even the illustrious Dr Peter Chamberlen had heard of the sectarian disputes among the Saturday-Sabbatarians in New England, and was willing to make his distinguished voice heard as well. "It is not without cause that you lament the fractions & disorders y^t are amongst

---

[130] Clarke to Hubbard, 5 May 1678: Hubbard MSS, pp. 119-20.

[131] Hubbard to Stennett, 29 June 1678: *ibid.*, pp. 120-4. Backus claims that Hiscox and Hubbard visited the Rogers family yet again at this time, and held worship with them on Saturday, 23 Nov. 1677, two miles out of town. Hiscox was then preaching in town and was arrested there and brought before the constable and Bradstreet the minister. "You are a young man," Hubbard admonished Bradstreet, "but I am an old planter of about forty years, a beginner of Connecticut, and have been persecuted for my conscience from this colony, and I can assure you, that the old beginners were not for persecution, but we had liberty at first." The Rogers family and Hiscox were then released, re-imprisoned, and finally released again: *History*, i. 474-5.

[132] Notice of letters recorded in Hubbard MSS, p. 126.

the saints'', he wrote. One of the reasons for this was that ''no sooner gets into a small assembly of honest men among one, but they presently put on breeches & call it the authority of Christ for whatsoever they do, and usurp authority''. These are ''the little horn men'', the ''babe sprinklers'', those ''y^t turning night into day, call any meat of the day supper''. Chamberlen tried to encourage them as well: ''we know our calling'', he wrote, ''he that accounts every day his last lives one day more every day than he expected.'' More practically, he offered that if ''y° send me the names of the persecuting governors I will (if you please) advert a line or two unto them, in the name of the Lord, & by the authority of King and parliament''.[133]

Good as his word, several days later Dr Peter Chamberlen wrote to the governor of New England, describing himself as ''senior Doctor of both Universities, and first and eldest physician in ordinary to his Majesty's person''. The letter is somewhat vague. Chamberlen ascribed the love he always felt ''for the intended purity and unspotted doctrine of New England'' to the fact that Cotton and Hooker were contemporaries of his at Emmanuel College, Cambridge ''and I never knew them, but of a holy life and conversation.'' Chamberlen testified that he also knew Sir Richard Saltonstall, Hugh Peter, and Sir Henry Vane, all of whom were connected with New England and ''had some share in the foundation of your government.'' Chamberlen reminded the governor that ''certainly the first intentions were never to debar the truths of Scripture and liberty of conscience guided thereby: but to suppress sin and idolatry, and prevent all the adulteries of Rome, to whom all things are lawful, especially lies and hypocrisy, to promote their most damnable doctrines, covetous superstitions, and blasphemous supremacy.'' In this regard, Chamberlen stressed that whatsoever ''is against the ten commandments is sin . . . and he that sinneth in one point is guilty of all''. Chamberlen pledged his humble assistance to the governor if he would be ''pleased to inquire about these things, and to require any instances or information''.[134]

Chamberlen's letter was sent by the Newport church to Connecticut, in the hope of having some ameliorating effect on the condition of the Sabbatarians at New London. They received a reply from Governor William Leete of Connecticut, sent from Hartford on 8 October 1678, thanking them for Chamberlen's letter, and especially, but certainly sarcastically intended, for the numerous scriptural references with which the Sabbatarian physician buttressed his case. Nevertheless, Leete wrote,

---

[133] Chamberlen to Newport, 28 Aug. 1677: *ibid.*, pp. 129-32.
[134] Chamberlen to Gov. N.E., 1 Sept. 1677: *Seventh Day Bap. Mem.*, i (1852), 88; Backus, *History*, i. 476-7.

What yourselves, or that worthy gentleman intend, or who or what he refers to, is not so easy to guess at. We have of late had to deal with Rogers and his of New-London, towards whom the authority have shewn all condescension imaginable to us; that if they would forbear to offend our consciences, we should indulge them in their perswasion, and give them no offence in the seventh day, in worshiping God by themselves. We may doubt (if they were governors in our stead) they would tell us, that their consciences would not suffer them to give us so much liberty; but that they must bear witness to the truth, and beat down idolatry, as the old good kings did in scripture; they judging so of our Lord's day worshiping.

Leete concluded his frank account of the problem at New London by asking the Sabbatarians at Newport to try to bring Rogers and his group within the bounds of permissible religious dissent: "It may be that your counsel may be more taking with them, to make them forbear, than ours".[135]

The Sabbatarian church at Newport did indeed make some attempt to keep the Rogerenes in line. William Gibson, lately of the Bell Lane church in London, was sent to New London to preach to the Sabbatarians there, but ended up quarrelling with the brethren instead. The Rogerenes remained adamant in their refusal to use medicine or seek medical help. Even when the elder Rogers injured his leg as a cart went over it, he refused to get medical attention, and was rewarded when the leg healed anyway.[136] By the beginning of 1680, Hubbard could write that "Many of the ch^h look at those at N. London as broke off from this ch^h except Jonathan [Rogers] and Naomi [Burdick, Samuel Hubbard's grand-daughter, who had married Jonathan Rogers]".[137]

Like Peter Chamberlen, so too did Francis Bampfield seek to reconcile the divisions among the brethren in New England. At the beginning of 1679, Bampfield suggested to the Newport Sabbatarians that they participate in a general meeting of all such churches in the New World, in England and Holland. Edward Stennett wrote a postscript to Bampfield's letter supporting such an idea, which in the event died with Bampfield himself in prison a few years later.[138] Chamberlen sent another letter to Governor William Leete, care of the church in Newport, noting that although the governor had a reputation as a "wise and understanding man", his recent persecutions of the Sabbatarians showed him to be other-

---

[135] Leete to Newport, 8 Oct. 1678: *ibid.*, i. 477-8.

[136] Hubbard to John Thornton, 8 Nov. 1679: Hubbard MSS, pp. 133-4. Hubbard herein speaks of things he had heard on a recent visit to New London. John Thornton, formerly of Newport, had recently moved to Providence. Hubbard sends regards to Roger Williams in this letter and in a previous one to Thornton on 9 Feb. 1678-9: *ibid.*, pp. 132-3.

[137] Hubbard to Clarke at Westerley, 7 Feb. 1679-80: *ibid.*, pp. 136-8.

[138] Bampfield to Newport, 12 Feb. 1678-9: noticed only in Hubbard MSS, p. 133.

wise. "Beware of smiting your brethren," he warned, "lest the ecclesiastical power of England invade you. A parliament is near at hand, when just grievances will be previously resented: I hope there shall be none during your government."[139] But these English interventions seem to have had little effect on the course of events in the New World.

Yet the correspondence with England continued to flourish, usually but not always concerned with the problematic Rogerenes. Hubbard wrote to Bampfield on 16 October 1680, noting that they had twenty-two members in the Newport Saturday-Sabbatarian church, and two months later had a letter in return from Joseph Davis, William Saller and others in the name of the Sabbatarian congregation at East Smithfield in London.[140] The following year, Samuel Hubbard wrote a somewhat longer letter to Edward Stennett recounting the story of the conversion of two Indians, an old man and his son, who had already been baptized at Nantucket and then sent out to spread the gospel among his people. "These 2 Indians came to brother Hiscox house," Hubbard recounted, "and they had a reasoning together". The old Indian had a Bible in his own language and was found to be sound in what he knew. "After much discourse they reasoned about Jehovah's 7th day sabth &c after much discourse the old man said, I tho^t a little water sprinkled was bap^m, but God have opened my eyes, now I see it is not; God can open my eyes to see the sabbath also." By the end of the discussion, the pair of Indians were won over to the Saturday-Sabbath. They were baptized by Hiscox in Newport, and had hands laid on them, and broke bread with the church. Their initiation completed, they returned to Martha's Vineyard, where they lived: "They thro' grace do stand fast," Hubbard reported to Stennett, "wth one brother & 2 sisters".[141] The Sabbatarians' mission among the Indians seems to have prospered, for the following month Hubbard wrote to John Thornton at Providence that on that day he had a visit of "a brother here of Martha's Vineyard one Isaac Takhamme a Indian" who sent best wishes from "David Ockes a Indian & how they stand fast in faith. And bro^r Isaac saith his brother & his wife will be next for baptism and the sabbath".[142]

Samuel Hubbard had trouble with the Rogers family yet again in the summer of 1682 when he received a letter from John Rogers informing him that himself, his father and his brother James were yet again in prison. The purpose of the letter was ostensibly to ask for a few lines of Scripture,

---

[139] Chamberlen to Leete, 2 Sept. 1679: Backus, *History*, i. 485-6.
[140] Hubbard to Bampfield, 16 Oct. 1680: notice only given in Hubbard MSS, p. 142; East Smithfield to Newport, 21 Dec. 1680: *Seventh Day Bap. Mem.*, i (1852), 119-120.
[141] Hubbard to Stennett, 7 Dec. 1681: Hubbard MSS, pp. 154-7.
[142] Hubbard to Thornton, 28 Jan. 1681-2: *ibid.*, pp. 157-9.

but his real aim seems to have been to ask for help.[143] Joseph Clarke mentioned the problem to Hubbard at the end of the year, and finally he was moved to act.[144] Samuel Hubbard sent a letter to Governor William Leete of Connecticut. "Sir, it seemeth strange to me an old planter of your colony," he wrote, "one of the first, before mr. Hooker came there ... but not long so stood after the Bay persecuted mr. Williams & others". While not mentioning the Rogers family by name, Hubbard reminded Leete that he himself "can witness by my own experience: for I was forced to remove for my cons^ce sake, for Gods truth".[145]. Three years later the problem of the Rogers family had still not been settled, and Hubbard wrote to Reeve in Jamaica reporting that the "church have sent bro. Hiscox, brother Joseph Clarke & bro. Maxon, to declare against 2 of them that was of us or more, which are declined to quakerism". These two were named as John and James Rogers, and Hubbard wanted his friends in Jamaica to be forewarned of them, for they "by their principles will travel by land & sea to make disciples, yea, sorry ones too".[146] The Newport church also wrote at this time to London, and they may have touched on their difficulties with the Rogerenes there as well, who plagued the Newport Seventh-Day men just as they had harried the town's Baptists years before.[147]

The last letters from London to Newport which have been preserved were sent in the summer of 1685. The church in London wrote to Hubbard on 22 August[148], and eight days later Joseph Davis wrote as well, warning that "the shadows of the evening seem to be streached out upon Great Britain, & tho' thro' grace I am carried above the fear of w^t man can do unto me, yet its a question to me who as to particular persons shall live: the devil being come down in a great rage full of wrath, knowing y^t his time is but short to scatter the holy people." Davis asked the Sabbatarians of Newport to "simpathize with our lamentable condition", for "the

---

[143] John Rogers to Hubbard, from New London prison, 7 Aug. 1682: *ibid.*, pp. 162-3.

[144] Clarke to Hubbard from Westerley, 7 Dec. 1682: *ibid.*, p. 163.

[145] Hubbard to Leete, 20 Dec. 1682: *ibid.*, pp. 163-5.

[146] Hubbard to Reeve, 10 May/4 June 1685: *ibid.*, pp. 181-2. Hubbard also asked Reeve to enquire after an Indian friend of Isaac the Saturday-Sabbatarian Indian of Martha's Vineyard.

[147] Hiscox, Hubbard, Thomas Ward, John Williams, Roger Baxter, and Thomas Burge in the name of the Newport church, to London, 4 May 1685: noticed only in *ibid.*, p. 181. Backus notes that the Rogerenes were famous for keeping the Saturday-Sabbath, and for refusing medical treatment, while continuing the practice of adult baptism and the Lord's Supper. During the smallpox epidemic of 1721 in Boston, John Rogers deliberately travelled there to demonstrate his divine immunity, but caught the disease nevertheless and spread it throughout his family on his return. The sect still existed when Backus wrote in 1777: *History*, i. 479-80.

[148] John Belcher, Henry Cooke, Robert Hopkins, John Waters, Joseph Parkham, Giles Ray, Simon Blunt, John Laboura, Christopher Williams to Newport, 22 Aug. 1685: noticed only in Hubbard MSS, p. 184.

glory is departed from England, the zealous for reform^n and y^t are faithful in their testimon^y are in great affliction & reproach." When Davis looked around him, all he saw was that a "flood of ungodliness is come in upon us, and popery, that hateful idolitry, is following after it I fear. The whole protestant interest in the world will be in great hazard."[149] This was England at the dawn of the reign of James II as seen by the Saturday-Sabbatarians. In New England, what was apparent to Samuel Hubbard and his friends was God's great mercies, in preserving their sect for decades against all odds.

V

Towards the end of his life, Samuel Hubbard had cause to reflect on the spiritual journey which God had set for him. "What marvelous rich grace to call us out of darkness, into his holy way", he wrote to his old friend Reeve in Jamaica,

> yea hath bro^t me into a howling wilderness, & kept me these 50 years, to try me, & make me thro' many trials to know my own hearts (which I hardly do yet as I ought) a valley of visions of his divine ordinances, & hath made known his holy sabbath to such poor worms: first to my wife, I next, the first dwellers or planter in N.E.[150]

Two years before his death, Hubbard summed up his life in yet another way:

> My wife and I counted up this year 1686: my wife a creature 78 years, a convert 62 years, married 50 years, an independant & joined to a church 52 years, a baptist 38 years, a sabbath keeper 21 years. I a creature 76 years, a convert 60 years, an independant & joined to a church 52 years, a baptist 38 years, a sabbath keeper 21 years.

"O praise the Lord," he concluded, "for his goodness endures for ever!"[151] The church founded by Samuel Hubbard and others in 1671, then, was clearly the seed from which grew the modern movement of the Seventh-Day Baptists. Their antecedents, which previously had only been asserted with reference to spiritual precursors, can therefore be seen as stretching back in a clear and direct chain to the Sabbatarian agitation of John Traske himself during the reign of James I, who now finally has claim

---

[149] Davis to Newport, 30 Aug. 1685: *ibid.*, pp. 183-4.
[150] Hubbard to Reeve, 23 May 1684: *ibid.*, pp. 174-7.
[151] Hubbard to Thornton, 19 Dec. 1686: *ibid.*, pp. 189-92. The last reference to Tacey Hubbard in the church records is dated 12 Sept. 1697: *Seventh Day Bap. Mem.*, i (1852), 127.

to be included in the list of Seventh-Day founding fathers.[152] This expansion of belief from Newport to many towns in the north-east ensured their institutional survival in the eighteenth and nineteenth centuries while the original movement in England suffered a sad decline. Yet as we shall see, the Mosaic ideas of Bampfield and his spiritual heirs in the following decades provided the ideological background for the re-uniting of Seventh-Day Baptism with millenarianism in the middle of the nineteenth century, to produce the hybrid form of Seventh-Day Adventism, and the religious atmosphere which helped spawn the Fundamentalist movement as a whole.

---

[152] See L.A. Platts, ''Seventh-Day Baptists in America Previous to 1802'' in *Seventh Day Baptists in Europe and America* (Plainfield, N.J., 1910), pp. 122-5; W.L. Burdick (a descendant of Hubbard?), ''The Eastern Association'', in *ibid.*, pp. 589-610.

CHAPTER SIX

EPILOGUE:
THROUGH THE HUTCHINSONIANS
TO THE SEVENTH-DAY ADVENTISTS

I

William Henry Black, the Victorian shepherd of the Seventh-Day Baptists, was convinced that if only the history of the Saturday-Sabbatarians might one day be written, it would "serve to show that we are not the simpletons, or hypocrites, or Jews, or nobodies" that they had often been painted.[1] Certainly these epithets would hardly fit the leading figures of that persuasion who promoted and institutionalized the Saturday-Sabbath in seventeenth-century England. Even in purely numerical terms, the presence of Saturday men was felt outside the walls of Pinners' Hall and Mill Yard. According to a remarkable list of Seventh-Day churches copied into the church book of a Baptist congregation in Wales, by December 1690 the strictest understanding of the fourth commandment had spread to many different parts of the country. This "account of some Sabbath-keepers in England" notes

> In the citty of london three congregations
> 1 one to whom Mr. John Belcher & Mr. Henry Cooke be ministers or Elders [at Bell Lane]
> 2 another to whom young Mr. Stennett is minister [at Pinners' Hall]
> 3 the others have Mr. Henry Shorsby to ther minister [at Mill Yard]
>   In the county of Essex
>   ther is a congregation in the citty of Coltchester [where Thomas Tillam preached]
> and at a seaport called Harwich ther is a Remnant
> In the county of Southffolke
>   At Woodbridge & Melton there beth A Remnant
> In the county of Norffolke
> There is a congregation at Ingham and Northwalsham,
>   and therabout, Mr. John Hagges ther minister
>   a also A little Remnant at great Yarmouth
>   In Lincolnshire
> Att A seaport called Boston ther be A small Remnant
> In the citty of Nottingham & therabouts be A Remnant
>   in the county of Bucks or Buckinghamsheire

---

[1] *The Last Legacy of Joseph Davis, Senior*, ed. W.H. Black (London, 1869), p. ii.

There be a congregation William Charsley & henry Cock
ministering Brethren
    at Wallingford in Barksheire
    Ther be a congregation Mr Edward Stennet ther elder
at Watleton in Oxffordsheire
        ther be also A Remnant Relating to the sayd Mr Stennet
    at Salisbury in Wiltsheire
Ther is a congregation John Laws & John Hall
    ministering Brethren, but ther Elder lives at Southampton
whose Name is, Michell Aldridge
    in Dorsetsheire ther is also a congregation
        som at the Citty of Dorsetor & some at Belmister som at Sherbor
[where Francis Bampfield ministered]
        & som at Sturmister all market towns
Joseph Newman and
    some other Brethren to minister to them
Robert   In Glostersheire Ther be two
                congregations that have
    each of them an Elder and
Robert Woods   severall Ministering Brethren
    In the county of Surry ther is at A market
    town called Cherssey Mr William
Burnet ther elder
    & Mr Thom Stickland a ministering Brother
December
1690

Even if some of these congregations were very pitiful "remnants" indeed, this list certainly shows that the Saturday-Sabbatarians commanded at least as much support as sects which are far more well-known to early modern historians today.[2]

But far more important than the establishment of another Restoration religious sect was the fact that by this means one solution to the problem of the Old Testament had been offered to those who worried about it. As William Black explained, "if the fundamental principle of Protestantism be right and true, that 'the Bible alone is the religion of Protestants,' then *the Seventh Day must be the true and only Sabbath of Protestants*; for, unless that day of the week be kept by them, they have no *scriptural* Sabbath at all."[3] Such literal and total dedication to the Ten Commandments as demanded by the Seventh-Day Baptists was unusual. But the problem refused to go away, and surfaced throughout the succeeding years until it found a more

---

[2] E.A. Payne, "More About the Sabbatarian Baptists", *Bap. Qly.*, xiv (1951-2), 164-6: repr. from volumes then in the possession of the Llanwenarth Baptist Church, Monmouthshire, with some suggestions for identifying the obscure names.

[3] W.H. Black, *Plain Reasons for the Religious Observance of the Seventh-Day-Sabbath* (rev. edn, London, 1870), pp. 4-6, 14.

evangelistic expression in the evolution of the Seventh-Day Adventist and Fundamentalist movements of the mid-nineteenth century.

Significantly, it was Francis Bampfield who pointed out the direction the Mosaic problem would take in the century after his death. We have already seen how Bampfield, the most important organizer of Saturday-Sabbatarianism, devoted the last years of his life towards demonstrating that "All Useful Sciences and profitable Arts" might be found in the Old Testament, that "one Book of *Jehovah Aelohim*". Bampfield suggested that the Mosaic scripture might be a guide to everything from map-making to dietetics. Bampfield's plan was to institute a "House of Wisdom" based on the study of the Hebrew language and the literal meaning of the Old Testament, within which the answers to all of mankind's problems could be found. Bampfield's utopian scheme was neglected during his lifetime and nearly forgotten after his death. But his application of the literal observance of the Old Testament in the widest sense, not only in regard to Sabbath regulations but more generally as the divine answer-key given by God himself to Moses for mankind, presages the development of the problem of the Mosaic law in the eighteenth century, and foreshadows the resurrection of both aspects of Bampfield's vision – Saturday-Sabbath and Old Testament literalism – in the nineteenth.

Apart from Francis Bampfield, another Englishman in the seventeenth century who thought along similar lines was Theophilus Gale, fellow at Oxford during the Commonwealth and nonconformist tutor afterwards. It was Gale's life work to prove that all languages, philosophy, and learning ultimately derived from the Old Testament and the Jews. Even the ancient philosophies could be shown to trace their roots back to this origin. Plato was "reported to have lived fourteen years with the *Jews* in *Egypt*; and, we need no way dout, derived the choisest of his contemplations . . . from the Jewish Church". The Hebrew language itself was the key to this divine knowledge, having remained pure and unadulterated since its creation for the Garden of Eden. So too was Greek merely a degenerated form of biblical Hebrew. Gale's sources included the standard Jewish commentaries in the sixteenth-century rabbinical Bibles, as well as classical authors and kabbalistic commentators. But Theophilus Gale lacked the utopian drive of Francis Bampfield, and his interests were rather more scholarly than reforming.[4]

Both Bampfield and Gale, like the Saturday-Sabbatarian movement in

---

[4] Theophilus Gale, *The Court Of The Gentiles* (Oxford, 1669-77), i. sigs. *3ʳ⁻ᵛ, **3ʳ⁻ᵛ, ****ᵛ; pp. 51, 53-4, 59; iii. 117-18. For a more modern reversed echo of Gale's linguistic views, see J. Yahuda, *Hebrew is Greek* (Oxford, 1982). See also S. Hutton, "The Neoplatonic Roots of Arianism: Ralph Cudworth and Theophilus Gale", in *Socinianism and its Role in the Culture of the XVIth to XVIIIth Centuries* (Warsaw & Lodz, 1983), pp. 139-45.

general, essentially were arguing for the continued validity and application of the Old Testament in reformed Christian life, and thus helped to
keep the problem a vital one. In the eighteenth century this principle was
magnified so as to encompass nearly every query that had been thrown up
by the scientific revolution. To the necessity of observing all of the Ten
Commandments, which continued to dominate the thoughts of the
Seventh-Day Baptists, was added an amplification of Bampfield's view
that the Old Testament might provide the answers to problems in almost
every field. Nowhere is this turn of mind more clearly exemplified than in
the establishment and continued popularity of the followers of John Hutchinson (1674-1737), those fervent opponents of the Newtonian universe
whose theories came to dominate intellectual and religious life at Oxford
during the middle of the eighteenth century. From there they would spread
to Scotland and the New World, to link up once again with Bampfield's
confessional descendants, to help produce the controversial Seventh-Day
Adventists during the millenarian revival that preceded the rise of American Fundamentalism.

II

The Hutchinsonians, as anti-Newtonians in what was supposed to be the
Age of Enlightenment, have generally suffered from the neglect of historians, despite the fact that their writings and those of their opponents generated scores of books and pamphlets during the eighteenth century. Leslie
Stephen, who also wrote John Hutchinson's entry in the *Dictionary of National Biography*, dismissed as a ''little eddy of thought'' this ''school which,
at the middle of the century, represented the influence upon theology of
the great University of Oxford''. Stephen discusses the views of the Hutchinsonians at all, he writes, ''only in so far as the crotchets of weak minds
may indicate the general current of speculation.''[5] Only recently have
some historians of science returned to look again at those figures who refused to accept unequivocally Newton's explanation of natural
phenomena, and who instead were content to derive their knowledge of
the natural world from the Old Testament and from the Hebrew language
itself. But even they have largely restricted their inquiry into the scientific
(and especially geological) views of the Hutchinsonians, and have mostly
overlooked his role in the development of Protestant theology.[6]

---

[5] L. Stephen, *History of English Thought in the Eighteenth Century* (3rd edn, London, 1902),
i. 389-92.
[6] A.J. Kuhn, ''Glory or Gravity: Hutchinson Vs. Newton'', *Jnl. Hist. Ideas*, xxii (1961),
303-22; M. Neve & R. Porter, ''Alexander Catcott: Glory and Geology'', *Brit. Jnl. Hist.
Sci.*, x (1977), 37-60; G.N. Cantor, ''Revelation and the Cyclical Cosmos of John Hutchin-

John Hutchinson was born in Yorkshire in 1674, and trained to be a land steward. At the age of about twenty he was given this position in the household of the duke of Somerset, and while managing a law suit for his employer in 1700 he chanced to make the acquaintance of John Woodward, physician to the duke. Woodward would soon become known for his attempt to reconcile the Old Testament with geological evidence, and in that capacity he employed Hutchinson to collect fossils during his travels between the duke's various estates. Woodward had already published his natural history of the earth before he had met Hutchinson, and clearly regarded the steward as a sort of research assistant, a role which Hutchinson was pleased to perform. At some point Hutchinson discovered that Woodward had been deceiving him consistently about the progress that he had made in using the fossils to verify the Mosaic account of Creation, and that the notebook which supposedly contained a draft of the learned study was in fact nearly empty. Hutchinson thereupon determined to complete the work himself, and applied to the duke of Somerset for permission to quit his service. When he explained his reasons, the duke instead generously gave Hutchinson a sinecure, a house, and the leisure to proceed with his research undisturbed. Robert Spearman, Hutchinson's follower and biographer, claims that ''he gave himself up entirely to a studious and sedentary life, which being so opposite to his former way of doing, by degrees weakened and broke his constitution, and at length laid the foundation of that disorder which carried him off.'' The duke also gave Hutchinson the right to present to one of his Sussex livings, and so the Mosaic geologist was able to place the Rev. Julius Bate, who with Spearman would edit his collected works and promote Hutchinsonianism after the founder's death.[7]

The labours of Spearman and Bate were essential, as Hutchinson's literary style was nearly impenetrable, and only cleared when he was launched into one of his immoderate attacks, usually against Isaac Newton. ''Let those who complain of the obscurity of Mr. *Hutchinson*'s stile consider,'' explained his editors, ''that he was writing no romance, nor fairy tale ... His work was to clear the way, and to lay in materials for such as should have more leisure to play the orator''. That being said, they admitted, '''Tis true, there are likewise long periods, longer sentences,

son'', in *Images of the Earth*, ed. L.J. Jordanova & R. Porter (Chalfont St Giles, 1979), pp. 3-22; C.B. Wilde, ''Hutchinsonianism, Natural Philosophy and Religious Controversy in Eighteenth Century Britain'', *Hist. Sci.*, xvii (1980), 1-24; M.C. Jacob, *The Radical Enlightenment* (London, 1981), p. 96; C.B. Wilde, ''Matter and Spirit as Natural Symbols in Eighteenth Century British Natural Philosophy'', *Brit. Jnl. Hist. Sci.*, xv (1982), 99-131. The Hutchinsonians also appear in H. Metzger, *Attraction Universelle et Religion Naturelle* (Paris, 1938), pp. 8, 197.

   [7] Robert Spearman, *A Supplement to the Works of John Hutchinson* (London, 1765), pp. i-v.

and more parentheses than one who reads to divert himself would chuse; yet whoever peruses him with care, will find his trouble well bestow'd, and abundantly repaid." The Hutchinsonian scheme in its most active form was an amalgam of the original words of John Hutchinson and the reworded abstract of Spearman and Bate. In essentials all three men were in perfect agreement, but without the reinterpreted text Hutchinson's views would have remained hidden in obscurity.[8]

The starting point for the elaboration of the Hutchinsonian system was their faith in the Old Testament as the continuing revelation of God, and in the Hebrew language as the medium of its expression. "In order to take a nearer view of the *Mosaic* philosophy," wrote Spearman of the Bible, "the original text must be consulted, simply as it stands, divested of those points or pricks for vowels which the modern *Jews* contrived". The Old Testament was the sacred word of God, but in its original form it was written without vowels, and so continues to appear on all scrolls of the Pentateuch today. Hutchinson knew that the vowels, which appear as points or lines above and below the string of consonants, were invented by a group of Jews who became known as the Masoretes, who examined closely the text of Scripture at Tiberias in Palestine as much as five hundred years after Christ. "The reader will be pleased to observe," Spearman explained, "that these points are a heap of almost imperceptible dots, placed under the *Hebrew* letters, to give the same word different sounds, and, by virtue thereof, a variety of different, nay opposite signfications, whereby the whole language is render'd vague and uncertain." These misleading vowel signs were invented only after the New Testament was written, once the Jews realized that the prophecies of the Old had been fulfilled: "after that, they turn'd masorites, rabbies, expounders, scribes, &c. patched up *talmuds*, *mishnas*, *cabbalas*, &c. . . . all to facilitate their main plot, the subversion of *Christianity*, to demonstrate their invincible hatred to the MESSIAH".[9]

So the Old Testament was certainly a guide book to God's divine plan, but it could only be understood by reducing the text to its original lines of consonants and then deciphering them according to a method untainted by the machinations of the enemies of Christ. Hutchinson's system was ingenious. As Spearman and Bate put it, the "principal thing the learner has to attend to, is, the proper meaning of the several roots, which he may obtain by comparison".[10] All students of Hebrew soon learn that the language is constructed around (mostly) three-letter roots, which are chan-

---

[8] [Robert Spearman], *An Abstract from the Works of John Hutchinson* (2nd edn, London, 1755), p. 4.

[9] *Ibid.*, pp. 42, 205-6.

[10] *Ibid.*, p. 211.

nelled into various paradigms by the addition of certain other letters to produce the full vocabulary of the Bible, or indeed of modern spoken Hebrew. Thus, the three-letter root for "open", פתח. by the prefixing of the letter מ . becomes the word for "key", as such a prefix usually denotes an instrument which will realize the promise of the verb. We now recognize that many words can only peripherally be connected to the root, or to each other: the various permutations of the root אמן. which gives us the English "amen", is a well-known example of this conundrum.[11] For Hutchinson, however, these sorts of puzzles provided the very key towards understanding God's sacred plan and the secrets of the universe. Grammar and the history of linguistic development were angrily thrust aside as Hutchinson and his followers argued that this, like all features of the Old Testament, had been planned by God himself. All of the permutations of the single Hebrew root were related and virtually interchangeable, as were all words with single consonantal spellings. This, in English, would be to argue that the words "bed", "bad", "bid", "bode", and "bud" were synonymous. The construction of such a complex biblical text was well within the abilities of the Deity; its deconstruction was mankind's only path towards divining the secrets of the universe.

John Hutchinson himself gave numerous examples of how this theory might be implemented, and of the dramatic consequences of its application. The word in Hebrew for the firmament described in Genesis is רקיע ("rakia"). Hutchinson's Hebrew lexicons revealed that in other contexts the root רקע ("rka") "signifies an opening, or dividing asunder, a drawing, or stretching out, according as where it is found, and what it is understood of – to expand, extend, distend, stretch." Kircher's concordance confirmed that the word implied "an Extension, Expansion, compact, and firm". On this basis, Hutchinson was able to discover that the firmament consisted originally of air and water, and was like "a Plate of ductile Metal hammer'd, of Wings expanded, or such Things, is extending one Edge one Way, and the other the other Way". To those who would object to the conclusions he drew from the extrapolation of a single root, Hutchinson explained that we "can have no Word in modern Language for it, because we have had no Idea of it." The conjunction of such ideas seemed strange only in English; in Hebrew it was the essence of clarity.[12]

So too did Hutchinson argue for the identity of the two Hebrew consonants שם. which can be read either as "a name" or "a place", or in the plural, "the heavens" (שמים). As Hutchinson explained, in his inimitable

---

[11] See R. Needham, *Belief, Language, and Experience* (Oxford, 1972), pp. 44-50.

[12] John Hutchinson, *Moses's Principia. Part II.*, in *The Philosophical and Theological Works*, ed. Robert Spearman and Julius Bate (London, 1749), ii. 264-5: first pub. 1727. The lexicons referred to are those by Marius of Calasio (1621) and Athanasius Kircher (1607).

prose, he believed "the Thing, to be the same as Place ... Place and Things are the same; and tho' שם be a general Name for Place, and Heaven be the Matter or Place which includes all".[13] But of course his most famous etymological demonstration was the emphasis on the common root of the words "glory" and "heavy", so that gravity could be seen as the product of the glory of God. "Glory does not appear to be a Root, or have a separate Idea;" Hutchinson surmised, "but to imply that the Root of Weight is applied to beneficial Purpose, or to valuable Actions, or Things, so Glory".[14] The ingenious application of unpointed and therefore unvocalized Hebrew enabled Hutchinson in his own mind and those of his followers to disregard Newton and to reject his principles, especially that which postulated gravitation as a non-mechanistic and therefore almost occult force. The problem was that Newton's knowledge of Hebrew was inadequate to understand the Old Testament in its original and therefore divine form. "One would think," Hutchinson's editors argued, "that such an one, born in a *Christian* country, who had access to examine books dictated by the Supreme Author of this system, would first have qualified himself to read and understand them, before he had dared to reject revelation, to set up a scheme in direct oppostion thereto, stolen from the worst and blindest of the heathens". Newton's experiments were misconceived from the start, and it was ludicrous to claim that "some children's gewgaws, a three corner'd piece of glass, a hole in a window, the pendulum of a clock ... may, it seems, become the foundation of mighty discoveries". These, in Hutchinson's view, "shew no more than a few very singular properties of the *names*", the last word being of course interchangeable with "the heavens".[15]

The physical universe according to John Hutchinson has already been explored by historians of science and its description need not be repeated here. His role as the founder of an anti-Newtonian scientific school has been stressed: Hutchinson's editors even claimed that while in London he had "much personal converse with *Newton* and his associates".[16] Hutchinson is primarily of interest here in connection with the problem of the Old Testament and the persistence of the Seventh-Day Sabbath, as a more extreme example of the sort of direct application of Scripture that Bampfield was advocating towards the end of his life, and one which provided at least passive support for the Seventh-Day men in eighteenth-century England and nineteenth-century America. Unlike Bampfield, and indeed nearly all

---

[13] *Ibid.*, ii. 79.
[14] John Hutchinson, *Glory and Gravity*, in *Works*, vi. 7: first pub. 1733-4.
[15] [Spearman], *Abstract*, pp. 148-9.
[16] *Ibid.*, p. 157.

of the Hebraists in the seventeenth century, however, Hutchinson was extremely, almost obsessively anti-Jewish, and saw the descendants of the Old Testament heroes as the authors of innumerable plots to subvert mankind and destroy Christianity.

Hutchinson was fond of repeating that when Christ told his disciples to search out the Scriptures he was referring to the original Hebrew copies extant in his time, not to the post-Christian Jewish commentaries, forgeries, and traditions. Indeed, he wrote, "every one knows, the *Jews* have not only grown more ignorant in these matters, but worse and worse ever since". Hutchinson understood that in rejecting the Jews as authentic interpreters of Scripture, he would incur the "Displeasure of those who have spent most of their Time in studying, and making themselves Masters of all their allegorical, or other ways of Evasion". But even Jesus decried the Jews of his own time for their lack of knowledge. "What great Knowledge can we expect from any of the Persons educated to understand this Rubbish," wrote Hutchinson, "when they are newly converted, save that they were sick of it."[17] So too did Hutchinson's editors continue this theme, denouncing "their *talmuds* . . . the grossest forgeries that ever were attempted to be imposed upon the world", and the Jews themselves, who claim that the Old Testament "cannot be understood without the interpretation of their *wise men*, who, at the same time, are perpetually contradicting each other in things the most trivial and foolish." Their nefarious invention of vowel points to pervert the meaning of scripture was just one of the diabolical plots of the Jews, "whose forgeries are the very *mystery of iniquity*, and themselves literally *Antichrist*." The absurd Jewish reverence for the pretended name of God, and indeed their very picture of the Deity, were all blasphemy, as they made God "the author of actions which any rational being would be ashamed of." Hutchinson's only consolation was that the Jewish rabbies "unluckily have not had wit enough to give their imprudent lies the air of probability".[18]

One of the most evil inventions that the Hutchinsonians laid at the door of the Jews was the creation of the Islamic religion and the Arabic language:

> Indeed, there are strong and certain presumptions, that the implacable enemies of CHRIST were all along the chief promoters of this dark business. It was transacted at the same time they were so indefatigably employed in the invention of pointing; *Talmuds*, grammars to suit their false interpretations, and the similitude between the two projects is obvious and glaring: the fabulous

---

[17] Hutchinson, *Principia. Part II.*, in *Works*, II. xxxviii-ix; *idem, Moses Sine Principio*, in *Works*, III. x-xi: first pub. 1749.

[18] [Spearman], *Abstract*, pp. 3, 199-200, 203, 205. Cf. John Hutchinson, *The Covenant in the Cherubim*, in *Works*, vii. 74: first pub. 1749.

stories of both are alike ridiculous, the *Hebrew* words taken in and wrested the same way, from plurals to singulars, letters varied, &c. and they say the two grammars agree as exactly in their features, as if children of one and the same father. What is said in praise of this suppositious language, this *Babel* of confusion, must sink it for ever with men of sense, that it has an hundred, nay, five hundred words for one thing. Could this possibly be the speech of one people? What imaginable title can it have to simplicity, certainty, or affinity with *Hebrew*, the most natural, distinct, and determinate of all tongues?

Hutchinson and his followers rejected the idea that Islamic sources might shed any light on biblical matters: "The sacred scriptures are able to explain themselves sufficiently; and it cannot be thought of without indignation, that it should be suggested, that they need *Mahometan* jargon to illustrate their meaning." As far as they were concerned, the Jewish invention of Islam and Arabic was merely the last stage in a more comprehensive plan: after the Jews fabricated the vowel points, the Mishnah, the Talmud, the kabbalah, and appointed their rabbis to expound these murky works, they "at last set up that outrageous impostor *Mahomet*, all to facilitate their main plot, the subversion of *Christianity*."[19]

What was needed now was a rededication of attention to the mysteries of the Old Testament, a rejection of Newtonian nonsense, and a purging of the Hebrew text of Jewish outrages. The Hutchinsonians regretted that although at least the Western churches had largely been spared the rabbinical contagion throughout the Middle Ages, during the Reformation the Protestants "appealed to the Scriptures: but as they had never studied *Hebrew*, the Jews were extremely forward to offer their services in this exigence, and they met with too, too favourable a reception." The result of this academic fraternization with the apostates, they claimed, was that "we find *Europe* over-run with *rabbinism* and the *talmud*, and no man admitted to preach the gospel before he had passed his courses under some avowed enemy of CHRIST. The consequence was, and a very natural one too, that the very fundamentals of *Christianity* were rendered precarious, and became the subject of public disputes." Those Protestants who were aware of the dangers implicit in such a course shied away from Old Testa-

---

[19] [Spearman], *Abstract*, pp. 115-17, 205-6, paraphrasing from John Hutchinson, *The Confusion of Tongues*, in *Works*, iv; and *Cherubim*. This theory may be original to Hutchinson, although it had long been suggested that Mohammed may have been influenced by a Jewish tutor. Hutchinson's explanation does not appear in the most profound defence of Islam, Henry Stubbe, *An Account of the Rise and Progress of Mahometanism*, ed. H.M.K. Shairani (London, 1911). Cf. P.M. Holt, *A Seventeenth-Century Defender of Islam: Henry Stubbe (1632-76) and his Book* (London, 1972); J.R. Jacob, *Henry Stubbe, Radical Protestantism and the Early Enlightenment* (Cambridge, 1983); S.C. Chew, *The Crescent and the Rose: Islam and England during the Renaissance* (New York, 1937); N. Daniel, *Islam and the West* (Edinburgh, 1960); *idem, Islam: Europe and Empire* (Edinburgh, 1966); *idem, The Arabs and Medieval Europe* (2nd edn, London, 1979).

ment study, with the result that "the *Hebrew* tongue, left to the ignorant
and vile comments of those who knew nothing of its excellency, is grown
contemptible even to a proverb". This was a situation which the Hutchinsonians aimed to put right.[20]

The Hutchinsonians, like so many subjects in the history of eighteenth-
century England, have suffered from historiographical obscurity, despite
the fact that they were the chief exponents of a comprehensive (if arguably
misguided) solution to the problem of the Old Testament for Protestants,
and despite the enormous number of their publications and the volume of
intense comment that they generated. It was especially in Oxford that
Hutchinsonianism was adopted with a fervour, as a sort of High Church
theological science that might combat the dangers of Newtonianism and
the new science which seemed so often to lead to Deism and worse. "Was
not I talking of religious sects?" wrote Horace Walpole, the famous author
and diarist, to a friend in the country during September 1753,

> Methodism is quite decayed in Oxford, its cradle. In its stead, there prevails
> a delightful fantastic system, called the sect of the Hutchinsonians, of whom
> one seldom hears anything in town [?London]. After much inquiry, all I can
> discover is, that their religion consists in driving Hebrew to its fountainhead,
> till they find some word or other in every text of the Old Testament, which
> may seem figurative of something in the New. As their doctrine is novel, and
> requires much study, or at least much invention, one should think that they
> could not have settled half the canon of what they are to believe – and yet
> they go on zealously, trying to make and succeeding in making converts.

Walpole admitted that "I could not help smiling at the thoughts of *etymological salvation*", but his estimate of the depth and potential of the movement
was considerably inaccurate.[21] When Edward Gibbon came up to Magdalen College in 1752, hoping to become an Orientalist, he was dissuaded
from the subject by his tutor. But he noted that (apart from himself presumably), the only serious student there was George Horne, then "a
young fellow (a future Bishop), who was deeply immersed in the follies of
the Hutchinsonian system".[22] Bishop Horne would become indeed the
central figure in the movement at Oxford as Hutchinsonianism actually

---

[20] [Spearman], *Abstract*, pp. 206, 231-2. Hutchinson's editors singled out for blame Buxtorf, Broughton, and Lightfoot. The proverb quoted was from *The Poems of Richard Corbett*,
ed. J.A.W. Bennett and H.R. Trevor-Roper (Oxford, 1955), pp. 56-9.

[21] Horace Walpole, *Correspondence*, ed. W.S. Lewis, *et al.* (New Haven, 1937-83), xxxv.
156. The same letter, to Richard Bentley, contains an amusing description of a riot in
Worcester over the Jew Bill.

[22] Edward Gibbon, *Memoirs of My Life* (Penguin edn, Harmondsworth, 1984), p. 80.
Magdalen was a centre of Hebrew studies at Oxford since the Civil War: see above, p. 60;
and D.S. Katz, "The Abendana Brothers and the Christian Hebraists of Seventeenth-
Century England", *Jnl. Eccl. Hist.* (forthcoming).

gained in strength in the second half of the eighteenth century, and kept the problem of the Old Testament before the public eye until it reunited with the Saturday-Sabbath and millenarianism in mid-nineteenth-century America.

That Hutchinsonianism survived to be lampooned by Walpole was due not only to the publication of the master's works in 1742 by his indefatigable disciples Robert Spearman and Julius Bate, but also by its adoption as a variety of religious creed by a number of prominent intellectuals. First among these was Alexander Stopford Catcott (1692-1749), whose sermon on 16 August 1735 at the mayor's chapel before the corporation of Bristol and Lord Chief Justice Hardwicke on the "Supreme and Inferiour Elahim" provoked the first serious debate about Hutchinsonianism and the scientific evidence contained in the Old Testament.[23] His son Alexander Catcott (1725-1779) promoted Hutchinsonianism at Oxford in the middle of the century, and later in Bristol as vicar of Temple Church.[24] But the creed became genuinely respectable with its adoption by Duncan Forbes (1685-1747), the well-known Scottish president of the court of session, who in 1732 made a public confession of his new-found faith. In his view, some coherent approach had to be found to deal with the fact that "Atheism, Deism, and the whole Train of Opinions that attend what is commonly called Free-thinking, flow from a settled Disbelief and Contempt of Revelation." Hutchinson's emphasis on the original Hebrew text of the Old Testament made his theology very nearly inaccessible, but Forbes testified that he found it well worthwhile, once he had "rubb'd up the little *Hebrew* I had, and address'd myself to a more careful Perusal of the Books". The Old Testament, argued Forbes, like Bampfield before him, might when properly understood provide the answers to nearly all of the important questions in God's Creation.[25]

In any case, it was not necessary to be a fervent supporter of all of Hutchinson's principles to recognize in his work a major contribution to biblical studies. As the poet Alexander Pope insisted in 1736, "Hutchinson is a very odd man and a very bad writer, but he has struck out very great lights and made very considerable discoveries by the way, as I have heard from people who know ten times more of these matters than I do." This was also the view held by Lord Bolingbroke. "Does Lord Bolingbroke un-

---

[23] Alexander Stopford Catcott, *The Supreme and Inferiour Elahim* (London, 1736). Many of the polemical works written in protest of Catcott's views are bound together as Bodl. Lib., G. Pamph. 250. See also, Neve & Porter, "Catcott" for his views on geology and the importance of field work in proving the testimony of the Bible – unlike Hutchinson, who seems to have given up active field-work after his initial disillusionment with Woodward.

[24] *Dict. Nat. Biog.*

[25] [Duncan Forbes], *A Letter to a Bishop* (London, 1732), pp. 3, 8, 33.

derstand Hebrew?'', Pope was asked. ''No, but he understands that sort
of learning and what is writ about it.'' These were hardly the views of fanatics. Their respect for Hutchinson derived from the same principle
enunciated by Francis Lockier, the dean of Peterborough, in 1730: ''The
one book necessary to be understood by a divine is the Bible'', he affirmed,

> any others are to be read chiefly in order to understand that. One must not
> read it through a system as a perspective, but bring our systems to our Bible,
> and not our Bible to our systems, as most of the divines in every church are
> too apt to do. Try to see its first natural sense, and consult comments after-
> wards – and that only where the nature of the thing makes them necessary.

This is exactly the sort of view that Hutchinson and his followers were trying to put across.[26]

Apparently through the influence of Forbes and the younger Catcott,
Hutchinsonian views found a strong foothold in mid-eighteenth century
Oxford, and were taken far more seriously than Walpole would suggest.
The most distinguished of these Hutchinsonians was Gibbon's fellow-
student George Horne (1730-1792), who became president of Magdalen
College in 1768, and bishop of Norwich two years before his death. His
tutor at University College, George Watson (1723?-1773) was also a believer, as was William Jones of Nayland (1726-1800), the celebrated
churchman who became Horne's chaplain at Norwich. So too was Walter
Hodges, the provost of Oriel College, a follower of Hutchinson. William
Stevens (1732-1807), the editor of the works of Jones of Nayland, carried
the principles of Hutchinsonianism into the nineteenth century, especially
among the members of ''Nobody's Friends'', the club founded by members of his group in 1800. Stevens, Jones of Nayland, and their associates
have often been seen as the link between the nonjurors of the seventeenth
century and the tractarians and leaders of the Oxford Movement in the
nineteenth.[27]

Hutchinsonianism penetrated outside of England as well, and was especially influential in Scotland. According to one clergyman who had been
ordained about 1820, at that time there was hardly a single non-Hutchin-
sonian minister in the diocese of Aberdeen.[28] Chief among these was certainly the Rev. John Skinner, the episcopal incumbent of Longside, Aber-

[26] Joseph Spence, *Observations, Anecdotes, and Characters of Books and Men*, ed. J.M. Osborn
(Oxford, 1966), pp. 124, 214, 294.
[27] See generally, William Jones, *Memoirs of the Life, Studies, and Writings of the Right Reverend
George Horne* (London, 1795); George Horne, *Works*, ed. William Jones (2nd edn, London,
1818); William Jones, *Theological, Philosophical and Miscellaneous Works* (London, 1801): 12 vols.
Cf. Kuhn, ''Glory''.
[28] W. Walker, *The Life and Times of the Rev. John Skinner* (2nd edn, London, 1883), p. 165.

deenshire for 65 years until his death in 1807. Skinner was imprisoned in 1753 for having conducted church services during the late Jacobite uprising, and while in jail had time to contemplate the controversy over the notorious Jew Bill of that year which would have given some of them limited emancipation. Skinner applied himself to Hebrew, in part to provide a moral and more scholarly set of arguments against Jewish emancipation, and soon was led to adopt the Hutchinsonian interpretation of Scripture.[29] Skinner's son of the same name became bishop of Aberdeen, and passed the see on to his own son afterwards.[30] All were Hutchinsonians, and made this the philosophy of Aberdeen diocese until the second half of the nineteenth century. From this nest came, among others, Alexander Nicol, appointed Regius professor of Hebrew at Oxford in 1822, who with his brother "read Hebrew without the points".[31] Another Scottish Hutchinsonian was the Rev. James Andrew, who in 1823 published his "Hebrew Dictionary and Grammar without points".[32] As in England, these Scottish Hutchinsonians were strict biblical literalists, and saw the Old Testament as being meant for Christians even more than for Jews, who deliberately misled the gentiles, "first with their *Mishna* and *Gemara*, then with their vowel-points, and *Keriketibs*, and in end, with their whole farrago of Talmudic nonsense, all with a view to obscure, and pervert the text, which they durst not alter or corrupt."[33]

Most importantly, Hutchinsonianism was successfully transplanted to America, where it became the ruling method of scriptural interpretation at King's College, New York, which after the Revolution would be renamed Columbia University. The conquest of King's was due to the conversion of its first president, Samuel Johnson (1696-1772), a leader in the revolt against Congregationalism at Yale in the 1720s, and later the most noteworthy disciple of George Berkeley in America. Johnson was at first much interested in science, and was drawn to Newton's discoveries, but about 1743 he chanced upon Duncan Forbes's *Letter to a Bishop*. Johnson was already a considerable Hebraist, and as he himself put it, Hutchinsonianism "opened to him a new scene of study and inquiry which as it depended on his favorite Hebrew was very engaging (with regard both to

---

[29] John Skinner, *Theological Works* (Aberdeen, 1809), I. xii, xiii, cvi-cxiii, cxxxii-cxliii, cliii-clxxv, cxcv; II. 1-8.

[30] W. Walker, *The Life and Times of John Skinner Bishop of Aberdeen* (Aberdeen, 1887); *idem*, *Rev. John Skinner*, p. 156.

[31] *Ibid.*, pp. 159-60. Alexander Nicol held the post for only six years before he died in 1828. Nicol was succeeded as Regius professor by E.B. Pusey, who held the chair for 54 years.

[32] James Andrew, *Hebrew Dictionary and Grammar* (n.p., 1823).

[33] Rev. John Skinner to Dr Doig, 15 Apr. 1796: repr. *Works*, I. cxl.

philosophy and theology).'' Johnson soon devoured the twelve volumes of
Hutchinson's works, with which he in the main wholeheartedly agreed,
though he could not be drawn to ''think so very hardly of Philo and the
Jewish Rabbis, however bad they were.'' Johnson also supplemented Hutchinson's books with works by Stillingfleet, Ralph Cudworth, and Theophilus Gale. His search seemed to confirm other contemporary philosophical works that he had read, and he asserted more than once that

> It is remarkable that Bishop Berkeley in Ireland, Mr. Hutchinson in Eng-
> land, and Abbe Pluch in France, the greatest men of the age, without any
> communication with each other should at the same time though by different
> media come into the same conclusion, namely that the Holy Scriptures teach
> the only true system of natural philosophy as well as the only true religion,
> and that Mr. Franklin in America should be at the same time without any
> design by his electrical experiments greatly confirm it.

This was a view he actively promoted for the last thirty years of his life.[34]

Samuel Johnson was very anxious to promote Hutchinsonian doctrine
and the study of the Hebrew language in America. In 1752 he put out his
Elementa Philosophica at Benjamin Franklin's press, the first textbook in philosophy published in America. In this he deliberately inserted digressions
about Hutchinsonianism, which to his dismay were excised from the English edition.[35] When he became first president of King's College the following year, he had more scope for spreading the new gospel. Indeed, he
left a paper to be read at his decease instructing the governors to elect as
his successor a man who acknowledged the Hebrew tongue ''as being the
mother of all language and eloquence as well as the fountain of all knowledge and true wisdom.''[36] Johnson wrote to Archbishop Secker in 1760 towards that end, suggesting as the next president of King's the famous Hutchinsonian George Horne, on the basis of that divine's statement of the
case against the followers of Newton.[37] But Secker rejected Horne out of
hand, describing him as ''a good man, but deeply tinctured with Mr. Hutchinson's notions in philosophy and Hebrew, both which I take to be

---

[34] Samuel Johnson, ''Memoirs'', in *Samuel Johnson*, ed. H. & C. Schneider (New York,
1929), i. 3, 6, 30-1, 45-6. Cf. Johnson to Cadwallader Colden, 19 Feb. 1753 in *ibid.*, ii. 303-4.
Generally on Johnson see also T.B. Chandler, *The Life of Samuel Johnson* (New York, 1805),
esp. pp. 2, 4-5, 76-85, 116-23, 201-4; E.E. Beardsley, *Life and Correspondence of Samuel Johnson*
(New York, 1874); T. Hornberger, ''Samuel Johnson of Yale and King's College: A Note
on the Relation of Science and Religion in Provincial America'', *New Eng. Qly.*, viii (1935),
378-97.
[35] Samuel Johnson, *Elementa Philosophica* (Philadelphia, 1752), repr. *Johnson*, ed.
Schneider, ii. 463, 510-11.
[36] *Ibid.*, iv. 115-16: dated Sept. 1659? Cf. Johnson to East Apthorp, 1 Dec. 1759: repr.
ibid., iv. 56.
[37] Johnson to Secker, 15 Feb. 1760: repr. *ibid.*, iv. 59-60.

groundless, notwithstanding a superficial attempt of his to prove a seem-
ing agreement between the former and Sir Isaac Newton, whom Mr. Hutchinson held to be an atheist''. Secker certainly knew that Johnson was a
follower of Hutchinson as well, but he was not about to promote the spread
of the doctrine any further: in the end, Secker's man, Miles Cooper, ''not
unskilled in Hebrew'', got the post.[38] After Samuel Johnson's retirement
from King's College, he devoted himself entirely to Hebrew, and after con-
sulting with Hutchinsonians in England produced his own Hebrew-
English grammar on Hutchinsonian principles. He also tried to find support for a Hutchinsonian professor of Hebrew in America.[39] As a Hutchinsonian, Samuel Johnson was first and foremost a biblical literalist,
and a year before his death he advised his ten-year-old grandson (who had
already been reading Hebrew since the age of six, like Johnson himself)
that ''When I am gone you must read over & over from time to time, to
keep fresh in your memory which I have taught you. The Lord's prayer
– The Creed – The Ten Commandments, The 3 first Chapters of
Genesis and then these Psalms.''[40]

For English Protestants worried about the continuing validity of the Old
Testament, the Hutchinsonians even in the nineteenth century provided
at least a point of reference. Samuel Taylor Coleridge was deeply troubled
by the first chapters of Genesis, especially by the significance of the term
''firmament'', and in his notebook wrote a memo to himself to ask his
Jewish friend Hyman Hurwitz, later first professor of Hebrew at University College London, the meaning of the original Hebrew word.[41] At the
same time, Coleridge clarified his views in print:

> We are far from being Hutchinsonians, nor have we found much to respect
> in the twelve volumes of Hutchinson's works, either as biblical comment or
> natural philosophy: though we give him credit for orthodoxy and good inten-
> tions. But his interpretation of the first nine verses of Genesis xi. seems not
> only rational in itself, and consistent with after accounts of the sacred histor-

---

[38] Secker to Johnson, 4 Nov. 1760: repr. *ibid.*, iv. 70-3.

[39] Samuel Johnson, *An English and Hebrew Grammar* (London, 1767), repr. 1771 and 1776.
Cf. Johnson to Parkhurst, 1765?: *Johnson*, ed. Schneider, i. 350; J. to W.S. Johnson, 8 Jun.
1767: *ibid.*, i. 405-6; J. to Lowth, 25 Jun. 1767: *ibid.*, i. 409-10; Lowth to J., 3 May 1768,
15 May 1770, 16 May 1771: repr. Chandler, *Johnson*, pp. 200-5 and last letter in *Johnson*, ed.
Schneider, i. 478; Parkhurst to J., 8 Jun. 1771: *ibid.*, i. 478-80; J. to P., 1 Nov. 1771: *ibid.*,
i. 480-1. See also I.S. Meyer, ''Doctor Samuel Johnson's Grammar and Hebrew Psalter'',
in *Essays on Jewish Life and Thought* [Baron Festschrift], ed. J.L. Blau, et al. (New York, 1959),
pp. 359-74, where he also reprints Stephen Sewall to J., 28 Dec. 1767 and J. to S., 1 Mar.
1768 about the grammar, pp. 372-4.

[40] *Ibid.*, p. 367.

[41] S.T. Coleridge, *The Notebooks*, ed. K. Coburn (London, 1957-   ), iii. 4418 (Aug. 1818).
For more on Hurwitz, see D.S. Katz, ''Coleridge and the Jews'' (forthcoming).

ian, but proved to be the literal sense of the Hebrew text. His explanation of the cherubim is pleasing and plausible: we dare not say more. Those who would wish to learn the most important points of the Hutchinsonian doctrine in the most favorable form, and in the shortest possible space, we can refer to Duncan Forbes's Letter to a Bishop. If our own judgment did not withhold our assent, we should never be *ashamed* of a conviction held, professed, and advocated by so good, and wise a man, as Duncan Forbes.

Indeed, Coleridge adopted the Hutchinsonian view of the Confusion at Babel, as summarized by Forbes, that it was in actuality a confusion of the single "lip" (*safah*) or religious confession, rather than of "tongue" (*lashon*), a fact obscured by allegedly inaccurate translations from the original Hebrew.[42] Coleridge's copy of Forbes's book is annotated and bears the marks of careful reading.[43] In sum, Coleridge saw "the Cabbala of the Hutchinsonian School as the dotage of a few weak-minded individuals" but adopted some of their interpretations and appreciated their emphasis on the Old Testament and on the Hebrew text.[44] He saw biblical scholarship as "a confirmation of the Position announced by several of the Jewish prophets, & which was received by all but the most bigotted of the Jewish Rabbis, that the ceremonial & political Laws of Moses were binding on the Descendants of Abraham only, while the moral & religious Commandments were obligatory on all men – a most important Truth, I admit".[45] Devotion to the Old Testament need not include strict observance of all the 613 commandments, but Coleridge argued that many were still valid.

So too did William Kirby (1759-1850) discuss Hutchinsonianism in his Bridgewater Treatise, arguing that only that school had made "inquiry as to what is delivered in Scripture on physical subjects, or with respect to the causes of the various phenomena exhibited in our system, or in the physical universe". The Hutchinsonians "perhaps have gone too far in an opposite direction", but they alone recognized the great truth with which Kirby began his treatise, that "in order rightly to understand the voice of God in nature, we ought to enter her temple with the Bible in our hands."[46] Hutchinsonianism even received poetic expression in the "Jubilate Agno" by Christopher Smart (1722-1771), a poem admittedly written

[42] S.T. Coleridge, *The Friend*, ed. B.E. Rooke, in *Collected Works* (London 1971-   ), iv. III. 502-3 (first pub. 1818). Cf. [Forbes], *Letter*, p. 31.

[43] S.T. Coleridge, *Marginalia, I*, ed. G. Whalley, *Works*, xii. 417.

[44] S.T. Coleridge, *Aids to Reflection and The Confessions* (London, 1884), pp. 313-14, from MS confessions in his notes on the Book of Common Prayer.

[45] Coleridge, *Notebooks*, iii. 4401 (Mar. 1818).

[46] William Kirby, *On the Power Wisdom and Goodness of God* [7th Bridgewater Treatise] (London, 1835), I. xvii, xlix-1, lxxi (disagreeing with Parkhurst and the Hutchinsonians on the meaning of the word "cherub"), lxxxiv-v (agreeing with their understanding of "firmament" as expansion).

when he was confined in a private madhouse in Bethnal Green, but notable for its complete rejection of Newtonian science by the use of proofs taken from the works of Hutchinson and his followers.[47] These favourable general references to the school helped spread its influence and encourage people to search the Old Testament for themselves. The reaction of Richard Chenevix, bishop of Waterford and Lismore, was typical when he received a set of Hutchinson's works: "Thô I can n't agree with him in many of his Conjectures, yet my Curiosity induces me to read yᵉ whole".[48]

The Hutchinsonians, then, like the Seventh-Day Baptists, were extreme biblical literalists who believed every nuance of the Old Testament to be divinely inspired. Unlike Francis Bampfield and the other Seventh-Day men, however, most Hutchinsonians were more interested in the philosophical implications of their views rather than in altering the form of worshipping the First Cause which underlay Newton's universe. But they kept the problem of the Old Testament alive and in the public eye throughout the eighteenth century when the Seventh-Day Baptists declined into being merely another non-conformist transitional stage between seventeenth-century bibliolatry and the scientific biblical criticism of the nineteenth. Their insistence on studying the text of the Old Testament, however misguided, was akin to the work of the alchemists whose search for the philosopher's stone yielded unexpected chemical dividends. At the very least, their intense promotion of Hebrew studies had the effect of popularizing the language, for even to be an opponent of the Hutchinsonians one had to know Hebrew well. We know of some scholars who took up Hebrew studies at a late age for exactly that purpose, and to defend Newtonian science. But unlike Bampfield and the Seventh-Day men, the Hutchinsonians coupled their study of Hebrew and the Old Testament with an intense hatred of the Jews and their imagined plots against Christianity, and deliberately shunned Jewish company. Instead, they sought to strip the Jews of their near-monopoly in the interpretation of the Old Testament and of the Hebrew language itself, and to eliminate them as competing arbiters of the Mosaic tradition.

Indeed, it is in this regard that the Hutchinsonians, as more academic scholars of the Old Testament than the Seventh-Day Baptists, met their most formidable opponents who undercut the entire school of thought. Chief among these was Benjamin Kennicott (1718-1783), the foremost biblical scholar of his age. Radcliffe librarian at Oxford from 1767, Kenni-

---

[47] Christopher Smart, *The Poetical Works*, ed. K. Williamson & M. Walsh (Oxford, 1980-3), i, with appx. pp. 131-2, "Smart and the Hutchinsonians". Cf. K. Williamson, "Smart's *Principia*: Science and Anti-Science in *Jubilate Agno*", *Rev. Eng. Stud.*, xxx (1979), 409-22.

[48] Chenevix to a lady, n.d. (after 1749?): bound in with Bodl. Lib., 8° Jur. R. 46.

cott's life work was the collating and comparing of all known manuscripts of the Hebrew Old Testament. Most scholars shared the view of (the English) Samuel Johnson, that "though the text should not be much mended thereby, yet it was no small advantage to know, that we had as good a text as the most consummate industry and diligence could procure."[49] But the Hutchinsonians opposed him tooth and nail, not only because he canonized with scholarship the hated vowel points, but because he seemed to tamper with the accepted consonantal skeleton of the Hebrew Bible itself. The version which the Hutchinsonians had subjected to their intense scrutiny was shown to be nothing more than the Hebrew Bible printed at Venice in 1524-5 from a late medieval manuscript. Kennicott sought to get behind this late text, not only by using Syriac and early Latin versions, but also the Septuagint and even the Samaritan Pentateuch, written in Hebrew and containing variant readings and alterations. Kennicott's parallel texts effectively undermined the biblical literalism of the Hutchinsonians and all those who were determined to adopt a highly complex academic approach to the Old Testament. His grammatical knowledge, used with great effectiveness against the Hutchinsonians in Oxford itself, supported this major blow against the school.[50] The final cut must have been the growing awareness about Sanskrit in the late eighteenth century, which laid waste to Hutchinsonian ideas about the origin of language.[51]

Ironically, in many respects the method used by John Hutchinson was very similar to that of Kennicott, Bampfield, and indeed Hebrew scholars in England and Europe since the Renaissance. Hutchinson's editors described how he would apply his principles when at work:

> In order to take a nearer view of the *Mosaic* philosophy, the original text must be consulted, simply as it stands, divested of those points or pricks for vowels which the modern *Jews* contrived: for this purpose our author chuses generally to follow the *Latin interlineary version, as the most literal, and fittest to show the order of the Hebrew* words; then, to investigate the true idea each word is intended to convey, he collates the different senses given it in the *Lexicons*. The authorities he makes most use of are, the *Roman* edition of *Marius de Calasio's concordance* of the *Hebrew* with other Eastern languages, *Castelli's lexicon heptaglotton, Schindler's pentaglot,* and *Buxtorff's large rabinical dictionary.*

[49] James Boswell, *Life of Johnson*, ed. R.W. Chapman (Oxford, 1980), p. 444: this remark was made in 1770.

[50] For Kennicott's succinct and anonymous reply to his critics, see *A Word to the Hutchinsonians* (London, 1756). Generally on the attempts scholars have made to find an older version of the Hebrew scriptures up until our own times, see *The Bible in its Ancient and English Versions*, ed. H. Wheeler Robinson (Oxford, 1940), pp. 30-32; and D.S. Katz, "The Chinese Jews and the Question of Biblical Authority in Eighteenth-Century England and After" (forthcoming).

[51] See generally, S.N. Mukherjee, *Sir William Jones: A Study in Eighteenth-Century British Attitudes to India* (Cambridge, 1968); R. Gombrich, *On Being Sanskritic* (Oxford, 1978).

This is the way any Christian Hebrew scholar would go about trying to understand the text of Scripture, although they would of course have the added advantage of the vowel points.[52] But Hutchinson's excessive searchings in lexicons and dictionaries seem to have led him to see Hebrew as a secret code, a system of symbols rather than as a complete language, a result well understandable to anyone who has tried to learn the Hebrew language, built as it is around roots which have to be isolated in every word before it can even be found in the dictionaries. Ultimately his linguistic views were recognized as far-fetched if not absurd. But by that time the emphasis on the Old Testament as the word of God had already in English America coupled once again with the belief in the Seventh-Day Sabbath, with far-reaching results.

III

At the same time that John Hutchinson and his followers were perfecting their method for understanding and applying the Old Testament to all problems from mining to the millennium, the churches founded by Francis Bampfield, Edward Stennett, Peter Chamberlen and others were trying their best to survive the rather different conditions of the eighteenth century. In 1692, soon after the Welsh list of Sabbath-keepers was compiled, the General Baptist (non-Calvinist) Saturday men, the church of John James and Dr Peter Chamberlen, was able to acquire a permanent meeting house at Mill Yard, Goodman's Fields. Their benefactor was Joseph Davis, and after the death of his son in 1731 the Mill Yard congregation was able to expand, laying out a burial ground and letting the hall out to Sunday Baptists when not in use. Between 1721 and 1727 the newly combined Particular Baptist (Calvinist) churches of Saturday observers joined with the others at Mill Yard and worshipped under the same roof. Now, with the addition of the late John Belcher's followers from Bell Lane, and with the Sabbatarians of Pinners' Hall once led by Francis Bampfield and the Stennetts, the Seventh-Day Baptists were briefly united. Doctrinal differences soon proved insurmountable, and the men of Mill Yard were left alone once again. The Calvinists moved to other meeting places, and seem to have held on to communal life until the middle of the nineteenth century, although no definite evidence for this has yet been found.

But of course it was the General Baptists at Mill Yard who were the most prominent Seventh-Day men in eighteenth-century England before the arrival of the Adventists in the late 1870s. Robert Cornthwaite led the flock between 1726 and his death in 1755. He was from Bolton, and passed

---

[52] [Spearman], *Abstract*, p. 42.

through Anglicanism, Presbyterianism, and the Baptist faith before becoming a believer in the Seventh-Day Sabbath and pastor of Mill Yard at the age of thirty.[53] Cornthwaite was known as a controversialist, and entered into a lasting dispute with Dr Caleb Fleming, a prominent Presbyterian divine.[54] The church in his day included some distinguished figures, among them Nathaniel Bailey, whose *Universal Etymological English Dictionary* went through thirty editions between 1721 and 1802. Bailey's definitions of the words "Sabbatarian" and "Sabbath" show that his lexicography could be profoundly influenced by his religious confession. Dr Johnson made an interleaved copy the basis of his own dictionary, and Lord Chatham was said to have read through it twice. Bailey himself became a Seventh-Day Baptist in 1691, and kept a boarding school at Stepney, where he died in 1742. Bailey taught his pupils Hebrew there as well as Greek and Latin, but his knowledge of oriental languages seems to have been rather rudimentary.[55] Another prominent member of Cornthwaite's congregation was Sir William Tempest, lawyer and fellow of the Royal Society, friend of Dr Samuel Clarke, Dr Benjamin Hoadley and others of advanced religious views. He also knew William Whiston, the celebrated translator of Josephus, who was himself a Seventh-Day man. Tempest was admitted to Mill Yard in 1732 and immediately became a trustee.[56] So Mill Yard under Cornthwaite was a fairly lively place, and Anne Arbuthnot, the sister of Dr John the physician and author, affirmed in 1744 that her "idea of a tour in London to see the different nations here" would have to include "the people at Goodman's Fields, etc. etc. (The seventh-day men, and sweet-singers of Israel there.)"[57]

[53] Joseph Davis, *The Last Legacy* (London, 1707); F.H.A. Micklewright, "A Congregation of Sabbatarian and Unitarian Baptists", *Notes & Queries*, cxci (1946), 95-9, 137-40, 161-3, 185-8; *idem*, "Mill Yard: The Joseph Davis Funds", *Notes & Queries*, cxcii (1947), 520; W.T. Whitley, "Seventh Day Baptists in England", *Bap. Qly.*, xii (1946-8), 252-8; [C.H. Greene], "The Bell Lane Church", *Trans. Bap. Hist. Soc.*, iv (1914-15), 127-8; *Legacy*, ed. Black. See also [Anon.], *The Seventh-Day-Man* (London, 1724) and Bodl. Lib., MS Rawl. D 1350, fos. 296-9.
[54] Daniel Noble, *The Christian's full Assurance* (London, 1755), pp. 23-5: funeral sermon for Cornthwaite, who died on 19 Apr. 1755, aged 59; Caleb Fleming, *The Fourth Commandment Abrogated* (London, 1736); *idem*, *A Plain and Rational Account of the Sabbath* (London, 1737); R. Cornthwaite, *The Romish Doctrine* (London, 1732). Cf. Micklewright, "Congregation", pp. 97, 161-3.
[55] N. Bailey, *Universal Etymological English Dictionary* (London, 1730), the folio edn: see also 1st edn of 1721 for boarding school advertisement; W.E.A. Axon, *English Dialect Words of the Eighteenth Century as shown in the "Universal Etymological Dictionary" of Nathaniel Bailey* (London, 1883), pp. vii-xv; *Gents. Mag.*, xii (July 1742), p. 3487; A. Neubauer, letter in *Athenaeum*, 2778 (22 Jan. 1881), 142; *Dict. Nat. Biog.*
[56] F.H.A. Micklewright, "A Mill Yard Layman – Sir William Tempest", *Notes & Queries*, cxcii (1947), 514; William Whiston, *Memoirs* (2nd edn, London, 1753), pp. 170-1.
[57] Spence, *Observations*, p. 363.

An even more distinguished congregant would be added during the pastorate of Cornthwaite's successor, Daniel Noble, who was born into a Seventh-Day Baptist family. As was common, Noble was sent to be educated among the Presbyterians, and during his pastorate at Mill Yard held an eldership at a first-day Baptist church as well, which was not thought to be objectionable. Noble guided this group until his death in 1783, and in his day the congregation numbered nearly one hundred faithful, with many others who attended in a chapel which seated 250 below and in a gallery for servants and liveried footmen. Noble was a schoolmaster as well, like his predecessor and his successors Peter Russell and William Slater. Although it has never been noticed by the great man's biographers, one of Noble's employees was none other than Thomas Paine, later to become the American revolutionary and outspoken opponent of revealed religion. According to George Chalmers, his earliest biographer, the young Paine was rather drawn to religion. When he set up in Sandwich as a master stay-maker at the age of twenty-two, according to some who remembered him, "in his lodging he collected a congregation, to whom he preached as an independent, or a methodist." Three years later, in 1762, Paine obtained a position in the excise, but he was dismissed in 1765 and not until three years later found suitable employment with them as an excise officer in Lewes, Sussex. During these lean years, according to Chalmers,

> he was about the same time obliged to enter into the service of Mr. Noble, who kept the great Academy in Leman-street, Goodman's-fields, at a salary of twenty pounds a year, with five pounds for finding his own lodging. Here he continued, teaching English, and walking out with the children, till Christmas, 1766, disliked by the mistress, who still remembers him, and hated by the boys, who were terrified by his harshness. Mr. Noble relinquished our author, without much regret

According to Chalmers, Thomas Paine obtained employment at another school in Kensington, kept by a Mr Gardnor, but he stayed there only from January to March 1767. "His desire of preaching now returned on him", Chalmers recounts,

> but applying to his old master for a certificate of his qualifications, to the bishop of London, Mr. Noble told his former usher, that since he was only an English scholar, he could not recommend him as a proper candidate for ordination in the church. Our author, however, determined to persevere in his purpose, without regular orders. And he preached in Moorfields, and in various populous places in England, as he was urged by his necessities, or directed by his spirit.

The picture of Tom Paine as an itinerant preacher is an unfamiliar one, but his application to Daniel Noble during these lean years is entirely understandable. Although a Seventh-Day Baptist, Noble had within his gift a Church of England living, that of Little Maplestead, Essex, by virtue of the advowson that was part of the Joseph Davis endowment of 1707.[58]

After Daniel Noble's death in 1783, the Mill Yard Seventh-Day Baptist congregation went into a decline from which it never really recovered. Noble was succeeded by Peter Russell, who had ministered jointly with him for the last 28 years, and then by William Slater, minister until 1819. Indeed, the church almost disappeared in the first half of the nineteenth century, ironically just as the faith was flourishing in the United States, where it would soon undergo a fateful transformation under the influence of the millenarian revival, as we shall see. That the English Seventh-Day Baptists did not entirely die out was due to the industry of William Henry Black, Slater's energetic son in law, who began as an afternoon preacher at Mill Yard in March 1840.[59]

W.H. Black (1808-1872) was born in the Hutchinsonian centre of Aberdeenshire, educated privately, and eventually found his way to London. In 1830 Sir Frederick Madden brought him to Oxford to catalogue the Ashmole manuscripts, and when he had completed the task, Black was offered a place at the British Museum. Black's archival talents recognized, he was sent to the newly established Public Record Office to survey the Welsh manuscripts, and finally in 1841 was offered a permanent post as assistant keeper, second class. Black stayed at the PRO for twelve years, and afterwards worked as an antiquary and cataloguer of manuscripts. In succeeding years he surveyed the records of Dr Williams's Library, the Arundel MSS in the library of the College of Arms, and other collections. His biographer in the DNB, who evidently was personally acquainted with Black, testifies that as "a conscientious and painstaking antiquary, he has had few equals in the present century." Certainly his antiquarian achievements are impressive as well. He was a member of the Camden Society, a fellow of

---

[58] Francis Oldys [=George Chalmers], *The Life of Thomas Pain* (5th edn, London, 1792), pp. 6, 13-15. Cf. [Anon.], *An Impartial Sketch of the Life of Thomas Paine* (London, 1792), p. 5; [William Cobbett], *The Life of Thomas Paine* (London, 1797), pp. 14-15. Noble is mentioned but not identified in A. Williamson, *Thomas Paine* (London, 1973), pp. 53-4; S. Edwards, *Rebel! A Biography of Thomas Paine* (London, 1974), pp. 23-4; E. Foner, *Tom Paine and Revolutionary America* (New York, 1976), pp. 2-3. For Tom Paine and the Jews see R.H. Popkin, "The Age of Reason versus The Age of Revelation: Two Critics of Tom Paine: David Levi and Elias Boudinot", forthcoming; *idem*, "David Levi, Anglo-Jewish Theologian", forthcoming. Cf. Daniel Noble, *Religion, perfect Freedom* (London, 1767), p. 28; Micklewright, "Congregation", pp. 97, 139, 161-3; E.A. Payne to the *Times Lit. Supp.*, 31 May 1947, p. 267.

[59] J.L. Gamble & C.H. Greene, "The Sabbath in the British Isles", in *Seventh Day Baptists in Europe and America* (Plainfield, N.J., 1910), pp. 39-40; W.H. Black, *A Course of Afternoon Lectures, in Systematic Theology* (London, 1868), p. 2.

the Society of Antiquaries who served three times on its council, and a founder of the Palestine Archaeological Society, the Anglo-Biblical Institute, and the Chronological Institute of London. He was also a member of the British Archaeological Society and those of Surrey, London and Middlesex, and Wiltshire. Apart from his numerous articles in the proceedings of the Society of Antiquaries over a wide range of subjects, his scholarly pinnacles are undoubtedly his revision of Rymer's *Foedera* and his discovery of Holbein's will, which pushed the painter's date of death back by eleven years.[60]

Perhaps not surprisingly, Black's obituary notice in the journal of the Society of Antiquaries omits the central fact that he was heir to the centuries-old tradition of Saturday-Sabbatarianism.[61] Admittedly, the congregation at Mill Yard had by Black's day fallen on very hard times. The legal troubles began about fifteen years before Black was even connected with Mill Yard, and indeed in 1831 the Seventh-Day Baptists were evicted from the premises for nearly a year when the heirs of Black's predecessor and father-in-law went over to the Established Church. Black fought the case at his own expense from 1841, and appealed to the Charity Commissioners in 1855. Part of the problem was that another Seventh-Day church at Natton in Gloucestershire had been receiving money from the Joseph Davis trust since its establishment, but in Black's eyes they no longer represented part of his own tradition. Not until 1869 was the entire issue finally resolved at the courts, as Black published the documents supporting his case and laid the problem before all those interested in the fate of his beleaguered sect.[62] According to a contemporary chronicler of London's religious life, by that time the English Seventh-Day Baptists had "dwindled down to two skeleton congregations, an endowment, and a Chancery suit. As there is money a form of worship is kept up, though for all practical purposes the cause is dead."[63]

---

[60] F.H.A. Micklewright, "W.H. Black", *Notes & Queries*, cxciii (1948), 228-30, 247-8, 274-7, 519-20; *Dict. Nat. Biog.*; *Proc. Soc. Antiq.*, n.s. ii (1861-4), 259, 399; iii (1864-7), 488; vi (1873-76), 3-4; and *Index*, vols. i-xx, p. 38. See also P. Levine, "History in the Archives: the Public Record Office and its staff, 1838-1886", *Eng. Hist. Rev.*, ci (1986), 20-41, esp. p. 39; D.C. Davies, *English Scholars* (London, 1939), ch. xi. Black's letters to Madden are now Brit. Lib., MS Eger. 2839, fos. 155, 190. Cf. Black to S. Grimaldi, Brit. Lib., Add. MS 34, 189, f. 27. Black's notes for the preface to the Ashm. MSS are now Bodl. Lib., MS Ashm. 1834, u 33549.

[61] *Proc. Soc. Antiq.*, 2nd ser., vi (1873-76), 3-4.

[62] *Legacy*, ed. Black; E.A. Payne, "W.H. Black, F.S.A., and the Mill Yard Meeting-House", *Notes & Queries*, cxcii (1947), 261-2.

[63] J.E. Ritchie, *The Religious Life of London* (London, 1870), pp. 159-66. "If you want to see what an endowment can do for religion, go to Mill Yard", Ritchie advised, "an endowment can but preserve a corpse which had better be put away. We bury our dead out of sight. As it is in the material world so it is in the spiritual world." (pp. 165-6).

That observation was not only unkind but substantially inaccurate. Despite the worrying legal difficulties, W.H. Black managed to keep his congregation intact, in the face of personal sacrifice. His manuscript diary reveals the great pressure he was under at the PRO, where Sir Francis Palgrave, the keeper of the records, was very unsympathetic to Black's religious persuasion. Palgrave himself was a convert from Judaism originally known as Cohen, and this background may explain his outright hostility to the Saturday-Sabbath. But Saturday was "God's Holy Sabbath", Black confided to his diary, no matter what Palgrave thought: "I have a right to be absent; & I pay dearly for the privilege too: but I don't refuse (when needfully to work on the idolatrous superstition &c.)". Black himself began to live in the house at Mill Yard from September 1844, and after his resignation from the PRO in 1853 was no longer forced to compromise his beliefs.[64] In 1860 he counted twenty followers; ten years later he ministered to only one man and three women, two of whom were his own daughters. One of the girls married Dr William Mead Jones, who would be Black's successor at Mill Yard; the other became the wife of the Rev. Solomon Carpenter, who was for many years a Seventh-Day Baptist missionary in China. Significantly, both of these men were Americans, for it was in the United States that the seventh day was flourishing by that time, as we shall see.[65]

Despite the implications of the sad condition of the Seventh-Day men in England, Black was sufficiently famous to be sought out by the *Daily Telegraph*, whose reporter the Rev. C.M. Davies, armed with a Post Office Directory and the advice of neighbours, had great difficulty nevertheless in locating that "unlikely-looking, unsavoury place" known as Mill Yard. Davies described Black as a "venerable scholar-like old man, arrayed in clerical black, and with a long white beard". Davies was impressed: "I expected to find some illiterate scholar, with a hobby ridden to death, when lo! I found myself in the presence of a profound scholar and most courteous gentleman, who informed me that he thought in Latin, said his prayers in Hebrew, and read his New Testament lessons from the original Greek!" In the service itself Black prayed equally for "all honest and sincere persons of whatever nation or profession: for Jews and Mahomedans and Christians: and that all may be fitted for nobler and purer state of society, and have their share in the First Resurrection." The congregation

---

[64] Black's diary is now Chatham's Library, Manchester; MS Division B, shelf 4, number 43. It covers the years 1844-5 and seems to be one of a set: see F.H.A. Micklewright in *Notes & Queries*, cxcii (1947), 76-9. For Palgrave, see L. Edwards, "A Remarkable Family: the Palgraves", in *Remember the Days*, ed. J.M. Shaftesley (London, 1966), pp. 304-8.

[65] Ritchie, *Religious Life*, pp. 161, 163; Micklewright, "Black", p. 274. Cf. J. Moseley, *Modern Reasons for Observing the Seventh Day Sabbath* (London, n.d. [?1860]).

only numbered fourteen persons, including three children, apart from the reporter. Davies was nevertheless quite taken with the dignity of worship and the standard of exposition at Mill Yard, and suggested that "it would be no harm if some of our Sunday preachers would take a quiet run out on Saturday to Goodman's Fields" to see the Rev. Black at work.[66]

Black was succeeded at his death in 1872 by his son-in-law William Mead Jones, an American who had become a Saturday Baptist when a missionary in Haiti twenty years before.[67] "The Church is more prosperous to-day under the labors of Mr. Jones than it has been probably for a century", claimed a Baptist historian in 1888.[68] But according to another informed observer of this flock,

> I am afraid that during the greater part of the 19th Century, the congregation can scarcely be said to have existed. When I was there the congregation consisted of the Jones family, my party, and a number of old people who were in receipt of compensation for loss of wages by not working on the Sabbath, an old charity belonging to the church.[69]

When Jones died in 1895, some members wanted to close the chapel, which in any case was no longer at Mill Yard, for in 1885 the entire premises were sold to the London and North-Eastern Railway Company which put a train track through it, moving the graves to another site. The courts at that time decided that they could not permit the whole of the sale price to fall into the hands of the few faithful who were left at Mill Yard. Help from their thriving progeny in the United States was sought and received in the form of an American pastor, who himself looked after the flock only three years.[70] In 1905 the church was reorganized at Highbury by T.W. Richardson, who combined Saturday-Sabbatarianism with other eccentric interests. He was Grand Arch Master and Past Provincial Grand Master of the Loyal Orange Institute, and was very active in Freemasonry. He was also the founder of the Order of Danielites, a group which abstained from meat, alcohol, and tobacco, and he edited its journal. Vegetarianism was indeed a life-long passion, and Richardson was an ardent contributor to the *Vegetarian Messenger*. During the First World War, he rose to the rank of Lieutenant-Colonel, and contributed to the problem of food shortages

---

[66] C.M. Davies, *Unorthodox London: Or Phases of Religious Life in the Metropolis* (London, 1873), pp. 227-37. Cf. W. Wilson, *The History and Antiquities of Dissenting Churches* (London, 1808), ii. 584-608; G.H. Pike, *Ancient Meeting-Houses* (London, 1870), pp. 159-207.

[67] Gamble & Greene, "Sabbath", p. 40; Micklewright, "Congregation", pp. 186-7.

[68] T. Armitage, *History of the Baptists* (New York, 1888), p. 552.

[69] Ernest Axon to Micklewright, 22 June 1946: repr. Micklewright, "Congregation", p. 187. But see the Mill Yard organ during this period, *The Sabbath Memorial*, 1875-81 in Brit. Lib.

[70] Micklewright, "Congregation", pp. 97-9, 139-40, 163, 185-8; *idem*, "Davis Funds"; Payne, "Black".

by suggesting in print that people chew their food twice as long as usual. But the courts ruled that Richardson's flock was the rightful descendant of Mill Yard and entitled to enjoy some of the Joseph Davis trust, which itself was reorganized in 1901, giving the Natton congregation its share of the profits. After Richardson's death in 1920 the church drifted on the point of dissolution once again until in 1929 the Rev. James McGeachy became minister, and indeed continued to lead the church on Fundamentalist principles almost to our own day.[71]

IV

Two elements in the sad history of the decline of the English Seventh-Day Baptists point to the more interesting changes which had taken place in the early nineteenth century. When W.H. Black met with the reporter from the *Daily Telegraph*, he very early on in the discussion informed him ''that the body of Seventh-day Baptists, though so small in point of numbers in England, is largely represented in America, where the University of Alfred belongs to them, and two colleges.''[72] It was the spiritual children of Stephen Mumford and Samuel Hubbard at Newport who carried the torch by Black's time. Secondly, it was well known that the Rev. James McGeachy who took over in 1929 was originally a Seventh-Day Adventist. McGeachy was born in Glasgow, brought up a Baptist and in 1913 joined the Adventists as a missionary, first in England and then in Egypt. Only in 1927 did he leave the Adventists over doctrinal matters and join the Seventh-Day Baptists.[73] The connections between the two groups have often been assumed, merely on the basis of their common adherence to Saturday as the Sabbath, but they now indeed can be shown to have had common roots, thus making it possible for the rather larger and more influential sect of Seventh-Day Adventists to claim historically their origins in men like Traske, Chamberlen, and Bampfield.

We have already seen how the Seventh-Day keepers of Newport's Baptist Community withdrew from communion with the others on 7 December 1671 to found the First Seventh-Day Baptist Church. Their influence was soon felt outside of Rhode Island. In 1684 a certain Abel Noble came to the New World and bought a large tract of land near Philadelphia. Noble drifted through the Baptists, joined with some former Quakers, and eventually was drawn to Seventh-Day observance through a chance meet-

---

[71] *The Sabbath Observer* of Mill Yard, 1905-35 in Brit. Lib.; Micklewright, ''Congregation'', p. 187.

[72] Davies, *London*, p. 229.

[73] Personal testimony of McGeachy, in Micklewright, ''Congregation', p. 188.

ing with the Rev. William Gillette, a physician-missionary of the Newport church. Noble managed to convince others around him, and together they established another centre of Saturday worship here in Pennsylvania. So too in New Jersey, in the town of Piscataway, the deacon and preacher of the local Baptist church became convinced in 1702 of the continued validity of the fourth commandment after having sought and failed to find arguments against it when attempting to reprove one of his parishioners. Three years later those who agreed with their minister split with the main body of the congregation to form a third Seventh-Day Baptist church with seventeen members. These, then, were the three centres of faith in the New World; from them grew many more smaller congregations. By the organization of the Seventh-Day Baptist General Conference in 1802, the sect numbered about 2,000 members divided among twenty churches in ten states or colonies.[74]

Another independent strand of Seventh-Day observance was that of the German Baptists who came to Pennsylvania and settled near Lancaster in a town they called Ephrata. The keeping of the Saturday-Sabbath was only part of a wider communal and social theory, but it nevertheless was an important aspect of their message. They made a celebrated pilgrimage to Philadelphia in 1735 where they proclaimed the validity of the Old Testament Sabbath from the steps of the city courthouse, and they followed up this initial success with similar demonstrations in New Jersey (1738) and New England (1744).[75]

But the entire question of the Sabbath was not yet of paramount importance for the most prominent of American millenarians during the nineteenth century, the followers of William Miller (1782-1849).[76] Miller, a New York farmer who served as an officer in the United States Army during the War of 1812, devised a Baptist theology based on the standard millenarian texts of Daniel and the book of Revelation. Miller's studies led him to believe that the Second Advent of Christ would occur on 21 March 1844, accompanied by unmistakable heavenly signs. The uneventful nature of that day compelled him to examine his calculations once again, and

---

[74] L.A. Platts, "Seventh-Day Baptists in America Previous to 1802", in *Seventh Day Baptists*, pp. 119-46, esp. pp. 124-5, 133; C.F. Randolph, *A History of Seventh Day Baptists in West Virginia* (Plainfield, N.J., 1905). See generally *The Seventh-Day Baptist Memorial* (New York, 1852-4).

[75] Conrad Beysell, *Mystyrion Anomias The Mystery of Lawlesness* (n.p., 1728); M[ichael] W[ohlfarth], *The Naked Truth* (n.p., 1729); L.E. Froom, *The Prophetic Faith of Our Fathers* (Washington, D.C., 1950-4), iv. 918-19; C.F. Randolph, "The German Seventh Day Baptists" in *Seventh Day Baptists*, pp. 935-1257.

[76] Generally on Miller and the Millerites, see W. Cross, *The Burned-Over District: The Social and Intellectual History of Enthusiastic Religion in Western New York, 1800-1850* (2nd edn, New York, 1965), pp. 287-321; E.T. Clark, *The Small Sects in America* (New York & Nashville, 1947).

Miller reluctantly produced the revised date of 22 October 1844, as his followers awaited the Day of Doom with great anticipation. "If Christ does
not come within twenty or twenty-five days I shall feel twice the disappointment I did in the Spring", Miller confessed early in the month. According to some estimates, there may have been as many as 50,000
Millerites during the tense weeks before the expect Advent.[77]

Other religious groups, while not convinced that they were living in the
last few months of this world, were nevertheless not entirely unaffected by
the quickening of religious impulses. There was a general feeling among
many religious thinkers that the American Republic had failed to live up
to their expectation of a new millennial nation of God's new Israel, des-
tined to lead the world to peace and prosperity. Recent Roman Catholic
immigration and the continuing failure to abolish slavery seemed to confirm the spiritual and moral decline of what Abraham Lincoln would describe as the "last, best hope" of mankind. The Seventh-Day Baptists were
also particularly worried about new legislation for the strict observance of
Sunday which was being introduced in various parts of the United States,
and set aside 1 November 1843 as a day of fasting and prayer for the Saturday-Sabbath. Many Seventh-Day Baptists were drawn to consider the distinct possibility that the literal observance of the Ten Commandments and
the Second Coming of Christ might be imminently related. Chief among
these was Rachel Harris Oakes (1809-1868), originally of Vermont, who although baptized in early life had passed through Methodism before coming under the influence of the Seventh-Day Baptists in 1837. Her
Methodist pastor tried to persuade her to observe her Saturday-Sabbath
within the bosom of his church, but Oakes left to join the Seventh-Day
Baptist congregation at Verona in Oneida County, New York. Later, taking a supply of Seventh-Day Baptist literature with her, she went to live
with her daughter Delight, a schoolteacher in Washington, New Hampshire. The town was a stronghold of Millerite beliefs, and Oakes's pleas
for the Saturday-Sabbath seemed as yet strikingly irrelevant in these last
days before Armageddon. Two local clergymen were however brought over
to observe the Saturday-Sabbath, not particularly surprising in this intense short period of shifting religious loyalties. Frederick Wheeler, a
Methodist circuit preacher with millenarian leanings, declared himself in
the spring of 1844, and was soon joined in August by Thomas H. Preble

---

[77] J. Butler, "Adventism and the American Experience", in *The Rise of Adventism*, ed. E.S.
Gaustad (New York, 1974), pp. 175-7. The year 1844 was determined as follows: the 2,300
days of Dan. viii-ix was seen as a reference to a group of years beginning in 457 B.C., with
an initial period of 70 weeks of years (i.e. 490 years). The cleansing of the sanctuary therefore begins in 1844, 2300 years after 457 B.C.

of East Weare, New Hampshire, formerly a Free-Will Baptist minister, but latterly a follower of William Miller.[78]

Their theological worlds were shattered along with those of tens of thousands of others when the appointed day passed quietly. This "Great Disappointment", as the non-events of 22 October 1844 came to be known, led to a fundamental reorganization of American millenarianism, but by no means caused its collapse. The Millerite revival was an historical fact observed by all, even without the expected *dénouement*. To deny the hand of Jesus in its success would be almost to deny the existence of God himself. These loyal Millerites began to argue that the right date had been set, but that the events that had indeed occurred had been interpreted incorrectly. They announced that on that day as predicted God had begun the "cleansing of the heavenly sanctuary", which when completed would be followed up by the pronouncement of the verdict and execution of God's judgement. Church leader Hiram Edson had a vision confirming this interpretation while standing in his unharvested field the morning after. The reviewing of all the names in the Book of Life began on 22 October 1844, and when this time-consuming task was accomplished, Christ would appear in His glory to begin His millennial reign.[79]

It was in Rachel Harris Oakes's town of Washington, New Hampshire that Adventist millenarianism and Saturday-Sabbatarianism were once again reunited for the first time since the demise of the Bell Lane congregation of Fifth Monarchy men. At the end of 1844, but after the Great Disappointment, William Farnsworth and his brother Cyrus, pillars of the community, announced their intention to keep the Sabbath on Saturday; by observing the fourth commandment along with the other nine they hoped to speed the Second Advent of Christ. They were joined by their families and a number of others to withdraw from the local church and to establish a new congregation dedicated to both principles. The three original founders were meanwhile at work making their views known. Thomas Preble published an article about the Sabbath in a new Adventist journal called the *Hope of Israel* which appeared in Portland, Maine in March 1845 and was soon reprinted in pamphlet form. This piece brought the doctrine of the Saturday-Sabbath to Joseph Bates (1792-1872), the sea-captain who himself wrote a book entitled *The Seventh Day Sabbath*, published at New Bedford, Connecticut in 1846. Captain Bates had been one of the prominent members of Miller's Advent movement before the Great Disappointment, and his book, and his conversion to the Saturday-Sabbath, brought about the enlistment of James (1821-81) and Ellen Harmon White (1827-

---

[78] Froom, *Prophetic Faith*, iv. 941-9.
[79] *Ibid.*

1915), the moving force behind the establishment of Seventh-Day Adventism. Mrs White had her first divine revelation about two months after the Great Disappointment, and throughout her life she would be regarded as the central figure in the church, although she never held any official position. These Millerites established their headquarters in Battle Creek, Michigan in 1855, and in 1863 became an official denomination under the name of Seventh-Day Adventists. At first they restricted their proselytizing to Millerites who had gone through the trauma of disappointment (the so-called ''shut door theory''), but certainly once they moved to Battle Creek and left the original Millerite homeland of western New York State, they were committed to a wider witness.[80]

There is no question, then, that the modern denomination of Seventh-Day Adventists is the product of the spiritual transformation experienced by a group of Seventh-Day Baptists across the religious watershed of the Great Disappointment of 1844. Historians of both Seventh-Day sects have claimed common spiritual ancestors without looking very deeply into the historical implications of such a view. Indeed, when the Seventh-Day Adventist missionary John N. Andrews made his first voyage to England in 1874 he was met by the Rev. William M. Jones of Mill Yard. The two men spent much of the visit touring round the sites of their common heritage: the route where Traske was whipped; Newgate, where Traske's wife remained faithful to the Saturday-Sabbath; Pinners' Hall where Bampfield preached; Tyburn, where John James was executed for his observance of the seventh day.[81] Four years later the Seventh-Day Adventists sent their first missionary to England to spread the gospel in the land where the light of the Saturday-Sabbath had first shined forth.[82]

Curiously, while not absolutely denying the origins of the Seventh-Day Adventists in the Saturday-Sabbatarian Baptists, the historians of the movement have given the impression that while happy to make the claim for confessional antiquity, they wished to be regarded as something quite new. ''Although the seventh-day Sabbath came to the attention of a group of Adventists through the Seventh Day Baptists,'' writes Le Roy Froom, the official historian of the sect, ''it was the light on the sanctuary and the prophecy of Daniel 7:25 coupled with that of Revelation 14:9-12 that in-

[80] *Ibid.*; T.M. Preble, *A Tract, Showing that the Seventh Day should be Observed as the Sabbath* (Nashua, N.H., 1845). For an interesting account of his early spiritual life immediately after becoming a Christian, see M. Ooley, ''The Logbook (1827-1828) of Captain Joseph Bates of the Ship *Empress*'', *Adventist Heritage*, v (1978), 2: 4-12.

[81] H.H. Leonard, ''John N. Andrews and England's Seventh-Day Baptists'', *Adventist Heritage*, ix (1984), 1: 50-6. Jones himself was originally an American.

[82] N. Barham, ''Opening the British Mission'', *Adventist Heritage,* ix (1984), 1: 12-18. The author claims that there were about 2,000 Millerites in Britain before 1844. See also D.S. Porter, *A Century of Adventism in the British Isles* (Grantham, 1974).

vested it with a significance and an importance that the Sabbath had never had under the Seventh Day Baptists.'' The morality of the Ten Commandments was not an idea that could grip the public's attention, Froom argues, and only when combined with the belief that men were living in the final hour and were to be tried by the great unchanging standard of judgement could they be brought to obey all of God's Ten Commandments.[83] This unemphasized connection between the two groups appears in other histories of the Seventh-Day Adventists.[84]

In fact, certainly in the early years, the two groups were very nearly indistinguishable in belief regarding the central importance of the moral law of the Old Testament and the Seventh-Day Sabbath in particular. W.H. Black, the pastor of Mill Yard, wrote a defence of the Seventh-Day Sabbath in 1838 which mirrors exactly Seventh-Day Adventist theology on that point. Both groups argue that the Saturday-Sabbath was instituted by God at the Creation, and was therefore not affected by the expulsion from Paradise or any subsequent ordinance. ''We therefore believe'', the Adventists affirm, ''that until the Sabbath is repealed by divine authority, and its change made known by definite Scripture mandate, we should solemnly 'remember' and 'keep' the unrepealed original seventh-day Sabbath of the Decalogue, which is explicitly on record.'' This precisely reflect's Black's view. Both maintain that the Sabbath is a part of the moral law, as durable for all generations as the remaining nine commandments. Jesus referred only to Jewish and pagan holy days, but not to the Sabbath, when he condemned the old religious order.[85] Indeed, the Sabbath theology of the two sects was so close, that when Rachel Harris Oakes eventually asked to be dropped from the list of congregants at the Seventh-Day Baptist church in Verona, she was refused on the grounds that despite having helped to found an entirely new religious denomination, she had not violated any of the church's beliefs.[86]

That being said, however, there were a number of theological differences between the Seventh-Day Adventists and the Saturday Baptists on

---

[83] Froom, *Prophetic Faith*, iv. 960.

[84] B.W. Ball, *The English Connection* (Cambridge, 1981); Butler, ''Adventism'', p. 178; Cross, *Burned-Over District*, p. 316; D.M. Young, ''When Adventists Became Sabbath-Keepers'', *Adventist Heritage*, ii (1975), 2: 5-10. The exception may be a book that I have not seen, R.J. Thomsen, *Seventh Day Baptists – Their Legacy to Adventists* (Mountain View, [Cal.?], 1971), but the review in *Adventist Heritage*, ii (1975), 1, reflects traditional Adventist historiographical views.

[85] Black, *Plain Reasons:* dated Oxford, 12 Aug. 1838 with the claim that it was published then and afterwards in the U.S.A.; *Seventh-Day Adventists Answer Questions on Doctrine* (Washington, D.C., 1957), selections in ''The Seventh-Day Adventist Church'', *Oecum. Rev.*, xix (1967), 17-28.

[86] Young, ''Adventists'', p. 5.

points regarding issues more distant from the basic fact of Seventh-Day observance. The Adventists argued that while it was certainly true that the Saturday-Sabbath was part of God's moral law and should be observed for its own sake along with the rest of the Ten Commandments, the keeping of the Seventh Day was more basically part of the eschatological testing in the period between 22 October 1844 and the Second Coming of Christ. This will become a more severe test when Sunday worship will become mandatory on pain of death, a situation which the Adventists in mid-nineteenth-century America thought was coming soon. At that time the "remnant church" will be gathered, from people in all denominations who observe all of the Ten Commandments. All the others will receive the "mark of the Beast" referred to in the Book of Revelation. Nevertheless, they would agree with the Seventh-Day Baptists that the foundation of Saturday worship was not its role as an eschatological test but rather in the opportunity it gave Christians to recognize God as the Creator, and in the demonstration of divine love when God gave mankind a day of rest. Unlike the Jews, the Seventh-Day Adventists emphasized not the biblical restrictions, but the opportunity the Sabbath gave to man to develop his spiritual and moral capacities and thus take part in God's plan of salvation. Ellen White hoped that in the final conflict between God and Satan all true Christians would see the need for "obedience to all the precepts of the decalogue". Of course, the Seventh-Day Baptists in William Black's English variety would be unsympathetic to such an apocalyptic version of events, and in any case denied the Adventist axiom of Ellen White's divine inspiration. Presumably Black and his followers would also not accept the Seventh-Day Adventist rejection of the immortal soul or spirit, although those who came afterwards would find common ground in the emphasis on the use of proper diet as a tool for religious piety.[87]

The Seventh-Day Adventists, then, are very much the apotheosis of the belief in the Saturday-Sabbath which began with renewed interest in the Old Testament during the Reformation, and which through the efforts of Chamberlen, Bampfield, Mumford and others in the New World survived to be replanted in the more fertile soil of mid-nineteenth-century American enthusiastic religion. From the Seventh-Day Baptists they absorbed their faith in the Saturday-Sabbath; from the Millerites they absorbed the millenarian tradition of the imminent Second Coming of Christ. Both of these strands were originally found in the Bell Lane church under Fifth Monarchy man John Belcher, which sent Stephen Mumford to the New World in 1665. The Seventh-Day Adventist claim to seventeenth-century origins is therefore more than anachronistic myth, although it has never

---

[87] "Seventh-Day Adventist"; Black, *Plain Reasons.*

been fully demonstrated before. Today the Seventh-Day Adventists claim over five million believers, 85 per cent living in the Third World. In the United States alone they number about 750,000 Sabbatarians spread over thousands of congregations. Thomas Tillam would have been very pleased.[88]

Of course, the millenarian impulse in religious thought was strong enough to survive even without the element of Saturday-Sabbatarianism. Hutchinsonianism, the eighteenth-century variant of the literal belief in the word of God as expressed in the Bible, was replaced in the era of the Seventh-Day Adventists by the Fundamentalist movement. This too was a reaction to the Great Disappointment of 1844: by the 1870s millenarianism was once again increasing in certain American Episcopalian, Presbyterian, and Dutch Reformed churches, and was institutionalized through the medium of the Niagara Bible Conference in New York. Most Fundamentalists would support the doctrines defined in 1878 there by James H. Brookes (1830-97), the Presbyterian minister from St Louis who edited one of their influential periodicals, *The Truth*. First among these was an affirmation of the inerrant inspiration of the Bible, preserved completely from error in the original manuscripts. Their defense of the biblical text against science, not now diabolized in the writings of Newton but in those of Charles Darwin, is most well known in the ''monkey trial'' in 1925 of John T. Scopes, a science teacher from Dayton, Tennessee, but their emphasis on the absolute authority of the Bible and the imminent coming of Christ has continued until the present day, in churches of several denominations calling themselves ''evangelical'' in order to escape the pejorative associations of the original name. The historian of the movement rightly stresses the millenarian background of the Fundamentalists, but by neglecting the Hutchinsonians and their own origins in the continuing controversy over the Old Testament, truncates the roots from which the movement grew, to form the enormously powerful group of churches that it is today.[89]

For the history of the Saturday-Sabbath shows above all else the significant practical consequences of a religious idea. After the Restoration, the belief in the Saturday-Sabbath was powerful enough to override the political alignments of the Civil War period, which now abruptly seemed strikingly irrelevant. The Presbyterians made this difficult transition by pathetically seeking ''comprehension'' within the Church of England; the

---

[88] *U.K. Christian Handbook*, ed. P. Brierley (1984), p. 116; *Statistical Abstract of the United States 1985* (Washington, D.C., 1985), p. 51.

[89] See esp. E.R. Sandeen, *The Roots of Fundamentalism* (Chicago, 1970); S.G. Cole, *The History of Fundamentalism* (n.p., 1931); L. Gasper, *The Fundamentalist Movement* (The Hague, 1963).

Quakers took the course of renouncing any political involvement in the temporal world. But the Seventh-Day men were the most politically disparate of groups, and possessing an astonishingly simple and powerful notion of the irrevocable truth of the Old Testament as well as the New, and the continuing validity of all the Ten Commandments, they stood fast against the engines of Restoration religious persecution, spread their gospel to the New World, and survived as a distinct religious sect until our own times. In the eighteenth century, the views of Francis Bampfield would be represented and echoed by John Hutchinson and his followers; in the nineteenth the Seventh-Day Adventists and the Fundamentalists would make the modern case using the same arguments for the absolute authority of Scripture.

INDEX

DATE DUE

HIGHSMITH 45-102   PRINTED IN U.S.A.